KU-183-892

Theorizing Social Work Practice

NEIL THOMPSON

palgrave
macmillan

© Neil Thompson 2010

All rights reserved. No reproduction, copy or transmission of this publication may be made without written permission.

No portion of this publication may be reproduced, copied or transmitted save with written permission or in accordance with the provisions of the Copyright, Designs and Patents Act 1988, or under the terms of any licence permitting limited copying issued by the Copyright Licensing Agency, Saffron House, 6-10 Kirby Street, London EC1N 8TS.

Any person who does any unauthorized act in relation to this publication may be liable to criminal prosecution and civil claims for damages.

The author has asserted his right to be identified as the author of this work in accordance with the Copyright, Designs and Patents Act 1988.

First published 2010 by
PALGRAVE MACMILLAN

Palgrave Macmillan in the UK is an imprint of Macmillan Publishers Limited, registered in England, company number 785998, of Houndmills, Basingstoke, Hampshire RG21 6XS.

Palgrave Macmillan in the US is a division of St Martin's Press LLC, 175 Fifth Avenue, New York, NY 10010.

Palgrave Macmillan is the global academic imprint of the above companies and has companies and representatives throughout the world.

Palgrave® and Macmillan® are registered trademarks in the United States, the United Kingdom, Europe and other countries

ISBN 978-0-230-55306-4

This book is printed on paper suitable for recycling and made from fully managed and sustained forest sources. Logging, pulping and manufacturing processes are expected to conform to the environmental regulations of the country of origin.

A catalogue record for this book is available from the British Library.

A catalog record for this book is available from the Library of Congress.

10 9 8 7 6 5 4 3 2
19 18 17 16 15 14 13 12 11 10

Printed and bound in Great Britain by
CPI Antony Rowe, Chippenham and Eastbourne

SHEFFIELD HALLAM UNIVERSITY
WL
361.32
TH
COLLEGIATE LEARNING CENTRE

101 969 873 X

Theorizing Social Work Practice

ONE WEEK LOAN

15 Aug 11

10/2/12

Sheffield Hallam University
Learning and Information Services
Withdrawn From Stock

For David and Helen

Contents

CONTENTS

Preface

Before starting my career in social work I had already developed an interest in politics and social issues and had read widely around these and related subjects. When I began my career in social work it was in the days when, as a residential child care worker, I was discouraged from asking questions or developing my knowledge base. I was simply urged to 'get on with the job', without any real clarity about what the job actually was or how to go about it. It was largely a case of copying what the other staff did and doing the best I could without any real depth of understanding. Some of the reading I had previously done helped cast some light on my working life, but for the most part there was a major gap between actual practice on the one hand and any sort of theoretical understanding on the other.

When I later went to university to undertake a professional qualification in social work, I was soon learning very fast and very enthusiastically – drawing out all sorts of important lessons retrospectively from my earlier experience. When I went out on placement I was fortunate enough to work with an excellent team – a team that was not only working at extremely high levels of professional practice, but also drawing on an extensive knowledge base. This proved to be a wonderful and formative experience, as it helped me to realize how important it was that practice should be *informed* practice, based on understanding, rather than habit or copying others. This was such an improvement on my earlier experience, so much more fulfilling, and it put me in a much stronger position to be able to help people.

The more I learned about the underpinning knowledge base of social work, the more I realized just how massive and complex that knowledge base was – and how important it was in casting light on the challenges of practice. Since then I have continued to explore the ideas that we can draw upon to make sense of the intricate and multi-level demands of practice. This book is based on that exploration and the lessons I have learned from putting its insights into practice in my own work as a practitioner, manager, educator and consultant over the years. It is intended as a guide for those beginning the journey of making sense of practice and for those who are already fully engaged in that endeavour and want to broaden and deepen their understanding.

It is not intended as a book that provides 'answers' in any simplistic or definitive sense – the world of social work is far too complex for that. However, what it should do is provide a set of ideas that encourage and support you in working out your own answers. In other words, this is a book intended to support and stimulate critically reflective practice (S. Thompson and N. Thompson, 2008). By this, I mean that it offers opportunities to develop a degree of theoretical understanding that can form the basis of further learning over time – a platform for high-quality practice premised on a professional knowledge base that is constantly growing and being re-evaluated in the light of new understandings and challenges to previous ways of thinking.

The book is premised on the idea that practitioners do not simply use a theoretical knowledge base in a direct way (what has traditionally been referred to as 'applying theory to practice' or what Schön, 1983, refers to as 'technical rationality') but, rather, go through a more complex process of 'theorizing' practice – that is, using a set of concepts to act as a framework for making sense of the situations we encounter in practice and how these relate to the wider context of social work and indeed of society itself. It is a challenging book, in so far as it contains a wide range of concepts, some of them quite profound and complex, but it should also be a rewarding book, as careful reading of it should help you to develop not only your understanding of the issues, but also your confidence in tackling theoretical matters, and thereby not being afraid to wrestle with some of the complexities involved.

It is to be hoped that you will feel the effort involved in studying will have been repaid in terms of the gains made and the understanding developed. It is strongly recommended that, once you have completed the book, you revisit it from time to time, both to refresh your memory and to make the most of the learning on offer by taking your understanding a step further in terms of both breadth and depth. The wealth of material covered here is such that it is unlikely that you will take in everything on first reading. But that is the nature of learning – not simply absorbing new information in a mechanistic way, but rather forming new understandings that enable us to broaden our horizons, make our analyses more sophisticated and appreciate more fully the links and interrelationships across the different elements.

I wish you well in your efforts to theorize practice and, in doing so, develop the highest quality practice we can, to ensure that we are able to offer the best level of service to those who need our help.

NEIL THOMPSON

Acknowledgements

Once again I find myself in a position where I have many people to thank for their contribution to the finished product. There are those who have offered helpful insights by commenting on all or part of an earlier draft of the book. I am therefore pleased to be able to thank Bernard Moss of Staffordshire University, Roger Sibeon of Liverpool University, Jan Pascal of La Trobe University, Denise Bevan of St Rocco's Hospice, Warrington, UK, Patrick Tomlinson, independent consultant and Sue Thompson of Avenue Consulting Ltd.

There are also those who have played a part in the production of the book, especially Margaret Holloway for her excellent audiotyping work and Penny Simmons for her equally excellent copyediting work. Both deserve praise and gratitude, not only for the quality of their work, but also the spirit in which they undertake it. Finally, there are those who have been a source of support in the background throughout the process. Catherine Gray of the publishers has been extremely helpful, as always, and Sue Thompson deserves a second mention for her supportive role too. This book is the last of the projects that Jo Campling was involved in developing before her untimely death. For me, then, this book represents the end of an era. I must therefore express my gratitude to Jo for this and all the guidance she gave me in my other publishing projects.

Introduction

This book builds on my work in two other texts, in effect forming a trilogy of books concerned with articulating what I see as the essentials of high-quality social work practice. The process began with the publication of my *Understanding Social Work: Preparing for Practice* book (initially published in 2000, with a revised edition appearing in 2005 and a third edition in 2009). That book provides a basis for understanding the nature and purposes of social work, and paints a picture of the challenges involved and potential ways of rising to them. This was followed in 2009 by the publication of *Practising Social Work: Meeting the Professional Challenge*, which took further the idea of practice challenges and related them specifically to the need to develop empowering, partnership-based forms of professionalism. To complement the discussions in these two books, *Theorizing Social Work Practice* now fills some of the gaps by showing that effective, high-quality practice needs to be informed by a sophisticated understanding of the practice world, drawing on a range of concepts that form an explanatory framework or, in other words, a theory.

The need for practitioners to theorize

Social work involves dealing with complexity. Its challenges are far too demanding and multi-layered to be amenable to simple, formulaic approaches. Social workers therefore need to be *thinkers* as well as doers – they need to be able to use their analytical skills to make sense of the complex situations they encounter (see Thompson, 2009a, Part II, for a fuller discussion of my views about this). Anything involving people is likely to be complex, and so situations that involve people who are distressed, in need, experiencing problems, in conflict and/or in crisis are likely to be even more complex.

Using analytical skills involves using ideas or 'concepts'. Making sense of complex situations by using concepts (or sets of concepts – a 'conceptual framework') is precisely what theorizing is all about. Theory and practice are often presented as opposites, but paradoxically what social workers are called upon to do in practice is to theorize. Indeed, as we shall explore in more detail below, this is the basis of reflective practice (S. Thompson and N. Thompson, 2008), using our intellectual faculties and professional knowledge base to develop coherent understandings of the situations we encounter and our role within them.

An essential foundation of my approach adopted in this book is that social work practice is based on *theorizing*. I am therefore rejecting the false and misleading idea that theory and practice can be seen as entirely separate entities – they are, in fact, two sides of the same coin. To undertake social work activities is not to choose between theory and practice, but rather to fuse the two – to engage in actions (practice) that are shaped by knowledge and understanding (theory). To attempt to practise without theory is to try to act without understanding, and can therefore be very dangerous indeed – it can so easily make situations worse. In reality, all our professional actions are based on some form of understanding. The major question is this: Is our understanding the best we can achieve in the circumstances or are we relying on untested assumptions, prejudices, habits and guesswork? Social work education and training involves helping students and practitioners to build up their knowledge base over time and to cultivate their skills in making sense of complex issues. In other words, education and training help us to theorize what we do, to develop understandings of our actions and their consequences and the various important aspects of the context in which they take place. In effect, to do social work is to theorize practice (to draw on sets of ideas to make sense of it) and to practise theory (to make use of those ideas in a practical context).

Beginning with practice

The traditional approach to writing or teaching about theory (whether in social work or any other professional discipline) is to present accounts of theory and then encourage readers or students to *apply* the theory to practice. However, there are some fundamental problems with this approach, in so far as the 'theory' often does not get as far as practice, partly because of limitations of memory, distractions and other such factors, partly because understanding a theory in the abstract and being able to draw on it in practice are two different things, and partly because the whole idea of applying theory to practice is flawed (what Schön, 1983, described as 'technical rationality', the mistaken assumption that there are simple, direct one-to-one links that can be made between theory and practice – see the discussion of reflective practice in Chapter 1).

Sadly, the limitations of this approach have led many people to see theory as being of little use because it can rarely give direct answers to the questions practice generates. However, 'abandoning' theory is not the only option. An alternative approach can be to begin with practice and then see how theory – the professional knowledge base, that is – can be 'drawn down' as and when required. This can be seen to offer a much more fruitful basis for integrating theory and practice, for connecting them in a meaningful way.

For this reason this book is concerned not with presenting theoretical approaches one after the other, but rather with looking at what a practitioner is likely to need to know in a range of practice situations. Inevitably a single book cannot cover all the eventualities and all the knowledge needed, but it can lay the foundations for further study and learning – and that is precisely my aim in writing the book.

Outline of the chapters

Given that my aim is to explain the importance of theorizing practice by seeing the work from the practitioner's point of view and what he or she needs to know, it would make sense to structure the book in a way that helps to do this. For this reason, the book is divided into three parts. The first part lays the foundations by exploring the nature and role of theory – in effect examining in more depth the issues touched on in this Introduction. The second part explores the nature of practice by discussing a range of issues related to the knowledge base practitioners need in order to be able to make sense of their work. The final part puts forward some suggestions for how our theoretical understanding as a profession can be developed, so that we can have an even better foundation of understanding to underpin our practice.

Within each of the three parts there are specific chapters, each of which makes a contribution to the picture I am trying to paint of high-quality professional practice premised on a well-developed understanding of the social world and our part within it. Part One sets the scene for the book by discussing the significance of theory as a foundation for well-informed practice. It has three chapters. The first is entitled 'The role of theory'. It examines the nature of theory and establishes why integrating theory and practice is such an important undertaking. It also clarifies what is meant by 'reflective practice' and argues that existing approaches to this topic tend to lack theoretical sophistication. Proposals for how reflective practice can be developed are also outlined.

The second chapter, 'Theory and postmodernism', is concerned with a critique of the contemporary emphasis on postmodernism and related ideas. The 'new wave' of theory can be criticized for a 'bandwagon effect' whereby some old ideas have been repackaged as new and some very questionable assumptions have been allowed to influence both theory and practice. This chapter highlight those aspects of 'new wave' thinking that are of value, while also pointing out the significant flaws to be avoided.

The final chapter in Part One is entitled 'Practices redefined'. Its subject matter is the changing definitions of practice. It begins with Payne's (2005a) tripartite classification before exploring such important issues as: care management and the 'dumbing down' of social work; social work as risk management; and the emergence of managerialism and bureaucracy as opposed to leadership and professionalism. Social work is also considered in its international context.

Part Two provides an overview of what understanding we need as social work practitioners. It has seven chapters, the first of which is 'The person'. This chapter examines the theory underpinning our understanding of identity and the existential challenges associated with it. It is therefore concerned with the significance of individual factors. It seeks to combine elements of traditional social psychology and social work theory with elements of new-wave thinking, linked together through existentialism.

Next comes Chapter 5 on 'Interpersonal interaction' in which communication, collaboration and conflict are the key topics. While individual factors can be very significant, we also have to consider the significance of interpersonal factors. This chapter explains why neither traditional approaches nor new-wave thinking are sufficient in themselves to give us an adequate understanding of this complex field.

The following chapter is concerned with 'Group dynamics and intergroup relations'. Communication, collaboration and conflict again feature as significant issues, but this time in relation to the significance of group factors. Individuals are members of many social groups and so, in order to understand the individual, we need to understand how groups influence their members and how groups both influence and are influenced by other groups.

Chapter 7 addresses 'Cultural contexts'. People do not exist in a cultural vacuum. We therefore have to develop an understanding of social and cultural norms and practices and frameworks of meaning. The significance of cultural factors cannot be overemphasized, although much of the theory base of social work has paid scant attention to them.

The next chapter is concerned with 'Sociopolitical structures and processes'. Cultural formations have to be understood in relation to wider issues of social structure, including such key issues as: social divisions; power relations; and social and political processes. This chapter is therefore concerned with the significance of the wider sociological factors that play such a key role in shaping human experience.

Chapter 9 explores 'The organizational context', another often neglected area. It includes questions about workplace cultures, structures and dynamics. The significance of organizational factors can be of major proportions, and so this chapter explores how such factors can play a significant role in relation to theoretical understandings and how we draw on them in practice.

The final chapter in Part Two is concerned with 'Morality and ideology'. It would be a serious mistake not to address values and ethics and the wider domain of social and political ideologies and their influence. This chapter therefore examines the significance of moral/political factors and how they play such a significant role in shaping policy, theory and practice.

Part Three is concerned with the importance of *developing* theory over time and not relying on a static knowledge base. It has five chapters. The first is entitled 'Developing coherence: drawing on existentialism'. It emphasizes the dangers involved in the postmodernist rejection of coherence. It also shows how existentialist concepts can be used in social work, so that the value of existentialism for developing theory can be appreciated.

The second chapter discusses 'The linguistic turn'. New-wave thinking in social work draws heavily in some place on the significance of language. This chapter explores the significance of language and communication and the need to develop understandings of them that avoid the mistakes associated with post-structuralism and post-modernism.

Next comes Chapter 13 with a focus on 'Spirituality and meaning'. The existentialist emphasis on meaning and perception links well with current concerns about spirituality in social work (see, for example, Moss, 2005). This chapter demonstrates how existentialism provides a sound foundation for understanding the significance of spirituality as a dimension of people's needs, problems and concerns and, indeed, as a dimension of their lives.

The penultimate chapter is concerned with 'Developing emancipatory practice'. The development of radical social work in the late 1960s and 1970s led to important developments in social work thinking and practice, especially in relation to anti-discriminatory practice. However, it also turned out to be seriously flawed in some ways. This chapter is concerned with demonstrating how the oversimplifications of radical social work can be avoided by a sociologically informed existentialism.

Finally we look at 'The challenges we face'. This final chapter contains an extended discussion of what needs to change to develop social work theory in line with existentialist thought: what strengths need to be built upon and what pitfalls need to be avoided. It uses the National Occupational Standards as a starting point for exploring the issues.

As this overview of the chapters shows, the book covers a very wide range of issues. In this respect, it reflects the social work world, which is highly complex and multifaceted. Indeed, a major aim of the book is to cast light on these intricacies and to lay the foundations for developing a fuller understanding of them.

This book represents a journey through some difficult terrain. It involves a number of concepts, many of which are complex in their own right, and which can therefore be challenging when combined. So, if at any point, you find that what you are reading is not as simple and straightforward as you would like it to be, please do persevere. Being an effective social worker involves being able to manage complexity, and so it is perfectly acceptable to find things difficult at times. It is not a sign that you are not up to it; it is more a sign that you are doing what social workers do much of the time: wrestling with complexity. The concepts presented here should ultimately make you better equipped for dealing with that complexity by giving you a basis of understanding.

The book will offer different things to different people, but everybody who reads it should be able to gain a great deal from it, to get a very high return on the investment of time, effort and energy that goes into studying what it has to say:

- *Students.* This book should help you lay a foundation for understanding the complexities of theory and for being able to use that theory positively and constructively as a basis for high-quality practice throughout your career. Ideally, it should also help to show that theory is nothing to be scared of – theoretical ideas belong to the world of practice and are used on a daily basis. A key message is that you should not let the sometimes obscure language of theory and theoreticians put you off and prevent you from gaining the benefits of having a strong theory base to draw upon.
- *Practitioners.* This book should help you to make sense of your practice and to avoid approaches that are based largely on habit, guesswork or copying others. In other words, it should help you to develop critically reflective practice. It should be especially useful for practice teachers and others involved in developing practice learning.
- *Managers.* Part of a manager's job is to try to ensure that standards of practice are at an optimal level. This book should support you in doing this by giving you a framework for helping staff understand the complexities that they are engaged with. As such, it should offer a basis for not only developing critically reflective management practice, but also supporting staff in developing critically reflective social work practice.
- *Educators.* Learners often struggle with the very notion of the use of theory in practice and often fall into the long-standing gap between theory and practice. This book, with its emphasis on *theorizing* practice should help to avoid that and provide a platform for more confident learning about ensuring that practice is *informed* practice.

Part One
Making Sense of Theory

Introduction to Part One: Theory into Practice

In Part One my aim is to 'set the scene' for the remainder of the book. In particular I want to take the opportunity to establish the importance of theory and the need to 'theorize' – that is, to draw on our theoretical understandings to make use of their insights in actual practice situations.

Clarke's comments are very relevant:

> We have enough theories that turn up to tell us what we will find. I have an interest in a more mobile and unfinished sort of 'theorizing' that orients us towards the problems of trying to understand the present – as a conjuncture of the complex and multiple routes that brought us to this point. It might also help us to see the different ways of the present that there might be (rather than following the carefully constructed motorway that dominant forces direct us to use to get to their future).
>
> (2004, pp. 4–5)

Theory is not about being told by an academic what the 'right' answer is or how a situation should be dealt with. Rather, theory provides the raw materials of the professional knowledge base and it is then the task of the critically reflective practitioner to transform those raw materials into usable information to cast light on the particular situation.

Part One also seeks to establish existentialism as a theoretical basis that provides a positive and helpful balance between the two unhelpful extremes of overly rigid approach of positivism and what Callinicos calls the 'extravagances and fallacies of postmodernism' (2007, p. 304).

Finally, there is a discussion (in Chapter 3) of how different understandings of social work generate different ways of carrying out social work duties. This is important, as it shows that theory is not just about understanding social work issues and thereby informing practice, it is also about defining or 'conceptualizing' social work. That is, our challenge as professionals is not only to theorize how to do our job, but also to theorize what that job is.

1

The role of
theory

Introduction

Theory is a subject that is often misunderstood, misrepresented and oversimplified. Partly as a result of that, it is also something that can cause a great deal of anxiety and unease, as if it were something to be afraid of. There is therefore a strong need to clarify what is meant by theory in order to establish a baseline from which to develop our discussions in the ensuing chapters. In this opening chapter my aim is therefore to clarify what is meant by theory, why it is important, and how it can sometimes be flawed and therefore unreliable. This will lead to a discussion of the importance of integrating theory and practice as a basis for sound professional practice in social work. Given that (i) theory can be flawed; and (ii) even the best theories cannot be expected to give a complete picture of the subject matter they aim to describe, then our approach to the whole question of theory needs to be a *critical* one – that is, one which does not take theoretical statements at face value as if they were 'gospel truth'. Indeed, as we shall see, this is the basis of critically reflective practice and this, in turn, is an important foundation for theorizing social work practice. This applies as much to the theoretical idea I will be presenting in later chapters (and have presented elsewhere in my writings). My aim is to stimulate debate as part of a process of exploring the complex issues involved, rather than to foreclose such debate by presenting 'the answer'. It will be important to bear this in mind as you work your way through the book. The ideas I use should be seen as a stimulus to critically reflective practice, not as a substitute for it.

What is theory?

Fundamentally, theory is an attempt to explain a phenomenon or set of phenomena by providing a structured set of concepts that help us to understand the subject matter concerned. If concepts can be understood as bricks, then theory is the wall that their interlinking produces – it is a conceptual framework. It can be used in a narrow sense to refer to a specific theory – for example, Freud's theory of the unconscious – or it can be used more broadly to refer to the professional knowledge base of a discipline. For example, we may talk of social work theory, by which we mean not just specific theories that attempt to explain social work issues, but rather the overall professional knowledge base that helps to shape practice. Chapter 3 of Thompson (2009b) provides an overview of some of the key aspects of that knowledge base, although it has to be recognized that it is a constantly changing foundation of understanding as new ideas are constantly being developed and older ideas being challenged and sometimes rejected.

Theory can also be divided into formal and informal categories. The former is more structured and explicit. Formal theory is likely to exist in published form, whether in books or journal articles, or both. It has a certain degree of intellectual credibility associated with it, even though it is likely that particular theories will be challenged and criticized by people from a different theoretical perspective (or people within the same theoretical perspective who prefer to adopt a different emphasis). Formal theory is also generally characterized by being explicit – that is, it generally makes its propositions open for discussion, challenge and verification. Informal theory, by contrast, is generally implicit. The term 'informal theory' refers to the way in which practitioners develop a tacit understanding of the phenomena they encounter in their practice. Generally, informal theory draws heavily on formal theory whether directly or indirectly, but is also mixed with 'practice wisdom' – that is, the knowledge that has been developed from reflective approaches to practice over the years.

It is commonly assumed that formal theory in some sense 'outranks' informal theory, and the latter is generally seen as less prestigious than the former. In reality, however, the situation is far more complex. Formal theory can at times be of little value, as it cannot realistically cover all practice eventualities. As we shall see below, formal theory can also be flawed in particular ways and therefore misleading. However, the picture relating to informal theory is also mixed. Insights gained from practice can sometimes be extremely helpful and cast significant light on the particular situation we are dealing with. But, what passes for 'practice wisdom' can also be quite problematic. For example, for many years the accepted wisdom took little or no account of the significance of discrimination in people's lives, due to the individualistic focus of social work at that time (see Thompson, 2006a). It is therefore important that we do not fall into the trap of thinking that one form of theory is necessarily better than another. They both have an important part to play, but neither should be accepted uncritically.

There has been much written and spoken about the gap between theory and practice (Habermas, 1986; Payne, 2005a; Thompson, 2000a) and it is perhaps inevitably the case that there will be some discrepancy between the two. This is because both theory and practice are highly complex entities, and the expectation that they will entirely coincide is certainly unrealistic. However, some people have unfortunately widened this gap by dismissing the significance of theory by making such comments as: 'I prefer to stick to practice', without recognizing that theory and practice are inevitably intertwined (this is a point to which we shall return below). It is largely because of this inevitable gap between theory and practice that we need reflective practice. This refers to forms of professional activity which draw on a professional knowledge base and which seek to make sure that practice is *informed* practice. This will be a recurring theme throughout the book.

Practice focus 1.1

Sarah was a newly qualified social worker who was keen to learn as much as she could in her new role. At university she had found theory very interesting and was keen to learn more about how to relate it to practice. She therefore took every opportunity to talk to her colleagues about their use of theory. However, she was surprised to find such a wide range of responses. Some colleagues were able to identify clear influences of formal theory on their work, and Sarah was able to learn a great deal from this. Other team members said little or nothing about formal theory, but were able to talk at length about how they had developed their understanding from their experience, while two team members were totally perplexed by her questions and seemed to find the whole subject a source of discomfort. Sarah could see now why her tutor had emphasized that the relationship between theory and practice was quite a complex one.

The tendency to reject theory and see it as unimportant has a long history in British social work (see, for example, Jones's 1996 work on anti-intellectualism). More recent and more general examples of this tendency to devalue theory are not uncommon. The failure to recognize the significance of the theoretical perspectives on which our ideas are based is a sad reflection on this long-standing tendency to see practice as important and theory as unimportant, without acknowledging that the two elements – theory and practice – are two sides of the same coin. It is a pointless and dangerous exercise to separate out theory and practice, although the tendency to do so is sadly a common one. As Butt puts it: 'It was Kurt Lewin who was reputed to have said "there is nothing as practical as a good theory"' (2004, p. 10).

This reflects the notion that theory is largely invisible to many people. That is, they have learned various concepts over time that have become embedded in their practice to the point where they no longer recognize how their practice is reflecting or drawing upon those concepts. In an earlier work (Thompson, 2000a) I referred to 'the fallacy of theoryless practice'. By this I meant the mistaken notion that we can act in a professional capacity without drawing on some sort of framework of understanding – in other words, a theory. This is a concept to which we will return at various points in the book, as it is unfortunately the case that the fallacy of theoryless practice is widespread.

Voice of experience 1.1

When I started doing my PQ [post-qualifying award], I knew I had to prepare a portfolio to show how I had consolidated my learning since qualifying. So I re-read some of my old textbooks to refresh my memory, and I was amazed to see how much of what I saw there was part and parcel of my day-to-day practice. I had not consciously been applying theory to practice, but it became quite clear to me that much of what I had learned previously had been influencing what I do without me even realizing it.

Linda, a social worker in a child care team

Why is theory important?

Probably the most important reason that theory should be recognized as important is that it shapes practice: knowing shapes thinking;

thinking shapes doing. Returning to the point made above about the invisibility of theory, we can see that so much of what we do draws directly or indirectly on theoretical concepts, so even if practitioners are not aware that what they are doing is reflecting a theoretical underpinning, it still remains the case that theory shapes practice. Consider the following examples:

- In working with people at various stages in the life course, especially children, practitioners will routinely draw on a knowledge of developmental psychology and even sociological aspects of development (Hunt, 2005).
- Work with families will generally take account of family dynamics, whether from a traditional family systems perspective (Burnham, 1986) or a more modern emphasis on narrative-based approaches (Vetere and Dowling, 2005).
- Professional interactions will generally be underpinned by a knowledge of communication theory – for example, in relation to observations skills, 'tuning in' to nonverbal communication and related matters (Moss, 2008; Thompson, 2003b).

This is not to say that the underpinning theoretical understandings will always be accurate or well developed, but to deny that they are there is to fall into the trap of the fallacy of theoryless practice. Even where the theoretical understandings cannot be directly articulated by a practitioner, they will still be there. That is, practitioners will be making assumptions about a range of factors (the nature and causes of human behaviour; how society works; the nature and causes of social problems; how best to communicate; how to recognize emotional reactions and so on) and basing those assumptions on concepts, wherever they have been derived from. Some sort of conceptual framework (and therefore theory) is therefore inevitable.

Theory is also important because it helps to build confidence – two types of confidence in particular. The first I shall refer to as 'subjective' confidence and, by this I mean the sense of self-belief that each individual has in him- or herself. There is also, alongside this, what I shall refer to as 'objective' confidence, and by this I mean the confidence that other people have in the individual practitioner, the faith and esteem that they attribute to that particular worker. A social worker who is able to show a good understanding of the professional knowledge base on which their work is built is much more likely to win the trust of fellow professionals, and indeed clients and carers, than somebody who appears to be basing their practice largely on guesswork, habit or simply following the lead of other people in an uncritical or unquestioning way. Achieving optimal standards of practice will depend on being able to rely on both these types of confidence, subjective and objective.

Theory is also important because it allows opportunities for challenge and critique. If practice is based on 'closed' forms of knowledge (that is, taken-for-granted assumptions that go unquestioned), then there is no facility to show up any false assumptions, misunderstandings or limited information on which the understanding (and therefore practice) are being based (S. Thompson and N. Thompson, 2008). By contrast, where somebody is openly using the theory base, the premises on which that theory operates are open to challenge and critique and therefore revision, growth and development over time. This is clearly a much better position to be in. It means that our approach to practice is based on openness and thus honesty and integrity.

Formal theory involves building up conceptual frameworks and making them explicit, so that they can be developed and/or challenged. Forte makes an important point when he argues that: 'Theoreticians are "structure producers" (Harre, 1978) and create a structure or "architectonic" (Rock, 1979, p. 2) for any approach to understanding human conduct' (2001, p. 25). There are therefore reasons why informal theory on its own is not a sufficient basis for practice.

Furthermore, it would be a mistake not to take account of the fact that the world in which we operate is constantly changing. Society is changing, the problems we face are changing, the legal context and related policy matters also continue to change, people's expectations of social welfare change, and so we have a significant context that is dynamic, rather than fixed and static. Theoretical understandings – particularly those based on dialectical reason – offer a much stronger basis from which to understand the significance of such movement and change and the inevitable conflicts that they bring (dialectical reason will be discussed in Chapter 2).

Linked to this is the importance of power. Where there are people there is power (Thompson, 2007a), and so we need to have a good understanding of how power operates if we are not to be in the position of reinforcing domination and the potentially oppressive workings of power. On the other side of the coin is the question of empowerment. If we are not attuned to issues of power and we do not have a good theoretical understanding of how they work, then we will be extremely ill-equipped to play a positive role in contributing to empowerment. Without a strong theoretical basis, there is a major danger that our actions will be based on dogma – that is, a fixed set of ideas that are being used uncritically without being open to scrutiny.

Practice focus 1.2

Patrick was struggling with the concept of empowerment in his work with older people. He was aware of the dangers of making people dependent by simply rationing services, and was keen to be genuinely helpful. However, he felt confused about how he could play a positive role in promoting empowerment. He therefore decided to raise the issue in supervision. He was fortunate to have a very knowledgeable and supportive team manager who explained that power is a very complex subject and, if we do not understand it, we will not be in a position to contribute to empowerment. She therefore suggested that Patrick should do some reading around power and empowerment and made some suggestions about suitable sources he could look at.

It would also be wise to recognize that, despite the importance of theory, there are often significant barriers to being able to draw on and learn from the theory base available to us. One of these is the use of 'academic code' in the literature. It is unfortunately the case that a tradition has developed in which so many authors feel the need to express theoretical understandings in forms of language that exclude people who are not members of that particular club. This is a common complaint from practitioners who feel alienated by forms of language that they struggle to grasp and which smack of elitism. It is important to recognize that different professional groups will develop different professional codes, and that there are often legitimate reasons for doing so – the use of 'academic' writing is therefore not a problem in itself, but it becomes problematic when such writing is taken to extremes. It is therefore the case that there can be significant problems in terms of linking theory to practice as a result of the use of unhelpful styles of language by a certain proportion of theoretical writers.

In addition to the use of academic style, there are also the obstacles presented by different writers using terms and concepts in different ways without clarifying precisely how they are using them or what they mean by them. Sunderland captures the point well when she comments that:

I am frequently aware not only in my reading of others' work, but also in my own writing and thinking, that a theoretical concept is often invoked, without making the particular concept clear – for example, the writer not saying how she and/or others understand it, or using it in different ways *without comment.*

(2004, pp. 167–8)

Similarly, Wittgenstein, the philosopher of language, argued that many deep philosophical issues are the result of the misuse of language and the confusion that this creates (Crossley, 1999). This aspect of the academic world can cause considerable difficulties in terms of (i) developing theory over time; and (ii) drawing on such theory in practice.

However, despite these problems, it is to be hoped that practitioners committed to promoting the highest standards of practice will be prepared to go through such linguistic barriers and make the effort to draw on the insights that are available from the theoretical literature. It would be very sad indeed if practice were to be impoverished by failing to address the knowledge to be gained from theory because of the limitations of communication evidenced by some theoretical writers. Similarly, it would be sad if the loose use of concepts without explanation that has become part and parcel of the culture of the academic world in many disciplines were to deter people from wrestling with the complexities that underpin our professional discipline.

Voice of experience 1.2

When I was a student I found so many of the books we were asked to read really difficult. It really knocked my confidence and made me feel that I must be too thick to be at university. Then, one day, we had a guest speaker on the course and he said that so much of the academic literature was badly written that we should not assume that, if we can't understand it, we are not very bright. If you struggle with what you read, he said, then that is probably telling you more about the way the book was written than it does about you. That made me feel so much better.

*Chris, a social worker in a team working with
asylum seekers*

A related barrier to the use of theory is that the academic world (in which theory generation generally occurs) tends to have a masculinist culture. That is, the way the work of the academic world is carried out is often quite 'macho' – very competitive and geared more towards winning or protecting 'territory' than to collaborating in developing a better understanding. This is evidenced by the common tendency for academics to attack each other's positions in their respective writings, rather than look for common ground. My view is that theory is too important to be left to theorists. As we shall see in Part Three, practitioners have a part to play in theory development. In addition, it should be noted that clients also have a part to play in developing our professional knowledge base, as their understandings are of course a crucial part of making sense of the practice situations we encounter (Beresford and Croft, 2001).

To sum up, then, there are clearly important reasons why we need to take theory seriously, why we should not fall into the trap of regarding theory as something separate from, or less important than, practice. Forte reinforces the point when he states that:

> A good theory points to a way of life. A good theory is socially relevant. A good theory is optimistic and affirms the possibility of social betterment. A good theory increases our political awareness. A good theory adds to our understanding of the particular obstacles that impede human development and undermine inclusive and participatory community life. A good theory contributes to the empowerment of all of society's members.
>
> (2001, p. 301)

These are important comments that I would fully endorse. However, they raise the question of what constitutes a 'good' theory. To explore this issue a little further, we shall turn our attention now to how theory can be less than good, how it can be seriously flawed and therefore unreliable as a provider of insights for practice.

Flawed theory

I mentioned above that theory is basically an attempt to ~
explanation. Some see theory as a means of findi~
a very problematic notion. The nin
Friedrich Nietzsche was very critical of
quest for truth (Wicks, 2002). He argued
such thing as Truth (with a capital T). Th
specific truths (with a lower-case t). This
well. Theory is not a matter of finding the 'a
itive Truth. It is more a case of looking for th

able at the time. This is not to say that one theory is just as good as another and that, in effect, it is all relative (Rorty, 1991). It is not the case that anything goes in terms of theoretical explanation. That would be a gross oversimplification of the reality of the situation.

While, at one extreme, there is no absolute truth or perfect theory, this does not justify going to the opposite extreme of saying that any theory is of equal worth when compared with another. Sibeon (2004) has produced a helpful categorization of what have come to be known as the 'cardinal sins' of theory. That is, he describes four ways in which theories can be flawed in some way. These can be summarized as follows:

- *Reductionism*. This refers to the way in which complex multi-level phenomena are treated as if they were simple, single-level issues. For example, discrimination can be seen to arise as a result of a combination of factors at different levels – for example, personal, cultural and structural (Thompson, 2003a; 2006a). However, many people see it as arising from a single source, such as personal prejudice or 'patriarchy' or 'imperialism'. Forms of reductionism that rely on psychological explanations without reference to wider cultural or sociopolitical factors are often referred to as examples of 'psychologism', while forms of reductionism that rely on sociological explanations without taking account of human actions tend to be referred to as 'sociologism'. In parallel fashion, biological reductionism is often referred to as 'biologism'. In order to avoid reductionism, we need to ensure that our theoretical explanations are multi-level – that is, they recognize the breadth of influences on human conduct and social processes.
- *Essentialism*. An essentialist explanation is one that presupposes an underlying 'essence' or unity. Psychological essentialism is premised on the assumption that individuals have a fixed personality and it is this that explains their behaviour: 'It is in my nature to be suspicious', rather than: 'A combination of my personal experiences and the social contexts in which I have lived makes me likely to be suspicious'. At a sociological level, the same type of (false) logic produces assumptions that 'men', 'women', 'black people' and other such social categories can be regarded as unified groups. For example, comments like 'white people are racist' are essentialist because they assume that white people can be regarded a homogeneous group in respect of racism (see also 'reification'). Such comments beg questions like: Does this mean that *all*

white people are racist? Or is it simply *most* white people or perhaps just *some* white people? And what, in this context, is meant by 'racist' anyway? Unfortunately, such essentialist views were not uncommon in the early days of anti-racist practice (see Chapter 8). Essentialism involves confusing explanation with 'explanandum' (explanandum means 'that which needs to be explained'). A claim that white people are racist is something that needs to be explained, and not an explanation in itself. Theories should therefore steer clear of essentialist assumptions by recognizing the fluid and interactive nature of both human experience in particular and the social world more broadly (see Chapter 2).

- *Reification.* To 'reify' means to treat as a thing (from the Latin word, 'res', a thing). A theory that relies on reification is one which makes the mistake of 'the illicit attribution of agency to entities that are not actors or agents' (Sibeon, 2004, p. 4). This means making the assumption that certain entities can make decisions or carry out actions in a purposive way. For example, comments like 'The working class are the driving force of history' assume that 'the working class' can speak with one voice or act in a unified way. While it would be legitimate to argue that 'the working class' *could* form a group that can collectively act and make decisions is a very different proposition from one which assumes that, without some process of group formation (as detailed in Sartre, 1982), the working class form a single entity capable of acting as one. Reification can combine with essentialism and reductionism, as when some people may claim that 'men' are responsible for sexism (rather than recognizing that sexism is a very complex phenomenon caused by the interaction of a range of forces and processes). The reality, as we shall see in Chapters 8 and 14, is far more complex than this reified conception would have us believe. To avoid reification we therefore need to make sure that we are clear about who can make decisions and engage in actions (be an 'actor' or 'agent' to use the social science terminology) – individuals, organized groups and organizations – and who cannot (categories or collectivities, such as 'men', 'women', 'children', 'black people' or 'Jews' or abstract entities like 'society').

- *Functional teleology.* This refers to the common process of assuming a purpose or intention where none exists. It involves confusing effects with intentions, purposes or even causes. For example, to say that the 'function' of social work is to prevent disadvantaged groups from rising up against an unjust social system is a gross oversimplification. To argue that social work *has the effect* of preventing such an uprising could possibly be a reasonable argument to put forward. However, to say that this is its *purpose* presupposes that there was a person or group who designed social work with this outcome in mind, and that is a much more difficult argument to justify. To avoid functional teleology, we therefore need to take care to differentiate between 'purposes' and 'effects'. This means avoiding using the term, 'purpose' too loosely.

There is also a fifth flaw that can be identified. Social work draws not only on sociology, but also (among other disciplines) psychology, and, due to the strongly individualistic emphasis in psychology, there is a danger that we fall into the trap of 'atomism'. This refers to the flaw of regarding individuals as isolated units, separate from society and not as part of a broader social whole. This is a common criticism of psychology. It reflects what Sibeon would refer to as 'methodological individualism'. Unfortunately, atomism has not been a rare occurrence in social work theorizing over the decades, and so this is a point to which we shall return from time to time throughout the book. An atomistic perspective is one that adopts a blinkered approach, seeing only the individual and taking little or no account of the very powerful influences of the wider social context. To avoid this we therefore need to make sure that we adopt a holistic perspective, seeking an overview of the situation that incorporates sociological considerations as well as psychological ones.

A sixth flaw identified in Sibeon's work is that of determinism. This describes the mistake of omitting 'agency' from our considerations. 'Agency' is the technical term for the capacity to act, to make decisions. It is the basis of human freedom. We are not puppets who are simply pulled in one direction or another. We make choices and perform actions, individually or collectively, that make a difference to our lives and to the people and social circumstances around us. Theoretical perspectives that paint a picture that does not include human beings as active participants in social life fail to do justice to the complexities involved. As such, they can be highly misleading and far from adequate as a basis for understanding.

Not so much a flaw in theory *per se*, but more in the use of theory is the tendency for theoretical perspectives to become a form of club. By this I mean that many people form an allegiance to a particular theoretical perspective and then bring down the shutters in terms of not being able to see other aspects of a situation. For example, somebody who is committed to a cognitive behavioural approach to practice may fail to become aware of significant factors in a situation that do not fit comfortably in a cognitive behavioural framework. This notion of the danger of a theory becoming a club is a topic to which we shall return in Chapter 3, but for now it should be noted that this can be a significant impediment to the effective use of theory when people adopt blinkers and see things from one theoretical perspective without being prepared to take on board that competing perspectives may also have valuable insights to offer in terms of developing our understanding. This 'club mentality' is, in effect, an example of reductionism as discussed above – reflecting a tendency to see just one side of the situation, rather than try to develop a more holistic approach that sees the overall picture.

The point was made earlier that practice is more usefully based on open, explicit theory, rather than the closed thinking of dogma. This is another way in which theory can be flawed where, in effect, what is presented as theory is basically dogma. In a later chapter, we shall be discussing the significance of discourse and ideology. Dogma is more closely associated with ideology than theory. No theory is perfect, and so we need to keep an open mind about the theoretical ideas we base our practice on. Being able to evaluate theory by reference to the flaws identified here can help us to do that. An understanding of the potential flaws in theoretical work helps us to keep our theorizing open and honest by steering clear of a dogmatic, uncritical acceptance of a particular theoretical perspective.

Integrating theory and practice

For decades, educators in social work have talked and written about 'applying theory to practice'. I prefer the terminology of *integrating* theory and practice. This is because, to my mind, the notion of 'applying' theory indicates a one-way approach. That is, while practice may have the questions, theory is likely to have the answers. In reality, it is better to see the relationship between theory and practice as a two-way street, in the sense that theory should inform practice, but practice should also inform and test theory. In this way, we can avoid the dangers of putting either of them on a pedestal. For example, some people are overly respectful of theory and assume that, because something appears in a textbook, it must necessarily be true (they are therefore adopting too uncritical an approach). On the other hand, as mentioned earlier, some people too readily reject theory and prefer to put practice on a pedestal as the more important side of the theory–practice equation. But, as Langan and Lee (1989) argued some time ago, theory without practice is useless and practice without theory is dangerous. What we have in effect, is a dialectical relationship between theory and practice. That is, our thinking shapes our practice and our practice shapes our thinking. The two enter into a relationship of mutual influence.

Integrating theory and practice is therefore what we need to aim for. It involves drawing on a wide range of theoretical understandings. Some people would use the term 'eclecticism' to refer to this. However, in my experience, the term 'eclecticism' is often used as a catch-all to refer to an uncritical approach to theory that just takes often unconnected concepts and muddles them together. What I am proposing is a much more sophisticated approach in line with critically reflective practice (S. Thompson and N. Thompson, 2008). This involves drawing on theoretical insights from a wide range of sources, but having the ability to integrate them into a meaningful whole that makes sense in relation to the particular practice scenario. This reflects the aspect of reflective practice epitomized by the notion of the reflective practitioner being a tailor cutting the cloth of the knowledge base to produce a closely tailored solution to the practice challenges being faced, rather than looking for a ready-made, off-the-peg solution.

Sibeon (2004) writes of 'intellectual diversity', by which he means the process of drawing on a wide range of perspectives, rather than being wedded to one particular school of thought (or theoretical 'club'). His comments are instructive:

> A reason for accommodating intellectual diversity is that, as well as ethical and political issues to do with freedom of academic expression, recognition of the legitimacy of theoretical pluralism is an appropriate way of acknowledging the probable inevitability of intellectual uncertainties and complex ambiguities surrounding both the contents of social theory and the relation of observers and social investigators to the social world (Alexander, 1987).
>
> (Sibeon, 2004, pp. 26–7)

What is significant here is the recognition that it is legitimate to draw on a range of theoretical insights – provided that they do not contradict one another. Joining one theoretical club to the exclusion of all other sources of understanding is therefore not the only option.

```
┌─────────────────────────────────────────────────────────────┐
│  ███ Practice focus 1.3 ███                                   │
│                                                               │
│  Gill was a student on placement in a youth offending team.   │
│  She was delighted when she found out that her practice       │
│  teacher was a keen family therapist, as she had become       │
│  quite interested in family dynamics after discussing it at   │
│  university. As the placement wore on she learned more and     │
│  more about how useful family therapy could be. She was        │
│  really pleased about this. However, as the placement was      │
│  coming to an end, she started to realize how narrow her       │
│  learning experience had been. In talking to fellow students   │
│  about their placements she could see that they had been       │
│  learning about a much wider range of perspectives. This       │
│  made her decide that she should try to ensure that her next   │
│  placement exposed her to a much wider range of theoretical    │
│  ideas and was not limited to just one school of thought.      │
└─────────────────────────────────────────────────────────────┘
```

In the Introduction to this book, the point was made that the approach adopted is one of starting with practice and therefore lived experience, and using theoretical insights to develop an understanding of it, rather than the traditional technical rationality approach of trying to take a theory and apply it to practice. What should be happening in critically reflective practice is that we look carefully at the situation and seek to illuminate it by drawing on relevant parts of the professional knowledge base and integrating these into a meaningful whole that is applicable to the current practice scenario. This is a highly skilled job, and one that takes experience over time, but that is the challenge of theorizing practice.

Reflective practice can be seen as parallel with the concept of pragmatics used in linguistics. Grammar is the study of how parts of language relate to one another and produce recognizable sentences or 'utterances'. Semantics is the study of how meanings are formed through grammar. Pragmatics is the study of how language is used in practice – how speakers (and writers) translate their knowledge of grammar and semantics into actual language use (Huang, 2007). The study of reflective practice is concerned with identifying how practitioners put their professional knowledge base (their equivalent of grammar and semantics) into action – actual social work practice. Grammar and semantics change over time, reflecting changes in language use. Similarly, social work theory changes over time in part in response to changes in practice. This, in effect, is what integrating theory and practice is all about – seeing how knowledge informs practice and how practice changes and develops that knowledge base over time.

Tools, models or frameworks can be very useful ways of linking theory and practice (Doel and Shardlow, 2005; Thompson, 2006b; S. Thompson and N. Thompson, 2008). However, it is wise to note that the use of tools is not a substitute for theory, nor is it a replacement for critical analysis. If we are to use frameworks and models as practice tools, then we need to understand the theoretical premises on which they are based and be able to use them critically. There is a direct parallel here with the use of tools in a practical sense. The tools will not do the job; the person using the tools still has to have an understanding of their purpose and the craft skills to be able to use such tools effectively and appropriately.

Voice of experience 1.3

I always struggled with the idea of linking theory to practice. It didn't bother me unduly, but I did have a feeling sometimes that I could perhaps do better in my job if I had a better grasp of theory and how to use it in practice. However, when my colleague, Priya, joined the team I was delighted to see how she used various tools like transactional analysis and ecomaps to make sense of complex situations. She taught me that frameworks like this are a really useful bridge between theory and practice.

Mal, a social worker in a multidisciplinary learning disability team

The work of Pietroni (1995, p. 129) captures some important aspects of reflective practice when he argues that the reflective practitioner:

- recognizes that professional knowledge is imperfect and can always be improved;
- realizes that technical expertise is necessary but that there are no formulaic answers to complex questions – Schön's 'indeterminate zones of practice';
- operates within an integrated personal/professional/political value-base which uses an analysis of power relations and commitment to anti-oppressive practice, that seeks to understand and change the social and political context affecting practice;
- 'builds in a cycle of critical reflection to maximize the capacity for critical thought, and a connection with rather than a distance from clients' (Pietroni, 1995, p. 43).

The passage above from Pietroni serves my current purpose well, in so far as it puts down a strong foundation for *theorizing* practice – drawing critically on an incomplete knowledge base in order to ensure that our practice is as well informed as it can be in the circumstances.

Conclusion

Having clarified some key issues about the nature and importance of theory and how theory can be flawed, we were able to discuss the significance of integrating theory and practice and link this to the fundamental concept of critically reflective practice.

Now we have established some key concepts and premises in this discussion, we are ready to move on and deepen and broaden our understanding of theory as a basis for practice. In the next chapter we turn our attention to how new forms of theory have challenged traditional approaches in recent years. From this we will be able to see how we can safely disregard much of the 'new wave' of postmodernist theorizing (given, as we shall see, that many of its concepts are not new and therefore not specifically 'postmodern'), while benefiting from some of its insights and also retaining some useful concepts from the traditional theory base that it has sought to displace.

Points to ponder

1. What ideas did the term 'theory' bring to mind for you before reading this chapter? Has your view changed now?
2. In what ways might theory be useful for practice?
3. What might prevent you from drawing on theory in practice? What can you do about this?

Further reading

For general texts about social work theory, see Beckett (2006); Forte (2001); Healy (2000); Payne (2005a); Thompson (2000a); N. Thompson and S. Thompson (2008). Sibeon (2004), although not specifically about social work, is also none the less an important text.

In relation to reflective practice, the following are helpful: Fook and Gardner (2007); Schön (1983); S. Thompson and N. Thompson (2008); and White, Fook and Gardner (2006).

2

Theory and postmodernism

Introduction

This chapter explores the significance of postmodernist thought for contemporary social work theory. As will become apparent in the pages that follow, I am not advocating postmodernism as a basis for social work practice. Some readers may wonder why, if I am not proposing postmodernism as a theoretical foundation for practice, I am devoting a whole chapter to it. The reason is that postmodernism and the related concept of post-structuralism have become very influential in recent years. My aim is to add my voice to the growing list of critics of this approach to social understanding and to pave the way for presenting an alternative in later chapters (especially Chapters 8 and 11) premised on existentialist thought.

Contemporary social thought has been overtaken by a wave of postmodernist thinking. It has been argued that postmodernism is now having a major influence across the social sciences. As Callinicos puts it: 'For better or worse, we live in an era where postmodernism has come to set the terms of intellectual and cultural debate' (2007, p. 2). This chapter explores the rise of postmodernist thinking, draws out some points about why it is seen to be so attractive, but also highlights some major flaws in postmodernist thinking. My basic argument is twofold:

1. While there are elements of postmodernism that are worth engaging with, the overall perspective is one that is highly problematic due to flaws in some of its basic premises.
2. I shall also be pointing out that, to retain the positives of postmodernism, it is not necessary to make a commitment to a postmodernist perspective, as so many of the useful ideas associated with postmodernism have long since existed in other schools of thought,

especially existentialism. Consider, for example, the comment by Walter and McCoyd about 'the postmodern understanding that there are many truths, each created within the context of that individual's social and historical milieu' (2009, p. 14). There is nothing specifically postmodern about this notion. It is to be found in the work of Nietzsche writing in the nineteenth century and existentialists (Frankl, 1984) and phenomenologists (Gadamer, 2004) in the twentieth century, as well as many other writers.

However, before considering postmodernism in any detail, it is wise to consider what led up to it in terms of the critique of positivistic thinking being a major factor (albeit not the only one) in driving this theoretical perspective forward, and so it is with this topic that the chapter begins.

The rejection of positivism

The term 'positivism' is used to refer to approaches to science which argue that it is possible to establish objective truths, hard facts that do not depend on any element of subjective interpretation. In the social sciences, positivism is seen as an attempt to apply the principles of the natural sciences to society to discover the 'laws of society' parallel with the idea of the 'laws of nature' with which the natural sciences are concerned. While there are still many people who adhere to this model of social science, it has been heavily criticized. This is because people and society (and the subtle, multi-layered interactions between the two) are far too complex and changeable to be pinned down to relatively simple 'laws of society'. The natural sciences are concerned with being able to identify the causes of particular events in the physical world. In the social sciences, what we are concerned with is reasons and meanings, rather than causes. As Taylor puts it, in discussing the work of the philosopher Gadamer:

> But bracketing out human meanings from human science means understanding nothing at all; it would mean betting on a science that bypassed understanding altogether, and tried to grasp its domain in neutral terms, in the language of neurophysiology, for instance.
>
> (2002, p. 132)

A key term here is that of 'agency' (Archer, 2000). This refers to the fact that human beings are 'agents', in the sense that we make decisions and engage in courses of action – we are not simply puppets carried along by external forces. This is not to say that a person's agency (that is, their capacity to act and make decisions) is unconstrained, as clearly wider social and political factors construct major limitations to what we can do and how we can do it (we shall discuss these issues in more detail in Chapter 8), but it is important not to go to the other extreme and ignore the fact that individuals have choices – for example, in terms of whether they go along with social influences (their culture, for instance) or reject them.

Nature is a set of impersonal forces. Human existence is a mixture of impersonal (natural, psychological, social and political) forces *and* the decisions and action active human agents (that is, people) carry out in response to those forces. Because our 'response' is so important in this equation, then, how we *interpret* the situation is a central factor. It is for this reason that the social sciences need to concern themselves with meanings and reasons, rather than simply with 'causes'. Positivism would have us look for causes and therefore grossly oversimplifies what human experience is like. Social science can only ever deal in probabilities, and so the idea of finding absolute truth or objective fact separate from subjective interpretation is something that can be highly problematic. Adopting a positivistic approach to human affairs can be seen as an attempt to look for certainties that are not there, a failure to recognize that human reality is characterized by a mixture of risk and insecurity on the one hand, and relatively predictable (but never entirely so) patterns of behaviour on the other.

Also implicit in the notion of positivism is that, through the establishment of objective scientific truths, society can progress; it can move forward based less on superstition and irrational beliefs and more on hard evidence and rational scientific understandings. Postmodernism takes issue with this set of assumptions and, as we shall see below, the rejection of this notion of science-based progress is a central plank of postmodernist thought.

Early sociology was very positivistic, and writers such as Comte were concerned with finding scientific ways of understanding society along the lines of the natural sciences (Gane, 2006). Much psychology continues to be of a positivistic nature even today, but in both disciplines there is increasing emphasis on meaning and narrative – trying to understand human experience by reference to the 'stories' we use to shape our lives and make them meaningful – see Chapter 13. In this way, both sociology and psychology are moving more in a direction consistent with existentialism and its phenomenological roots, which emphasizes the significance of understandings and perceptions rather than absolute truths (phenomenology can be defined as the study of perception, and is therefore concerned with issues to do with interpretation and meaning making – it is a concept that we will draw upon in later chapters).

Practice focus 2.1

Bill had a degree in physics, but decided not to pursue a career in that subject as he wanted to work more with people. He therefore registered for a degree in social work. At first he found the studying very difficult. He was used to reading about natural science phenomena and having fairly clear-cut factual information to draw upon. He found the social science materials he was reading very difficult to adjust to at first. He complained to his tutor that he found it all very 'wishy-washy' and all just a matter of opinion, with no real science underpinning it. However, with the support of his tutor and the other members of the teaching team, over time he began to appreciate that social science is different from natural science, and has to be because people are conscious 'agents' and therefore a lot more difficult to pin down than physical forces which are much more predictable and therefore easier to deal with. He still longed for the relative certainty of physics, but realized that the new challenge of learning he faced was a necessary one if he was going to be able to cope with the complexities of social work.

In this context, this notion of truth is particularly important. We return to Nietzsche's concept of the rejection of Truth. Nietzsche is one of the most influential thinkers in western thought. His ideas were very influential, not only in relation to postmodernism and post-structuralism, but also in relation to existentialism and Freudian psychoanalysis – a very diverse range of theoretical perspectives. In his writings he was at pains to point out that it makes no sense to think in terms of one overall, overarching truth, only smaller truths specific to particular sets of circumstances. This is something that has particularly influenced postmodernist thinking, a topic to which we shall return below. His argument was that everything needs to be seen from a particular perspective (his approach came to be known as 'perspectivism' for this reason) and, as there is no one who can see reality without doing so from a particular perspective or point of view, there cannot be a purely 'objective' reality. Gadamer (2004) adopted a similar perspective in his writings in using Nietzsche's term 'horizons', by which he meant that each of us sees the world from our own perspective – we each have our own 'horizon' or point of view. This is not to say that there is no objectivity at all, as Nietzsche would see a complete reliance on subjectivity as equally flawed. We shall return to these complex issues in Chapter 11 when we discuss existentialism, a philosophical approach that occupies similar territory.

Rorty introduces the very useful concept of 'redemptive truth', which he defines as 'a set of beliefs which would end, once and for all, the process of reflection on what to do with ourselves' (2007, p. 90). He goes on to make the important point that:

> Redemptive truth, if it existed, would not be exhausted by theories about how things interact causally. It would have to fulfil a need that religion and philosophy have attempted to satisfy. That is the need to fit everything – every thing, every person, event, idea and poem – into a single context, a context that will somehow reveal itself as natural, destined and unique. It would be the only context that would matter for purposes of shaping our lives because it would be the only one in which those lives appear as they truly are. To believe in redemptive truth is to believe that there is something that stands to human life as elementary physical particles stand to the four elements – something that is the reality behind the appearance, the one true description of what is going on.
>
> (Rorty, 2007, p. 90)

As we shall see, this is not the sort of 'truth' that social work can realistically be based on. A more critical perspective on what is meant by truth is called for.

What the critique of positivism teaches us is that there is a place for *science* in social work where this is social science based on probabilities and attuned to the nature of human experience, but there is no place for *scientism* (or positivism), with its rigid limitations and false notion of progress towards absolute ideals and redemptive truth.

Up to this point I would be happy to endorse postmodernism, as I too would be unwilling to accept a positivist approach to understanding human experience. However, postmodernism goes far beyond this basic rejection of positivism and, in my view, goes too far in the opposite direction, in effect taking us from too *objective* an extreme to another unhelpful extreme, this time to one that is too *subjective*.

The Siren call of postmodernism

In ancient Greek mythology, the Sirens were temptresses who, through their beautiful and mysterious singing, attracted sailors towards them, with the result that their ships were sunk on the rocks nearby. I am therefore using the term 'Siren call' to refer to the fact that postmodernism has certain attractive features, but I shall be arguing below that these are ultimately unacceptable (Noble, 2004). In effect, the metaphor is based on the idea that the appeal of post-modernism amounts to a form of seduction that can be disastrous in its consequences, just as the Siren call was for those who paid heed to it. First, let us look at the attractions of postmodernism. Let us consider what makes it seductive, before considering its weaknesses and the reasons why, ultimately, I believe it should be rejected as a theoretical underpinning for social work.

Consistent with what I was arguing above, postmodernism rejects the scientistic notion of progress. It is highly critical of the Enlightenment idea that science would bring more and more progress over time, that society would get better because of the increasing reliance on rationality in general and science in particular. This led to an approach known as anti-foundationalism. This is similar to the point made earlier about Nietzsche's rejection of absolute Truth. According to anti-foundationalism, there are no absolute foundations of knowledge of society or of reality. This is very similar to the notion of 'social constructionism' – the idea that our sense of reality owes much to how it is presented to us through social conventions and processes (Berger and Luckmann, 1967; Burr, 2003). That is, reality is not simply laid out in front of us for all to see directly, uninfluenced by social and cultural forces. Our sense of reality is shaped ('constructed') by a range of social processes, such as the operation of the media, the use of power and ideology and so on. There is, then, no ultimate, absolute reality unmediated by the workings of society. There is no ultimate 'foundation', hence the term 'anti-foundationalism'. A commitment to anti-foundationalism, then, involves a rejection of the idea that scientific or theoretical inquiry can uncover ultimate truths.

One of the significant consequences of adopting an anti-founda-tionalist understanding of social reality is that there can be no ulti-mate reality or sense of absolute Truth. It is for this reason that the postmodernist adoption of anti-foundationalism stands in opposition to positivism. However, there is a very real danger that, in postmod-ernist hands, anti-foundationalism throws out the baby with the bathwater by going too far in the direction of rejecting the foundations of knowledge on which the social sciences are built.

Voice of experience 2.1

To begin with I found postmodernist thinking quite attractive and a breath of fresh air compared with some of the very stuffy traditional theories I had come across. But it wasn't long before I started to feel uncomfortable with it and felt it went too far. I don't want theories that are set in stone, but I don't want them built on sand either. There must be a happy medium somewhere between the two.

Anita, a development worker with foster carers

Another key feature of postmodernism is what has been labelled 'incredulity towards meta-narratives' (Lyotard, 1968). This refers to the rejection of the idea of overarching theories and the notion that there can be 'grand theories' which offer a broad understanding of society, humanity or whatever the object of study is. Examples of such metanarratives would be marxism and Freudian psychoanalysis. Postmodernists argue that such approaches create a view of the world that excludes other insights. This is similar to my use of the term theoretical 'club' in Chapter 1.

In place of metanarratives, there is an emphasis on fragmentation and 'local narratives'. That is, instead of trying to explain things in terms of one grand overview, it is necessary to limit ourselves to looking at specific issues in finer detail, to have more of a micro-level focus than a macro one. There is some benefit in this approach but, as we shall see below, there are also costs, in so far as it oversimplifies some complex issues in terms of levels of theory and their validity as explanatory frameworks.

In terms of costs, one of the most significant, as far as I am concerned, is that postmodernism rejects the validity of attempts to bring about emancipation, to bring about a society based on social justice, rather than discrimination and oppression. Postmodernists would argue that it is idealistic and unrealistic to be able to think of being able to change society on a large enough scale to bring about emancipation from social disadvantages and injustices. Again, I recognize a kernel of truth and value within this, but also some major difficulties. However, this is a key part of what makes postmodernism attractive to some people – the fact that it frees them from a commitment to large-scale social change. To some people this makes it a more realistic and manageable theoretical perspective and calls for less of a personal, professional or political commitment to social justice and social change.

Practice focus 2.2

Kaldip had been qualified for three years when she decided the time was right for her to do some more studying. She therefore registered for a part-time Master's degree in advanced social work at her local university. One of the modules was on social work theory and, as part of it, she was introduced to the idea of postmodernism. While most of the students found it quite interesting (albeit difficult and challenging), Kaldip did not feel comfortable with it at all. She had been actively involved in feminist and anti-racist initiatives, both in her professional role and her private life. She struggled to see how postmodernist analyses could provide a foundation for her work when it lacked a fundamental commitment to the idea of emancipation and significant social change. She was aware that there were postmodernist feminist texts in particular, but could not see how these could be reconciled with a rejection of the idea of emancipation. She found the whole thing quite confusing.

One further feature of postmodernism worthy of mention at this point is the idea that society is fundamentally unstable, that we need to understand it in terms of flux and instability, rather than enduring structures and institutions. Postmodernism, under the influence of post-structuralist thinking, is therefore critical of any theoretical perspectives that incorporate the notion of enduring structures – whether social structures of power or (cultural) structures of meaning. Postmodernism, unlike existentialism, fails to recognize that flux and enduring structures are *both* aspects of social life, aspects that inter-act dialectically, rather than competing concepts to choose between. This failure, as we shall see, is a serious problem when it comes to making sense of the complexities of the social world in general and the social work world in particular.

The rocks of postmodernism

Here I am returning to the analogy of the Siren call. My argument is that, in many ways, postmodernism is seriously flawed. It has been criticized for being, in effect, new wine in old bottles and for offering a far from defensible theoretical approach. For example, Sibeon's (2004) criticisms have been quite telling, as have those of Clarke (2000):

> postmodernist claims about flux and fluidity tend to conflate different levels of analysis. It may be true that abstractly, everything is contingent, polyvalent, contestable and changeable. In concrete situations, however, social arrangements have differing densities, proving more or less resistant to change. They are also more or less contested: some pass themselves off as natural features of the social world for generations. Similarly, everything may have different potential meanings, but this is empirically only significant in the process of contestation: the struggle to articulate alternatives to the dominant, established and heavily sedimented meanings.
>
> (2000b, p. 6)

In other words, although postmodernism is right to highlight the fluidity of social reality and thereby be critical of many of aspects of traditional social thought which emphasize fixity, it is not helpful to lose sight of the fact that much about human experience does have a strong degree of stability, predictability and structure. Although Clarke is not writing from an explicitly existentialist position, his approach is entirely consistent with the existentialist outlook I shall be developing in later chapters. Existentialism recognizes flux and fluidity as central features of human existence, but also takes account of the fact that this 'flow' of experience takes place within the parameters of fairly stable cultural and structural patterns, processes and institutions. From an existentialist point of view, everything is changing, but the key to understanding this is the notion of the *pace* of change. Cultural and structural formations are *relatively* stable because, while they are certainly changing, they are doing so quite slowly when compared with, for example, the pace of change individuals often encounter in their lives, especially at critical times (for example, adolescence or giving up one's home to become a resident in a care home for older people – see N. Thompson and S. Thompson, 2008, for a discussion of crisis theory). To say that everything is characterized by change is therefore not to say that there is no stability or no enduring structures.

Voice of experience 2.2

It was something I found quite confusing at first, this thing about continuity and change. Things are changing all the time and yet so much stays the same. But that's what social work is like. Social work has changed a lot since I first came into it 12 years ago, yet so much of it is just the same too. But then that's just a reflection of life, isn't it?

Gill, team manager in an older people team

Sibeon's criticisms are equally strong if not more so:

postmodern thought lacks an adequate theory of agency and of the actor or agent, and subscribes to a flawed conception of agency-structure ... Postmodern theorists have a tendency to employ deterministic conceptions of the actor, conceptions that ... are curiously reminiscent of the social determinism and reification associated with reductionist modernist paradigms such as Marxism, radical feminism, and Parsonian structural-functionalism.

(2004, p. 18)

His view echoes the approach I am adopting here, especially when he argues that: 'while aspects of postmodern thought are a source of potentially useful analytical precepts, the postmodern genre as a whole is seriously flawed' (p. 21).

It has been pointed out by many writers that there is an inherent contradiction in postmodernism, as the very idea of postmodernism is itself a metanarrative, in the sense of a theoretical club or camp, an overview for understanding rather than a specific, substantive theory. I would want to go a step further and argue that the notion of postmodernity (as the new era that we have allegedly entered or are in the process of entering) is also, in itself, a metanarrative. The idea that the highly complex, multi-level realities of a particular historical period can be characterized by one simple notion is, to my mind, wholly simplistic and a distortion of the subtle and intricate realities involved. It could be argued that this is an example of reification, as used in Sibeon's (2004) important work referred to in Chapter 1.

Other critics of postmodernism include Callinicos (2007); Ferguson (2006); Ferguson, Lavalette and Mooney (2002); Ife (1999); Midgely (1999); O'Neill (1995); Powell (2001); and Sardar (1998). One critic who focuses specifically on social work in this regard is Noble, who makes the important point that:

Social work needs to wake up from the enticing, almost mesmerizing, effect of postmodern discourse and take another look at the way economic, gender and colonial issues continue to lie at the root of injustice and impoverishment. Focusing on the local and the contextuality of the specific takes attention away from the continuance of the pervasive power of structural forces. Anti-racism, and the new social movements for gay and lesbian rights, disability equality, and ecological sustainability, dramatically draw attention to the ongoing oppressive and exploitative nature of capital and patriarchal ideologies. Postmodern social work, if unchecked, has the potential to further undermine these more progressive movements in contemporary societies.

(2004, p. 302)

Postmodernism can also be criticized for offering an easy means of rejecting competing ideas. Ideas that do not fit with the postmodernist view of the world are often simply labelled as 'modernist' and therefore seen as inherently valueless. For example, Hollinger (1994) rejects existentialism as 'modernist' without providing any argument or evidence whatsoever, even though, as Howells (1992a) has pointed out, many of the key ideas of postmodernism (especially the valuable ones) were apparent in existentialist thought long before postmodernism came along as a theoretical bandwagon to be jumped on. For example, the postmodernist emphasis on flux and the variability of human experience has been known in existentialist thought for decades as 'the contingency of being'.

Practice focus 2.3

Natalie was a senior social worker at a hospice. Before becoming a social worker she had trained as a counsellor and had been particularly interested in the existentialist school of counselling and psychotherapy. She had been surprised when she trained as a social worker to find that existentialist ideas were not equally influential there too. When she was joined in her team by a social worker who was interested in postmodernism, she had some interesting discussions with her. However, the more she learned about the subject, the more parallels she could see with existentialism, although she also recognized that there were some significant differences. It reminded her of how stimulating she had found discussing theoretical ideas when she was a student.

There is therefore a built-in protection that makes postmodernism, at one level, invulnerable to attack. Anything that is out of line with postmodernist thinking can simply be rejected as 'modernist'. There is a parallel here with cruder, less theoretically sophisticated versions of marxism which dismiss opposing ideas as 'bourgeois' or as examples of 'false consciousness', or more dogmatic approaches to psychoanalysis which dispose of competing perspectives as mere examples of 'unconscious resistance'.

An example of this in action is the way in which the criticism that the whole idea of postmodernism being flawed and incoherent is fended off by postmodernists decrying 'coherence' as a modernist idea and thereby rejecting its value (we shall discuss this point in more detail in Chapter 11). In this way, postmodernism seeks to avoid criticism by moving the goalposts.

Another major problem with postmodernism is that it shows no respect for the history of ideas. It presents often long-standing ideas as if they were new. There is a great irony here, in so far as what commonly happens in postmodernist thinking is that some old, well-established ideas are revamped and yet, at the same time, ironically other ideas are simply rejected as modernist. The use of repackaged existentialist concepts, as mentioned above, is an example of this.

Given this school of thought's rejection of emancipation as a viable goal to pursue, this form of postmodernist thinking can be seen as an obstacle to progressive practice. How can social work make a contribution to promoting social justice, for example, if, according to postmodernism, that is an unrealistic goal? In terms of postmodernism as a basis for social work practice, Cunningham and Tomlinson make an important point when they argue that:

> Suffice it to say that a metanarrative (for of course, as several critics have noted, postmodernism is itself a metanarrative) which refuses to 'privilege' any discourse over any other scarcely provides a firm foundation for a critical social policy. As Crook has noted:
>
> > When radical social theory loses its accountability, when it can no longer give reasons, something has gone very wrong. But this is precisely what happens to postmodern social theory, and it seems very appropriate to use the over-stretched term 'nihilism' as a label for this degeneration. The nihilism of postmodernism shows itself in two symptoms: an inability to specify mechanisms of change, and an inability to state why change is better than no change.
>
> (1990: 59)

It would be ironic indeed if social policy as an academic discipline, having finally shaken off the phoney neutrality of the tradition of empiricist social administration, should now opt for the even more pernicious 'ironic detachment' of postmodernism.

(2006, p. 170)

There are 'weaker' (or more moderate) forms of postmodernism that have developed which can be seen to move in a helpful direction. Healy's comments on this point are helpful. She argues that: 'Postmodernists reject visions of massive social transition as a chimera and demand, instead, greater caution and constraint in the formation of critical practice objectives and processes' (2000, p. 2). This is an example of the weaker form of postmodernism which can be seen to differ from the stronger version by virtue of the fact that the latter rejects not only large-scale social change, but also the whole idea of emancipation. However, I would want to argue that the weak version is also problematic.

Pease and Fook, in the introduction to a book on transforming social work practice, argue that:

we side with those expressions of postmodern thinking that do not totally abandon the values of modernity and the Enlightenment project of human emancipation. Only 'strong' or 'extreme' forms of postmodernism theory reject normative criticism and the usefulness of any forms of commonality underlying diversity. We believe that a 'weak' form of postmodernism informed by critical theory can contribute effectively to the construction of an emancipatory politics concerned with political action and social justice.

(1999a, p. 12)

While I welcome the authors' attempts to move away from the difficulties that postmodernist thinking presents and their commitment to emancipatory practice, I feel it is necessary to develop an alternative perspective, rather than 'water down' the excesses of the stronger forms of postmodernism. My view is premised on the recognition that the very basis on which postmodernism rests is fatally flawed — regardless of whether we are considering strong or weak versions. Some of the key elements of postmodernist thought can be summarized, and critiqued, as follows.

Rejection of the notion of social progress through rationalism

The weak version claims that social progress is possible, but on a smaller, less ambitious scale. However, this contradicts the postmodernist idea that one perspective cannot be better (more 'privileged') than another. How do we define progress if one perspective cannot be seen as being preferable to another? The key term here is 'ironic detachment' (as mentioned in the quotation above from Cunningham and Tomlinson – the key postmodernist notion of remaining detached or 'uninvolved'. The key issue here is the philosophical notion of 'relativism'. Space does not permit a discussion here that would do justice to the complexities involved. Interested readers are therefore advised to consult Rorty (1989) for an interesting exploration of the debate.

Sibeon is critical of postmodernism for, in effect, creating a cul de sac. The logic of postmodern thought brings us to a dead end:

> In place of empirical enquiry involving explicit theoretical criteria and rules of methodological procedure, postmodernists prefer 'pastiche', 'irony', 'parody', theoretical 'mischief', deconstructive 'playfulness', and the like (Featherstone, 1988). Impulses of this kind represent, in my opinion, a somewhat whimsical aestheticism that enjoyed its heyday at the height of the postmodern turn during the late 1980s and early 1990s; they are not impulses that have any useful part to play in the contemporary reconstruction of sociological theory 'after postmodernism'.
>
> (Sibeon, 2004, pp. 21–2)

I would also want to add that such impulses have no useful part to play in tackling social problems and helping to empower people facing major personal and social challenges in their life. In other words, they are not appropriate premises on which to build a theoretical basis for social work practice. Developing weaker forms of this approach that none the less retain these elements would not help, and to remove them altogether takes away some of the defining features of postmodernism, so what would be left could not then accurately be called 'postmodernist'.

Rejection of metanarratives

Sibeon (2004) accepts the value of rejecting 'grand theories' and the theoretical flaws on which they are premised (reductionism, essentialism and reification, in particular). However, he argues that postmodernists take this too far by also rejecting any overall theoretical approach (what Sibeon calls a 'metatheory'). Also called 'sensitizing' or 'nomothetic' theory, metatheory is concerned not with the specifics of theoretical explanation, but rather with the philosophical underpinnings of the particular theoretical investigation in question (we shall discuss this further in Chapter 11).

It can be argued that rejecting metatheory as a 'metanarrative' once again leads us into a dead end. All theoretical inquiry requires an underpinning metatheory or set of philosophical assumptions about the nature of reality (ontology), the nature of knowledge (epistemology), and the appropriateness or otherwise of the methods of inquiry used (methodology). Even a weaker version of postmodernism would struggle to achieve theoretical coherence without some degree of clarity about these issues (but see the discussion of coherence below).

An emphasis on 'indeterminacy'

As noted earlier, this aspect of postmodernist thought provides a further example of its extreme nature. While I would agree that change, flux and indeterminacy are characteristic of human reality (as acknowledged in the existentialist concept of the 'contingency of being'), there are dangers in failing to acknowledge the other side of the coin – the relative stability of enduring structures and institutionalized patterns. Individual lives and society more broadly are indeed characterized by 'indeterminacy', by a lack of certainty and stability. However, they are also characterized by a high degree of probability and well-established patterns of interaction and behaviour. Language is a good example of this. It is constantly changing. New items of vocabulary and new linguistic forms emerge and old ones die out. However, language could not work as a basis of communication if it did not have, alongside that 'flux' and variability, a degree of predictability and stability.

Any postmodernist theory, whether weak or strong, that continues to focus on the change and variability aspects of human existence without also considering the high degree of predictability and stability is therefore doomed to be inadequate as a basis for understanding.

An emphasis on fragmentation

Once grand theories or metanarratives are cast out, then what fills the void previously occupied by them is an emphasis on fragmentation – an understanding of human experience as being characterized not by a coherence that knits together disparate elements into a meaningful whole, but by disjointed fragments. Again this is problematic, as such a conception renders theory impotent. Vincent argues that postmodernists:

> oppose all closure, totalizing discourse and erasure of difference. They do not believe in truth, rationality, knowledge, subject-centred inquiry or the search for a coherent epistemology ... Contradiction, difference and incoherence are welcomed.
>
> (1992, p. 188, cited in Sibeon, 2004, p. 16)

Without coherence, theoretical efforts to develop understanding are doomed to failure. Postmodern theory's acceptance of incoherence invalidates it as a theory – it is self-contradictory. Ironically, though, self-contradiction is also something that postmodernism accepts as a legitimate part of its approach.

A further irony is that, despite a strong subjective element to postmodernism, it fails to recognize that it is through human subjectivity and the meaning-making processes involved (see Chapter 12), that the world is not experienced as fragmented – it is experienced as 'making sense' in terms of a particular narrative. That narrative is a *self*-narrative – that is, it is the sense of self or identity (within a cultural context that informs it) that provides a unifying thread (see Chapter 4). However, the notion of self is also something that postmodernism seeks to undermine, and so the way forward is blocked there too.

While the efforts of some writers to 'salvage' postmodernism are understandable, the view I have presented here is that this is not the best way forward. Casey's comments are helpful in this regard:

> Against apparent social systemic intractability, and the decomposition of a sense-making life-world, postmodern thought offers as compensation a playful, though never satisfying, *jouissance*. Although some theorists try

to reclaim postmodernism for leftist critical theory it is difficult to discern from a linguistic playfulness and discarded subject, imperatives to social action beyond bewilderment and quietism.

(2002, p. 116)

This does not mean that we are therefore left with the sole option of going back to positivism. As we shall see in later chapters, there are other alternatives that can be explored.

Beyond postmodernism

As we have seen, key aspects of the postmodernist project can be seen as highly problematic. The net result of this can so easily be conceptual confusion. My basic argument is that there is much more to be gained by taking the positive elements of postmodernism and relocating them in a form of theoretical understanding that is not tainted by the weaknesses of postmodernism, rather than try to rehabilitate postmodernism to make it into a theoretical perspective that gives scope for promoting social justice. These are important points to which I shall return in Chapters 11 and 12, but for present purposes it is worth emphasizing that the basis of my argument is that postmodernism is *inherently* flawed. Attempts to improve it cannot be fully successful unless they change some of the fundamental premises – at which point what is left would no longer, in effect, be postmodernism. I am not therefore rejecting postmodernist *ideas* in themselves. Rather, I am dividing them into two categories, helpful and not so helpful. Once the latter are rejected, it becomes apparent that the former are not original to postmodernism, and so the term 'postmodernist' has little value.

There are clearly concerns about postmodernism as a social theory in general, but perhaps what is the most telling criticism from a social work point of view is its pessimism towards social change and the potential for reducing discrimination and oppression and promoting social justice and equality in their place. Casey links this with political protests and dissatisfaction that, in their day, did not lead to substantial progress:

Philosophies revealing the indeterminacy of meaning and the arbitrariness of grand narratives and truth claims, including those of the sovereign subject, have attracted a significant intellectual following. Many of the philosophers and intellectuals associated with postmodernism personally witnessed the failure of leftist social movements in which they had had some degree of involvement. At a time when there appeared to be no oppositional social actors and when the old ones, especially the workers' movement, had been converted into apparatuses of power, the new critics rejected modern politics altogether and turned to either excoricative or ironically celebratory criticism. They looked to cultural arenas and identity practices for counter-politics.

(2002, p. 116)

The question we now face is whether we can develop a politics of emancipation (what Casey describes as 'leftist') that can be more effective than previous versions, but without falling into the distractions of postmodernism. It is not necessary to become a member of the postmodernist 'club' and be associated with its extreme forms of analysis or have to wrestle with its inconsistencies and internal contradictions.

Voice of experience 2.3

I don't feel comfortable with so many people's attitudes towards politics these days. There seems to be so much defeatism and apathy. People seem to just accept that there is nothing that can be done. I wouldn't want to go back to the days of constant industrial unrest, but I think the current level of resignation is not doing us – or our clients – any good.

Sam, a social worker and trade union representative

Conclusion

In this chapter, I have shown that a return to positivistic approaches to practice is not a worthwhile option. I have indicated that postmodernism, in rejecting positivism, was a step I welcome, but that has brought problems too. My argument has been that we should not reject postmodernist insights altogether, but reconfigure them to (i) do justice to the history of ideas; and (ii) avoid the rocks on which our ship of theory can easily be sunk. However, once we strip away the unhelpful aspects of postmodernism, what remains bears a striking resemblance to existentialism.

With this in mind, in Chapter 11 I shall be arguing that existentialism can be seen as a constructive balance, a positive middle ground between the two extremes of positivism on the one hand and post-modernism on the other. These issues will therefore be revisited in more detail at that point.

By exploring in this chapter a range of reasons why we should be very sceptical about postmodernist approaches to social work, I have paved the way for developing alternative theoretical understandings. In effect, what this chapter has done is to outline a pendulum swing from one unhelpful extreme of an overly rigid, *objectivist* positivism to an equally unhelpful extreme of a theoretically flawed, *subjectivist* postmodernism. If we are to take seriously the notion of *theorizing* social work practice, then it will be important to steer a path that avoids each of these destructive theoretical extremes.

Points to ponder

1. What do you see as the limitations of adopting a *scientific* approach to social work?
2. Which postmodernist ideas, as discussed in this chapter, do you find helpful and why? Which ones do you not feel comfortable with?
3. How realistic do you think it is to be able to work towards social progress?

Further reading

N. Thompson and S. Thompson (2008) is a useful starting point for discussing some of the ideas discussed in this chapter. Tew (2002) provides a helpful critical introduction to postmodernist and post-structuralist ideas, as does McDonald (2006). Pease and Fook (1999 a,b) present the case for a weaker version of postmodernism. Once again, Sibeon (2004) is a useful text to explore, as are Parton and O'Byrne (2000) and Healy (2005).

3

Practices redefined

Introduction

Theory can be understood as a window on the world – a way of making sense of aspects of our experience. To a large extent, theory not only explains practice, but also *defines* it in terms of how it creates a particular understanding of what it is all about. Different theories conceptualize practice in different ways. That is, they have different understandings of what it is all about. For example, in an earlier work (Thompson, 2009a) I have described social work in terms of a process of promoting well-being and social justice through empowerment which, in turn, is promoted through processes of problem solving. However, this is clearly not the only way to conceptualize social work, and other authors and thinkers will have their own approaches. Theory develops a set of conceptual understandings and therefore creates a framework for making sense of the practice situations we encounter. In doing so, it also establishes a framework of meaning and therefore definition. Consequently, in this chapter we are going to be exploring how the way we conceptualize social work affects the way it is understood, and therefore the way it is practised. We begin by looking at different ways in which social work can be conceptualized and follow this with a discussion of how social work is understood in different terms in different countries. And finally, we explore how managerialism, a feature of neoliberalism that has come to dominate social work (and public services more broadly) in recent years, can be understood as a threat and challenge to social work professionalism.

The approach adopted in this chapter reflects a recurring theme of the book, namely the significance of narrative and meaning. Developing a theory, as we noted in Chapter 2, is not a matter of finding the definitive truth. Rather, it is a process of developing a framework of understanding that helps us make sense of whatever aspect of the world it addresses. In this sense, a theory is a narrative – a 'story' that attempts to provide a coherent set of meanings that serve as a basis for informing (and thus shaping) practice.

This is the final chapter in Part One of the book. It therefore plays an important role in conveying the fundamental message underpinning Part One, namely the need to have a sound understanding of the nature of theory (and thus 'theorizing') before exploring in Part Two some of the core elements of the theory base we need to draw on in practice. In this sense, this chapter acts as a bridge between what has been discussed so far in Part One and what is to come in the next part.

Conceptualizing social work

The work of Freire (1972a; 1972b; 2007) has proven very influential in the world of education. He was critical of what he called a 'banking' model of education which mainly involved 'depositing' information (facts, figures and conventional understandings) in learners. He argued that this traditional approach to education produced passive, compliant learners who would then be ripe for exploitation by more powerful groups and forces in society. He proposed a more emancipatory approach in which people are helped to 'learn how to learn'. Such an approach is intended to give learners a foundation for continuing to learn and for questioning taken-for-granted assumptions in order to enable social progress – a conceptualization of education as a force for actively developing knowledge rather than passively accepting the current social and political arrangements – the status quo. Compare this with the development of critically reflective practice (Fook and Gardner, 2007; S. Thompson and N. Thompson, 2008; White, Fook and Gardner, 2006).

This very brief account of Freire's work provides an example of how the way a professional field (in this case, education) is defined or conceptualized shapes how it is subsequently practised. A different conceptualization produces a different set of professional practices. The same logic can be applied to any professional discipline, including social work.

In terms of conceptualizing social work, first it has to be recognized that it is a contested entity (Thompson, 2009b). That is, there is no single unifying definition acceptable to all. While the International Federation of Social Workers' definition (see below) is widely accepted by a large proportion of people within the social work world, it is still not an entirely agreed definition. As we shall see, there are various ways of considering what social work is and therefore how it should be practised.

One traditional way of understanding social work is in terms of a tripartite distinction as follows:

- *Casework*. This refers to work with individuals and/or families. This is currently the most common form of social work practice in western societies. It involves a worker engaging with an individual, a couple or a whole family, depending on the circumstances, forming a picture of the situation and attempting to move forward accordingly.
- *Groupwork*. This involves working with groups of people either on a structured, planned basis or, more loosely, as part of a therapeutic process. This is now less common than it once was and tends to take place mainly in specialist settings. It involves a skilled worker seeking to influence the group dynamics in the direction of helping the participants move forward in clarifying their needs and finding ways of achieving them. High-quality groupwork can be a very powerful and effective way of contributing to empowerment and helping people solve their problems (Doel, 2005; Doel and Sawdon, 1999; Preston-Shoot, 2007).
- *Community work*. This refers to dealing with whole communities through, for example, community development initiatives. This involves the development of programmes of work that enable members of communities (usually neighbourhoods with high levels of poverty, deprivation and disadvantage) in order to capitalize on the potential for mutual support and communal ways of addressing common problems within that community (Stepney and Popple, 2008; Twelvetrees, 2008).

However, this is not the only way of understanding how social work can be divided into different sections. There are also tripartite models developed by Payne (2005a) and Beckett (2006). Payne's model identifies the following three types of, or approaches to, social work:

1. *Reflexive-therapeutic*. This is the traditional view of social work as a process involving therapeutic interaction between a worker and a client, couple or family. Payne describes it as follows:

   - This process of mutual influence is what makes social work reflexive, so that it responds to the social concerns that social workers find and gain understanding of as they practise. In these ways, clients gain power over their own feelings and way of life. Through this personal power, they are enabled to overcome or rise above suffering and disadvantage.

(2005, p. 9)

2. *Socialist-collectivist.* This refers to approaches geared towards promoting social justice through processes of empowerment, especially for the most disadvantaged and oppressed groups in society. It reflects a more explicitly political understanding of the role of social work as a means of helping people escape the problems associated with an unequal and exploitative society.

3. *Individualist-reformist.* According to this approach, the major role of social work is to maintain social order by seeking to ensure that the welfare needs of disadvantaged groups are met as far as possible. In its extreme forms it can be oppressive, in so far as its major focus can become one of ensuring that individuals 'accept their lot' and do not challenge the political or social status quo – the equivalent of the 'banking' model of education discussed above.

Beckett's model comprises the following three elements, which he describes in terms of sets of roles:

1. *Advocacy roles.* This includes both direct advocacy (speaking on behalf of the client) and indirect advocacy (helping the client to speak out on their own behalf). These involve helping the client to have a voice and trying to ensure that their voice is heard.

2. *Direct change agent roles.* This covers a broad range of activities, such as counsellor, mediator, educator or catalyst. The focus here is on the social worker playing a role in bringing about change in the client's life and circumstances.

3. *Executive roles.* Beckett captures the idea of an executive role in the following passage:

> The executive roles are concerned with making things happen in a practical sense. They could actually be called *indirect* change agent roles, since they are about bringing about change not as a result of a personal interaction, but by recruiting external resources of one kind or another, whether they be material resources, legal powers or the services of others.

(2006, p. 10)

What these tripartite models have in common is an attempt to try and develop a structure for understanding the boundaries of social work. In this respect, they are attempts to define the territory of social work and therefore have an important part to play in conceptualizing the entity that has come to be known as 'social work'. Consistent with my arguments earlier in the book about the nature of theory, we can see that it is not a question of working out which is the 'correct' or 'true' conceptualization of social work. Rather, it is a case of recognizing that how we understand social work will shape how we practise it. *Theorizing* social work therefore needs to incorporate an understanding of the nature and purposes of social work (Sibeon, 1991). Simply wanting to know 'how to do it' is not enough. We shall return to this point below.

Practice focus 3.1

Joan had been a social work assistant for four years before she started her degree in social work studies. She had never really thought about the nature of social work; she had simply done what was asked of her to the best of her ability. So, despite her extensive experience in the field, she really struggled when, as part of her degree course, she was involved in a group exercise in which the students were asked to come up with a definition of social work. She came to realize that being able to do it and knowing what it was she was doing were two different things! Although it proved to be a difficult exercise, she found it very helpful, in so far as it made her think about how important it is to be clear about what we are doing and why we are doing it, rather than simply getting stuck in routinized practices and losing sight of the bigger picture. It made her realize that, as a professional, she needed to have a fuller understanding of the wider scene of which her work formed a part.

The point I wish to emphasize is that defining and conceptualizing social work are not simply intellectual matters; these processes also have significant implications for practice. This is because different theoretical conceptualizations will have different implications for how practice is carried out. Consider, for example, the following three theoretical perspectives and the implications for practice in terms of the precepts on which they are based:

- *Cognitive behavioural therapy*. This theoretical approach is geared towards changing behaviour by changing the core beliefs on which such behaviour is based (Kinsella and Garland, 2008). It is widely used in a variety of settings, but especially in the mental health field. This is a popular and, in some ways, very effective social work method. However, it is based on the idea of *changing behaviour*, and so some people in the social work world object to it on the grounds that they do not see social work as a process of changing behaviour. Others have no such objection, provided that such behaviour change is what the client wants and is part of a process of empowerment rather than a 'treatment' that is done *to* people in a medicalized, disempowering way.

- *Family therapy.* This involves working with whole families to attempt to change the family dynamics in order to resolve the difficulties that are being caused by how the family currently operates. There are various schools of thought or traditions of practice in family therapy (Burnham, 1986; Byng-Hall, 1995; Carr, 2000), but what they all have in common is an understanding of their practice based on the idea that the family needs to be the 'unit of intervention' – that is, the focus of attention. This represents a very different perspective from approaches that focus on individual casework on the one hand and community development on the other. For some social workers, family therapy is one method among others that can be used in certain circumstances, whereas for others, there is a very strong tendency to specialize in family therapy to the exclusion of other practice modalities.

- *Care management.* This is an approach that has grown in importance since the implementation of the NHS and Community Care Act 1990 in England and Wales and similar developments in other countries. Developed as a response to addressing community care needs, it involves the social worker carrying out an assessment of needs and circumstances and, from this, developing a 'package of care' – a set of supportive services and other interventions that are geared towards attempting to prevent the need for institutional care (Thompson and Thompson, 2005). Here there is no emphasis on behaviour change or on family dynamics. This is a very different conceptualization of the role of the social worker. If practised uncritically, it can easily become a routinized rationing of scarce resources, rather than an empowering approach to addressing social need and social problems (Thompson, 2009a).

These are just three examples from a wide range of possibilities. They illustrate well the point that there is a strong relationship between how social work is understood (defined, conceptualized) and how it is practised.

What is also important to recognize is the important contribution made by England (1986). He made the very significant point that everybody has difficulties in their life. This is part of being human. But, there are also groups of people who have difficulty dealing with their difficulties because of certain complicating factors. These include disability, frailty in old age, poverty, stigma, discrimination, trauma and other such factors. Whichever model of social work we choose to adopt, it seems to me that England's idea can and should remain constant across them all, that what social work is doing at heart is recognizing that, without assistance, certain people will 'fall behind'. Promoting social justice for all involves addressing these issues in a constructive way. This is an important point to which we shall return below.

Voice of experience 3.1

I started my career working with adults with learning disabilities and I had a fairly clear idea of what my role was in terms of helping them to do things they struggled to do because of their condition. However, when I moved to work in a child care team, I was really confused to begin with. Many people seemed to want me to do things that they seemed perfectly capable of doing themselves. Some parents seemed to want me to run errands for them; it was as if they wanted to make themselves dependent on me. I had to resist that very strongly and focus very clearly on what was preventing them from dealing with their own difficulties and not get drawn into being a general family helper. I had to keep reminding myself of what I had read in Hugh England's book about everyone having difficulties of some kind and remembering that it would be unrealistic for social workers to try and help everybody with their problems – and it would be inappropriate anyway.

Jack, a team manager in a children in need team

My aim in drawing links between conceptualizing social work and practising it is not to 'sell' a particular model of the social work world (my own views of social work are made explicit in Thompson, 2009a; b, and will inevitably influence my comments in this book). However, my argument is that it is wise to have a clear picture of what understanding of social work we are basing our practice on if we are to ensure that such practice is ethical (that is, not running counter to our value base) and as effective as possible (not going in the wrong direction, for example). The comments of Karvinen-Niinikoski in this regard are helpful:

> Open expertise recognizes uncertainty and, instead of claiming to be the only one to possess proper knowledge and professional skills, it will be ready to question communication and even polemics as well as a willingness to negotiate and reconstruct expertise according to the different contexts of action.
>
> (2004, p. 25)

This takes us back to critically reflective practice – drawing critically on a knowledge base rather than attempting to (i) practise without a knowledge base ('It's all common sense'); or (ii) to find the 'definitive' truth or guaranteed 'right answer'.

Having explored some of the complexities of the relationship between how we understand social work and how we practise it, let us now turn to an understanding of social work in international context before considering how social work has been pushed in a particular direction by recent political developments.

Social work in international context

The International Federation of Social Workers has defined social work in the following terms:

> The social work profession promotes social change, problem solving in human relationships and the empowerment and liberation of people to enhance well-being. Utilizing theories of human behaviour and social systems, social work intervenes at the points where people interact with their environments. Principles of human rights and social justice are fundamental to social work.
>
> (http://www.ifsw.org/en/p38000208.html)

This is an important definition but, as with most definitions in general, they are just as significant in terms of what they leave out as what they put in. Indeed, it is in the nature of providing a dictionary-style definition that information will be collapsed into a small space. Definitions in themselves may not be very helpful in terms of shaping our understanding. However, it is important to recognize that social work is practised differently in different countries. For example, Payne (2005b) makes the point that social work in developing countries generally has more of a community development focus, while social work practice in the more industrialized areas of the world is more likely to have a casework focus.

Another significant factor is that in some countries (the UK for example) 'social services' and 'social security' are separate entities, while in other countries (many nations in continental Europe, for example) the social work role is combined with a social security role. Given that social work can be seen as a branch of applied social policy (personal social services), then it is understandable that different social policy contexts in different countries will produce different models of social work. This is consistent with the work of Esping Anderson (1990) who has produced a model of different types of welfare state and the implications of these for how social policy is put into practice. The details of this need not concern us here, but the basic point illustrates how conceptions of 'welfare' and (therefore of social work) vary across time and space.

Linked to this is the work of Clarke and colleagues (2000a) who have questioned whether it is a valid statement to claim (as many people do) that we no longer have a welfare state in the United Kingdom. They provide an interesting analysis of what it means to describe a state as a *welfare* state. This very question of what is welfare and what is the role of the state in addressing welfare needs, is a major one that requires a much closer analysis than I am able to give it here. Bauman (2005) is a good starting point.

Professionalism and the managerialist challenge

The political scene across the western nations in recent decades has been characterized by a political philosophy that has come to be known as neoliberalism. The liberalism element of the word refers to the traditional focus on the role of the individual in society, the strong emphasis on people as individuals and therefore the de-emphasizing of wider social factors, such as government and social policy. Neoliberalism is therefore a new form of liberalism. It has taken traditional liberal approaches, premised on a major focus on the individual and a preference for limited state involvement, and added a strong conservative element to it. In the early days of neoliberalism, it was referred to as 'New Right' thinking. It has a strong emphasis on the role of the market and the belief that the market should be a key factor in shaping society in general and government policy in particular. It is premised on the idea of having a minimal state – that is, government playing a minimal role in the workings of society, with market forces playing a much more significant role. As social work, in the United Kingdom at least, is primarily associated with governmental activities, then neoliberalism clearly presents major challenges, and could be seen as actually putting the role of social work under threat.

Many thought that the election of a Labour government in 1997 would herald a return to a focus on public sector values and a distinct move away from the individualism and market emphasis of the Conservative government. However, it was not to be. As Clarke, Gewirtz and McLaughlin comment:

> Although reform of welfare has long been a central part of the British political agenda, the changes begun in the 1980s by the Conservative governments of Margaret Thatcher inaugurated a period of 'permanent revolution' that has affected the scale, purposes, forms and social relationships of welfare. Subsequent reforms, initiatives and modernization programmes have been directed at the 'reinvention of welfare'. The New Labour government elected in 1997, following eighteen years of Conservative rule, proved to be just as enthusiastic about the reconstruction of welfare as a major political task, seeing it as a means through which a distinctively 'modern' British people might be constructed.
>
> (2000a , p. 1)

The implications of this move towards a neoliberal approach to social work have been quite significant (Ferguson, 2007; Ferguson, Lavalette and Mooney, 2002; Lavalette and Pratt, 2006). It is worth exploring them in a little more detail.

A key aspect of neoliberalism has been the development of 'managerialism'. Managerialism is premised on the idea that central government can and should control local government – for example, through performance indicators, targets and stars (with the punishment available that a star can be withdrawn from a department rating and with it a significant proportion of the budget). The net result of such an approach is a devaluing of professionalism and an increasing emphasis on bureaucracy.

Practice focus 3.2

Gwenan was a social worker in an older people team. She enjoyed her work, but over time was finding it less satisfying. This was because each new policy initiative that came forward seemed to place less emphasis on professionalism and more on meeting government targets. She was concerned that the people who really mattered – the older people they served – featured less and less in official thinking, while bureaucratic concerns were dominating more and more. She could also see that it was affecting morale, in so far as there had been a marked increase in moaning and negativity over time. She therefore decided to talk to the team manager about this, and she agreed that it was a concern. They therefore decided to put the matter on the team meeting agenda and see if, as a team, they could look at what strategies they could develop to challenge the increasingly bureaucratic nature of their work and reaffirm their professionalism.

Clarke and Newman capture the point well when they write of:

the capacity of bureaucratic coordination to deliver *routinized or predictable outputs*. The structuring principles of bureaucratic administration – emphasising the appropriate application of a body of rules and regulations by trained staff – turn complex tasks of assessment or calculation into routinized processes and guarantee that the outcomes of those calculations are stable or predictable.

(1997, p. 5)

This effort to 'proceduralize' practice is, of course, doomed to failure, as the issues at stake in social work are far too complex to fit into such a simplistic framework, hence the need for a professional approach that is sensitive to the complexities and subtleties involved (Thompson, 2009a). Making social work less effective, less professionally satisfying, less appealing to new recruits and more burdensome in terms of paperwork and (often unrealistic) 'targets' is clearly a dangerous direction to go in. These factors, combined with my comments above about neoliberalism undermining social work as a legitimate social enterprise, place a degree of doubt over the potential for social work to flourish unless and until the managerialist tide turns.

But even if this political philosophy does not result in the overall demise of social work, it has none the less presented significant difficulties for current forms of practice. I shall focus on three of these in particular: first risk, then professionalism, and finally the 'dumbing down' of social work.

Risk

It has been recognized in recent years that social work has had a tendency to overemphasize risk factors (Denney, 2005; Thompson, 2009a; Webb, 2006). Risk assessment and risk management have always been strong features of social work practice although, in the past, these were often dealt with at an implicit level without being specified in any particular detail. The movement in the past few years has been away from such an implicit model to one that makes risk factors a much more explicit feature of the work. While being more explicit about such significant factors is something that I personally welcome, and see as being a key part of critically reflective practice, the price we have paid for this is a tendency to become 'risk averse'. That is, to overemphasize the significance of risk. This can be seen to have produced forms of bad practice that I have previously referred to as defensive practice (Thompson, 2009b). I am not alone as an author in questioning the wisdom of such a strong emphasis on risk, particularly as it has often been the case that the understanding of risk on which such work has been based has tended to be oversimplified. What is needed, then, is a much more sophisticated understanding of risk, but also a recognition that it is no coincidence that risk has featured so heavily in our work over recent years. It represents a neoliberal shift from an emphasis on care and support for vulnerable and disadvantaged members of the community to a stronger focus on perceiving certain members of the community as a threat to wider society. Even where there is no strong social control element in terms of the emphasis on risk, the clear message is that social work should only be concerned where there is danger to an individual, thereby de-emphasizing the role of social work in supporting and empowering people. This is entirely consistent with neoliberal thinking, with its commitment to minimizing the role of the state and making welfare predominantly an individual and family matter.

Professionalism

Professionalism has also been hard hit by neoliberalism, mainly through the effects of what I referred to earlier as 'managerialism'. This concept is captured by the idea that 'managers have the right to manage'. There has been a shift of power away from professionals towards managers, thereby reducing the emphasis on professionalism and pushing social work in the direction of more bureaucratic forms of practice. While social work can be defined as a 'bureau-profession' as opposed to the traditional professions with their basis in private practice (Sibeon, 1991), the need for a commitment to professional knowledge, skills and values remains strong (Thompson, 2009a). However, the development of managerialism has had major implications and consequences in terms of a reduction in professional confidence and pride, producing feelings of being deskilled and devalued. Some of the consequences of managerialism I have noted through my training and consultancy work are raised levels of stress, increased levels of sickness absence, increasing problems with recruitment and retention, and other such related problems.

Underpinning these concerns is the basis of managerialism, which is fundamentally a lack of trust. By threatening to cut budgets in public bodies that do not meet their targets, central government is, in effect, giving a message that it does not trust local government to carry out its duties without a strong steer from the centre. In turn, local government is placed in a position whereby councillors need to impress upon senior managers the need to meet their targets, and so on. If councillors do not do this, then they can be held legally responsible for not meeting their statutory duties as local government elected members. The senior managers then have to ensure that middle and junior managers are 'on message' in terms of the targets. In turn, managers have to make sure that practitioners are hitting the targets as defined by 'performance indicators' (statistical data relating to number of people receiving services, the cost-effectiveness of those services and so on). The whole system is therefore premised on each layer not trusting the layer below and giving controlling messages in terms of what needs to be done and how it needs to be done. In this context, it is no surprise that we have had a crisis of confidence in terms of professionalism.

Voice of experience 3.2

I have seen so much change in recent years. In my early days we had more autonomy over what we did and it worked much better that way, because the situations we deal with are quite complex and messy (if they weren't, if they were quite straightforward, we wouldn't be involved in the case!). Nowadays we seem to be constantly fighting against efforts to practise in routine and standardized ways. We don't give in though, because we know that sort of approach is woefully inadequate for dealing with the type of work we do in our team.

Kim, a social worker in a mental health team

What this means is that social work now faces major challenges. Whatever theoretical perspective we choose to adopt, there is a significant challenge involved, in that we have to make sure that it is a *professional* approach, rather than a bureaucratic, managerialist one (Thompson, 2009a). That can be a major battle to fight but it is one that it is important to engage with.

'Dumbing down'

This is a phenomenon that, to a large extent, follows on directly from the movement from professionalism to bureaucracy. In some respects, the very notion of managerialism can be seen as a form of 'dumbing down' in its own right (that is, being a less-than-intelligent approach to subtle and varied problems of practice). However, managerialism also involves creating lower expectations in terms of the intellectual level required to carry out the work effectively and appropriately. This is an issue that has become a significant cause for concern in social work education in recent years.

This tendency towards 'dumbing down' can be seen to run counter to a commitment to critically reflective practice. Folgheraiter reports on the work of Elliot (1991), who offers apt comment in stating that:

Rather than operating as an infallible source of relevant knowledge, the role of the reflective practitioner is to participate in a process of collaborative problem solving through which the relevance and usefulness of his/her specialist knowledge can be determined and new knowledge acquired ... From the perspective of the 'reflective practitioner' model, professional competence consists of the ability to act intelligently in situ-

ations which are sufficiently novel and unique to require what constitutes an appropriate response to be learned *in situ*. Competence cannot
be defined simply in terms of ability to apply pre-ordained categories of
specialist knowledge to product [*sic*] correct behavioural responses.
Within this model of professionalism, stereotypical applications of
knowledge are to be avoided and this implies that any attempt to pre-
specify correct behavioural responses or 'performance indicators' is a
constraint on intelligence practice ... Learning to be a reflective practitioner is learning to reflect about one's experience of complex human
situations holistically. (Elliot, 1991, pp. 312–14; quoted in Brooks and
Sikes, 1997, p. 22)

(Folgheraiter, 2004, pp. 182–3)

In effect, the very notion of *theorizing* social work can be seen as a
counterbalance against dumbing down, in so far as it involves the
active use of intellectual skills (analytical skills and the explicit use of
a professional knowledge base, for example) and a commitment to
making sure that our practice is based on a relatively sophisticated
understanding of various aspects of the situations we encounter (to be
discussed in Part Two).

The development of managerialism in recent years has also been
accompanied by what can be seen as further efforts to counteract it.
For example, I feel it is no coincidence that, as managerialism has
become more dominant, the emphasis on critically reflective practice
has become stronger. This is because critically reflective practice can
be seen as a direct challenge to the uncritical, mindless practice associated with managerialist bureaucracy. Similarly, as managerialism
has grown in influence, so too has the emphasis on leadership.
Leadership emphasizes the need to inspire and motivate staff, rather
than push and drive them through control and sanctions. As such,
leadership can be seen as a further challenge to managerialism
(although some people have sought to hijack the benefits of leadership
as a means of ensuring that managerialist targets are met, thereby
defeating the object of leadership as a philosophical approach to organizational effectiveness). One important point to recognize in relation
to leadership is that leaders are not necessarily managers (Thompson,
2009c). Practitioners also have the capacity to lead – that is, to inspire
and motivate colleagues to move forward in meeting professional goals
and to ensure consistency with professional values. We shall return to
this point in Chapter 10, in which the organizational context of practice is our primary focus. However, for present purposes, it is important to note that, in trying to challenge neoliberalism in general and

managerialism in particular, social workers are presented with the opportunity to develop their leadership skills in order to be proud professionals working towards legitimate professional goals – rather than demoralized bureaucrats being pushed along by the current of managerialist thinking.

Practice focus 3.3

Gwenan was delighted when her team had the opportunity to discuss the increasing bureaucracy and possible ways of challenging it. To begin with some people were reluctant to engage with the issues, as they found them a little threatening. However, as others joined in the discussion, the whole team gradually felt more comfortable in acknowledging the situation. At one point Gwenan felt the discussion was becoming too negative, too much of a 'moaning shop', but then the team manager showed good leadership skills by gently steering the discussion towards identifying concrete steps they could take to try and improve the system and to resist the influences of managerialism. They were not able to identify any 'magic answers', but nobody expected that anyway. What they were able to do was to reaffirm their identities as professionals who had to wrestle with bureaucracy rather than resign themselves to being former professionals who had been reduced to being bureaucratic box tickers.

A further important dimension of the effects of managerialism on social work is the challenge of working within a multi-professional context. Social work has never been entirely isolated from the work of other professionals in the field but, increasingly, there has been an emphasis, and quite rightly so, on the need to work in partnership, not only with clients and carers, but also with colleagues from other disciplines. Given that managerialism has had the effect of undermining professional identity, confidence and pride, then it is easy to see that this will have significant implications for how we are perceived by other professionals. If we do not value ourselves as important players in the multi-professional arena, then we can hardly expect other professionals to value our contributions. There is therefore a further significant challenge of shaking off the managerialist influence and reaffirming professionalism as a key factor in promoting high quality multi-professional practice. For a fuller discussion of these issues, see *Practising Social Work*.

Voice of experience 3.3

I think we face a real challenge now. Some people have become so demoralized by the increasing bureaucracy that they do not come across well in the eyes of other professionals. I think those colleagues who have managed to keep a strong professional identity despite the difficulties we face are in a much stronger position to win the respect and co-operation of professionals from other disciplines.

Lindsay, a social worker at a health centre

Conclusion

This chapter has argued that it is important to be clear about how we are conceptualizing practice, as this will have a bearing on how we then carry out our duties in practice. We have also seen that there are different ways of conceptualizing social work, depending not only on theoretical or political perspective, but also across international borders. We have also noted that the dominant political philosophy of neoliberalism has emphasized managerialism and bureaucracy at the expense of professionalism. An important message from this chapter, and indeed from the book as a whole, is that it is important to reaffirm professionalism rather than allow managerialism to inculcate a sense of defeatism and cynicism.

A major theme of this book is that theory is an essential basis for understanding. However, what is also apparent is that theoretical perspectives can become a club for people to join, rather than a tool for people to use. As Part One of the book comes to a close, it is important to emphasize that the remainder of the book will seek to explore the significance of those theoretical understandings, while also outlining the dangers of defining practice too rigidly in accordance with a partic-ular theoretical persuasion. In particular, I shall be using existential-ism as a philosophy that allows scope for a variety of theoretical understandings to be fused together in a meaningful way. In a sense, existentialism as a philosophy is a meta-theory – that is, it is not a specific, substantive theory relating to a narrow field of work. It is, as discussed in Chapter 2, an overarching theoretical approach that helps to make sense of human existence, something which pits it against the theoretical assumptions of postmodernism. Chapter 3 has shown how practices can be defined by the theoretical premises we adopt. Existentialism seeks to ensure that we have a strong theoretical basis for our practice, but not a rigid or dogmatic one that excludes the insights that can be drawn from competing perspectives. This will be an important factor in Part Three of the book, where we look at how theory can be developed so that it can offer an even better basis for understanding the complexities of practice.

Points to ponder

1. If someone asked you 'What is social work?', how would you reply?
2. Why is it important to recognize the professional basis of social work?
3. In what ways does managerialism undermine such professionalism?

Further reading

N. Thompson and S. Thompson (2008) is a good starting point. Payne (2005b) and Thompson (2009b) both offer helpful discussions on the nature of social work. For a critique of managerialism, see Ferguson (2008); Ferguson, Lavalette and Mooney (2002); Lavalette and Pratt (2006); and Thompson (2009a).

Part Two
Making Sense of Practice

Introduction to Part Two:
Dimensions of the social work world

In Part Two my aim is to show how the knowledge we need for social work can be understood as a set of embedded levels of understanding, a bit like a set of Russian dolls. The person needs to be understood not in isolation or in static terms, but rather as constantly changing in response to interactions with other individuals and groups, in a context that includes cultural factors, sociopolitical and structural factors as well as organizational concerns – and all this needs to be understood in a wider context of moral and political values.

It is a complicated picture, but I have tried to present it as clearly as I reasonably can. However, I make no apology for the complexity of the issues involved, as that reflects the reality of what we encounter in social work. It would be unfair and misleading for me to 'dumb down' the intricacies of the social work world. However, by presenting different dimensions in different chapters, I hope that I will have made digestion of the complexities far easier than would have been the case by trying to gain an understanding without considering the dimensions separately. In practice, however, we do not encounter the dimensions separately – practice does not come in distinct, neatly structured chapters! This once again underlines the need for critically reflective practice, based on an ability to theorize practice and develop a well-informed way forward, rather than a simple reliance on the theory base to provide the answers.

4

The person

Introduction

It has been a recurring theme throughout my writings on social work that it is essential to recognize that everyone is a unique individual, but each of us is an individual *in a social context*. That is, each person's uniqueness is not a reason to disregard the wider social context. I have argued that it is necessary to take account of *both* – that is, recognizing, on the one hand, the fact that each of us is a unique person with our own wishes, feelings, history and plans, but, on the other, none of us exists in a social vacuum. We are all in part shaped by the social world we currently live in and were brought up in. To understand the person, we therefore need to understand not only the individual factors specific to him or her, but also the wider social factors, cultural and structural, that play a significant part in making us who we are. My work on PCS (personal, cultural and structural) analysis (Thompson, 2003a; 2006a) reflects this, with the emphasis on the need to understand not just personal, individual factors, but also the interaction of the three different levels (personal, cultural and structural) with the unique results that emerge from the complex interactions of these different levels, and therefore different sets of factors.

In this book, we have already discussed the danger of atomism – that is, the failure to see the person in their social context. To add to this we also need to be wary of the danger of the form of reductionism known as 'sociologism'. As noted in Chapter 1, this refers to the tendency to see society in terms of broad structures, processes and institutions, but lose sight of the actual *people* (what Archer, 2000, would call 'agents') within those frameworks. For example, the classic work of Wrong (1961) about 'the oversocialized conception of [wo]man' has taught us that there are dangers in failing to recognize individual factors alongside social factors. Wrong was critical of how, in criticizing individualistic models, sociologists had developed a tendency to go too far in the opposite direction and see the social factors, but not the individuals interacting with those factors.

We shall see below just how influential social factors are in shaping our sense of self. But, it does not matter how influential the social context is, it never entirely displaces the role of 'agency', the fact that individuals make choices and react to situations based on how they interpret them. An adequate understanding of people needs to be *psychosocial* – that is, it needs to take account of both the significance of the social forces that weigh on each of us, and how we respond to those forces. As I shall be emphasizing, we are not totally unrestricted individuals who can do precisely what we like, but nor are we puppets pushed here and there by wider forces. The reality, as we shall see, is a combination of both sets of factors and, of course, the interactions between them.

Sartre (1969) described human experience in terms of a mixing of coffee and cream, in the sense that, once the coffee and the cream are combined, they become a new entity in their own right and cannot be separated out. This analogy applies to individuals in society: personal and social factors merge together and cannot then be distinguished. The two sets of factors, unique personal ones and contextual social ones, become two sides of the same coin, in the sense that they are both aspects of the same reality. Unfortunately, much of the theoretical work about the individual in society has reflected approaches that conceive of the individual in society in terms, not so much of coffee and cream, but rather of soup and bowl (Elkjaer, 2005). That is, a common oversimplification of human existence is to see the individual contained within society in the way that soup is contained within a bowl, but the bowl does not become part of the soup and the soup does not shape the bowl. Sartre's analogy is a much more accurate and helpful one in terms of capturing the complexities of what it means to be an individual, a *person*.

Identity

Common-sense understandings of an individual's identity tend to reflect a rigid essentialist perspective. That is, it is commonly assumed that individuals have a 'personality' which is largely unchangeable. Unfortunately, much of the traditional psychological literature on the question of identity has tended to reinforce that view. However, we now have more sophisticated understandings available to us in terms of theoretical perspectives which conceive of identity not as a fixed entity, but rather as a journey or process.

Identity, then, is a fluid matter. It is not the starting point or the destination. It is the journey itself. This helps us to avoid essentialism and defeatist ideas such as: 'I can't change' or 'It's the way I am'. This is not to say that everything is within our control and that we can be exactly who we want to be. There will be, of course, strong influences on our identity, but it is important not to confuse influences with determining factors. We are free to reject influences. In fact, that is an important aspect of how influences operate, in so far as we can be influenced positively or negatively by other factors. Consider, for example, the religion in which a person is brought up. That religion can have a profound positive influence, in the sense that the individual embraces the religious beliefs and values and becomes a part of that religion, just as that religion becomes a part of him or her. Alternatively, their religion can be a negative influence, in the sense that the individual rejects that religion.

So, what makes that person who he or she is, is not the direct influence of the religion, but of that person's rejection of that religion. For example, someone brought up in the Catholic faith may become a devout believer, and his or her life may be strongly shaped by Catholic beliefs and practices, giving, in effect, that person a strong Catholic identity. On the other hand, however, some people will strongly reject Catholicism, and so their identity will in large part be shaped by their rejection of the Catholic faith. In a similar vein, somebody who has experienced poor parenting may in turn become a poor parent because he or she lacks the skills of parenting as a result of lacking a suitable role model in their formative years. However, others who have experienced poor parenting may become all the more determined to become excellent parents but, either way, whether the individual concerned becomes a poor parent or an excellent one, their identity as a parent will have been shaped by their upbringing and their personal acceptance or rejection of that influence. There is, in this sense, a dialectical interaction between the individual and the influences to which he or she is exposed (I shall explain the idea of 'dialectical reason' and its importance below).

Practice focus 4.1

Dwight was a staff development officer in a large voluntary organization. One day he was running a course on religion and spirituality as
part of a training programme in relation to equality and diversity. At one
point he was explaining how significant religion is in many people's
lives and how it can shape not only behaviour, but also actual identity,
our sense of who we are and how we fit into the world. He was about
to explain that this is an important dimension of spirituality when
Miriam, one of the participants, said that the situation wasn't so clear
cut. She went on to say that, ethnically she was Jewish and this was
an important part of her identity, but she had lost her religious faith
some years ago when her younger brother was killed in a stabbing
incident outside a youth club. Dwight found this fascinating and saw it
as a useful learning point for all the participants, and so he invited
Miriam to talk more about this if she was happy to. She went on to
explain that religion and ethnicity were both things that the individual
could accept or reject (albeit at a price in terms of social pressures),
and she had chosen to retain her ethnicity but not her religion. Dwight
was able to use this as an example of how complex such matters can
be.

One of the key influences on behaviour is childhood experience. For
example, the attachments we form to people in our early lives can be
seen to be significant factors in shaping who we are and how we deal
with our challenges in life (Howe et al., 1999). In social work, we are
often dealing with people who experienced childhood trauma and/or
deprivation in their early years and the harmful effects of these experiences on them. Some people would use the term 'damaged' to refer to
such situations. That is to say that their early life experiences
'damaged' them in some way, as it is often expressed in the literature.
However, I do not feel comfortable with such dehumanizing terminology. While it is clear that such experiences can be harmful, it is things
that are damaged, not people. The point remains, however, that early
childhood experiences can be a significant influence one way or the
other.

While it is clearly important to stress the importance of childhood
experiences, it is equally important to recognize that influences on
identity do not stop once we reach adulthood. There will be a whole
range of factors in our lives that can play a part in helping to shape
our sense of self: our relationships, our work experience, how we are

treated by other people, our experiences of loss, and so on and so forth. However, again it is important not to see such influences in too narrow a sense. There are also much broader influences in terms of cultural factors that shape such important issues as frameworks of meaning, symbolism, and so on. As Kallen puts it: 'one's personhood is not developed in a cultural vacuum, each individual's personhood is shaped by the cultural particularities of his or her socialization' (2004, p. 21).

Similarly, there will be structural factors in terms of, for example, class, race and gender, which will have a significant bearing on how we see ourselves and, indeed, on how the world sees us. In this regard, Parekh's (2008) work has been very helpful. He argues that it is important to see individual identity in the wider context of being human, being part of the human community:

> The human identity remains abstract unless it is anchored in and enriched by our particular identities. The latter, in turn, are embedded in – indeed made possible by – and nurtured and limited by our shared humanity. We are not homogenous instantiations or specimens of the human species. We are French or American, Hindu or Christian, mothers or fathers, and thus human in our own mediated and unique ways. And we are all these because we have certain distinctive capacities and needs by virtue of being human. We attain glimpses of our universal identity not by abstracting our various differences, but rather by comprehending imaginatively distant millions in their uniqueness, and thus as beings who are at once both similar and different, or rather similar by virtue of being different.
>
> (Parekh, 2008, p. 3)

While Parekh's work is quite recent, there is also important sociological understanding to be gained from more long-standing theory. For example, Goffman, a classical sociologist, wrote convincingly of the significance of stigma in developing what he referred to as 'a spoiled identity' (Goffman, 1990). His work has been influential in helping us to understand how certain social processes can lead to some people having a negative label attached to them; something which can be very significant in terms of how that person is perceived by people in the wider society and therefore how that person comes to see him- or herself. This is something that is very relevant to social work, as so many of the people we seek to help will be prone to being stigmatized in this way (because of mental health problems, for example).

A further important aspect of being a 'person' is that each of us will have a differing sense of self in differing social contexts. This does not mean we will not know who we are – indeed, the ability to retain a sense of a coherent self across very different social situations is very much what identity is all about. We generally have the ability to adapt different aspects of our identity to different situations. Having difficulties in retaining such coherence is commonly associated with people who are deemed to be 'schizophrenic' (a term that refers to having a 'fractured' sense of self, rather than – as is commonly believed – a 'split personality'). Parekh's comments are again insightful:

> Since human life is inherently plural in the sense that different areas of life are autonomous to different degrees and make independent claims, different identities cannot be subordinated to any one of them, however far-reaching it might otherwise be. The context decides which identity is relevant, and that identity, as socially defined, largely dictates appropriate behaviour.
>
> (2008, p. 23)

This is an important point for social work. It means that we cannot form a view of a person's identity from limited information. For example, it would be a serious mistake to assume that a man who is very pleasant, charming, considerate and well-mannered could not abuse a child ('He's far too nice and caring'). How he comes across in certain social situations may be very different from how he relates to children when he is alone with them and in a position of power over them.

Voice of experience 4.1

Maybe I was naive at first, but I had not realised just how 'ordinary' child abusers seem to be. I suppose I hadn't really thought it through, but I soon realized when I came into this type of work that there is nothing about an individual that stands out and says: 'Look at me, I'm a monster who abuses children.' The whole situation is much more complex than that.

Marie, a child protection social worker

Our understanding of identity has also been increased in recent years by an emerging emphasis on spirituality. This is evidenced in the work of Moss. He argues that spirituality:

is a sort of 'short-hand' way of asking the fundamental questions about ourselves – what makes us 'tick'; what is important to us; what gives us a sense of meaning and purpose in our lives. In short, it asks of people what is their world-view.

(2005, p. 12)

The work of Moss and others (see, for example, Coyte, Gilbert and Nicholls, 2007) is part of a growing awareness of how spirituality and its concerns with the existential issues we all face are very relevant issues not only for social work, but also for the helping professions more broadly – and, indeed for our understanding of human experience in general. We shall return to this important topic in Chapter 13.

In considering how an individual's sense of self can best be understood, it is also important to take account of Bourdieu's notion of 'habitus' (1984; 1992). This refers to the collection of habits and ways of understanding that become a deeply ingrained part of an individual's conception of their life. Crossley explains it as follows:

The concept of the habitus points to the pre-reflective nature of much of our action and indeed to the habitual structure of consciousness itself. How we perceive, think and feel is shaped by sedimented traces of our past experiences which we remain largely unaware of in Bourdieu's view, that is, by habitual expectations and assumptions.

(2005, p. 108)

This is an important concept because it links the individual's personal circumstances to the wider social sphere, in so far as habitus reflects that individual's engagement with the wider social world, rather than simply being (as much of the traditional psychological literature would have us believe) a matter of what happens in our own mind, separate from social factors. Callinicos offers an important perspective on this:

By *habitus* Bourdieu means a particular set of dispositions, consisting especially in the practical abilities required to apply categories that are means of perceiving and of appreciating the world, appropriate to a specific objective position within the class structure. ... The *habitus* constitutes the means through which individual actors are adapted to the needs of specific social structures.

(2007, pp. 295–6)

In developing our 'habitus', we adopt habitualized ways of understanding and behaving – but these do not occur at random, they reflect the social structure. Indeed, habitus can be seen as a fundamental means through which the structure is maintained and reproduced over time. Each individual 'connects' with the wider cultural assumptions and practices in his or her social environment. This cultural sphere acts as a link between the wider social structure (the cultural level is in large part shaped by the structural level) and the personal level. Habitus can be understood as the individual's connection with the cultural level (the means by which the cultural level helps to shape the personal level) – that is, the individual becomes 'socialized' into their culture (Rubinstein, 2001).

In trying to understand the 'person', therefore, we need to bear in mind that he or she will be a unique individual in their own right, but will also be 'embedded' in wider cultural and structural formations that are very influential, but which do not *determine* who or what the individual is (Thompson, 2003a).

It is also helpful to distinguish between identity and identities. This is, in a sense, a recognition of the fluidity of identity, that it is not something that is fixed and static. As noted above, we will have, to a certain extent, different identities in different circumstances. For example, someone who is a senior executive in a large organization may adopt a particular persona in that setting, while being a very different person in many respects when, for example, playing on the floor with his or her grandchildren. It is not without significance that the terms 'person', 'persona' and 'personality' are derived from the Greek word for 'mask'.

Subjectivity, objectivity and narrative

The concept of 'dialectical reason' has already been mentioned. I have previously explained this in the following terms:

> Analytical reason breaks things down into their component parts, and this is an essential first step in the process of understanding. It is, however, only a first step and needs to be followed by *synthesis* – the linking together of those parts into a coherent whole. The process of synthesis ... is the hallmark of dialectical reason. ... The dialectic refers to the process by which conflicting forces come together and produce change.
>
> (Thompson, 2000a, p. 68)

Fundamentally, adopting dialectical reason involves recognizing the limitations of forms of thought that neglect the significance of change and interactions and seeking to go beyond them by adopting a more sophisticated form of reasoning. Dialectical reason emphasizes the *dynamic* nature of society and indeed of human experience more broadly. It helps us to avoid static forms of understanding that neglect the significance of conflict, change, history and development.

Dialectical reason can be applied to the relationship between subjectivity and objectivity, in the sense that the two can be seen to interact and influence each other. This is an important point, because, in existentialist terms, there is neither pure subjectivity nor pure objectivity. The objective world 'out there' needs to be interpreted, made sense of; it cannot be understood 'directly' without being mediated by human consciousness – that is, subjectivity. And, in turn, subjectivity cannot exist unless there is an objective world to relate to. What this means is that no person's personal, internal thoughts can be entirely separated from the wider objective world, but nor is there any pure objectivity in the sense of an understanding of the world that is not in some way shaped by the perspective of the individual concerned. Subjectivity and objectivity interact and shape each other: my encounters with the (objective) world shape my (subjective) understanding of that world (for example, dealing with someone who has a drink problem can help me to understand the impact of alcohol abuse on families), but, by acting on the basis of that understanding, I may be able to change the nature of that objective world (for example, by helping the family to deal with the problems presented by excessive drinking). The technical term for this is 'the dialectic of subjectivity and objectivity'. It is an important existentialist concept to which we shall return later, but for now, it is important to note that 'the person' needs to be understood in the context of the dialectic of subjectivity and objectivity if we are to do justice to the complexities involved and not oversimplify it.

This is the basis of the philosophical discipline of hermeneutics which is, literally, the 'study of meaning'. An important figure in this regard is the philosopher, Hans-Georg Gadamer whose work on hermeneutics has been extremely influential (Dostal, 2002; Gadamer, 2004). Consistent with the existentialist emphasis on perception and interpretation, Gadamer's work teaches us to emphasize meanings, not causes. In trying to understand a person's behaviour, who that person is, how they fit into the wider world and so on, we should be looking for meanings, not objective causes. This is because the basis of identity is the dialectic of subjectivity and objectivity, the interactions, as discussed above, between the individual's perception and the wider world that he or she is perceiving – each influencing the other.

Practice focus 4.2

Anna was a social worker in a project working with sexually abused children. She enjoyed the work and found it rewarding, even though it was quite demanding, physically and emotionally. The longer she worked there, the more determined she was to understand what was happening to the children, what was going through their minds. She developed quite a few ideas about this and was particularly interested in issues to do with trauma. In addition, she developed an interest in how children's understandings were shaped by the abuser. For example, she became aware that many of the children she worked with had been led to believe that adult–child sexual encounters were perfectly normal and unproblematic. Anna wanted to develop a fuller understanding of how this happened and how the children who had been sexually abused came to perceive sexuality in very different terms from their peers. She wanted to have a clearer view of what processes were taking place that had such a profound impact on how they perceived sexuality. It was this perception, she believed, that enabled the perpetrator to persuade them that sexual contact was acceptable. In other words, she wanted to work out the mechanisms by which the *objective* occurrence of abuse came about through the *subjective* perceptions that such behaviour between adults and children was acceptable.

Much has been written about the social construction of reality, the way in which social formations shape an individual's experience of the world and how it is understood by that person. For example, the work of Berger and Luckmann (1967) has been of immense influence in shaping modern-day understandings of the relationship between individuals and society. Their notion that reality is socially constructed (that is, it is not simply 'given' as an absolute, but is developed through social processes) has led to some very helpful understandings. However, we should not allow an emphasis on the *social* construction of reality to mask the fact that there are also important issues in terms of the *personal* construction of reality, in the sense that no two people will have an identical sense of what reality is, because no two people will have identical experiences and identical perceptions of those experiences.

This is not to deny the usefulness of the concept of social construction, but rather to point out that it needs to be complemented by the concept of the personal construction of reality and a recognition of how the two sets of factors interrelate dialectically. To focus on the social construction of reality without also taking account of the personal dimension is to fall foul of reductionism, as discussed in Chapter 1, as it neglects the important role of agency. Archer makes the point that: 'we must neither under- nor over-privilege human agency in our analytical approach' (2000, p. 21). An approach to identity that focuses on social construction without personal construction would be an example of the former error.

This is partly reflected in the work of Parton and O'Byrne (2000) on 'constructive social work', as they call it. They emphasize the significance of meanings that are partly personal and individual, but also partly shaped by wider social forces. Their approach is a helpful one, particularly in terms of the emphasis on the significance of narratives. A narrative is a story, a relatively coherent understanding of who we are and how we fit into the wider world. In a sense, it is a further example of the importance of spirituality (see Chapter 13).

The notion of narrative is not a new idea. Historically it can be traced back to the time of the ancient Greek philosophers. As Crawford, Dickinson and Leitmann comment: 'Narrative as a form of researching, representing and understanding human experience dates back to Aristotle and is a strong thread throughout the history of Western scholarship' (2002, p. 175). As well as being historically significant, narratives are also theoretically important. This is because they become a foundation for our sense of self and, as such, they are an important factor in terms of our understanding of identity.

Voice of experience 4.2

My work often involves me in trying to help people change some aspect of their self they are not happy with – for example, by trying to boost self-esteem. It's not quite personality change that we go in for, but there is a strong emphasis on helping the women we work with to see themselves more positively and shake off the negative and demeaning images that they have had foisted upon them. In effect, we are helping them to write a new self-narrative, a more empowering one.

Loreen, a social worker in a women's empowerment project

Narratives do not exist in a social vacuum. If we want to understand personal narratives and how they relate to identity, we need to see them in their broader context. In particular, we need to appreciate the significant role of cultural meanings – that is, cultural influences on the development of our self-narratives. Parekh's comments help to cast some light on this:

> Culture refers to a historically inherited system of meaning and significance in terms of which a group of people understand and structure their individual and collective lives. It defines the meaning or point of human activities, social relations and human life in general, and the significance or value to be attached to them. It is embodied in its beliefs and practices, which collectively constitute its fuzzy but recognizable identity. To say that almost every modern society is culturally diverse or multicultural is to say that its members subscribe to and live by different, though overlapping systems of meaning and significance.
>
> (2008, p. 80)

This passage helps us to recognize that the individual needs to be understood by reference to his or her cultural context. These are important issues to which we shall return in Chapter 7.

One further important feature of our understanding of identity is the concept of alienation. It was used in the work of Marx to refer to how workers are alienated by capitalism, in the sense that their labour is taken from them but without full recompense, in so far as the capitalist class draws off the surplus profit. In other words, because the relationship between capital and labour is not an equal one, workers become alienated from their own labour. Other writers, for example Blauner (1967), have taken this idea further to extend it to other forms of alienation, other ways in which people can be left feeling separated or isolated from their sense of who they are and their value in the wider world. This is a concept that has also been taken up in the existentialist literature and is one that has important implications for social work (Krill, 1978). In an existentialist sense, alienation can be understood as a fundamental part of the human condition. However, social factors such as poverty, deprivation, stigmatization and discrimination can reinforce and amplify this fundamental alienation. On the other hand, factors such as solidarity and 'connectedness' (to be discussed in Chapter 13) can help to counter it.

Time and change

As we have noted, identity is not a matter of each of us being a fixed, immutable entity. People change over time as they are exposed to different influences and as they gradually grow, develop and change their perspective on issues. Such an understanding of the complexity of identity shows how inadequate it is to have a fixed notion of personality. If we are to have a good understanding of identity and the person, then we need to understand what the factors are that are significant in bringing about a change in a person's identity.

One of the most significant factors in promoting change is a crisis. A crisis can be defined as a turning point in somebody's life (Thompson, 1991). It is not to be confused with an emergency. The concept is much more sophisticated than that. A crisis is a point where a person can no longer go on as before. The point has been reached where the situation will either get worse or it will get better, but it cannot, by definition, stay the same. There are two types of crisis in people's lives. The first type is known as a 'developmental' crisis. This refers to expected crises relating to turning points in our lives. These are often fully explored in the literature relating to human development. For example, adolescence can be seen as a crisis in which the child can no longer continue to be a child and faces what is in reality a series of crises, rather than one major one. Other life crises would include leaving home, getting married or establishing a marital-like relationship, one's children leaving home, retirement and so on.

Alongside these developmental crises will be a set of unexpected ones that are linked to particular events arising from the circumstances we encounter. Such crises will generally include a strong element of loss, and so examples of such crises would include the death of someone close to us. However, it is important not to equate crisis with death, as many crises have no direct connection with death (Thompson, 2002a). Such examples would include the breakdown of a relationship, being made redundant or becoming disabled as a result of a road traffic accident. 'Crisis' is therefore an important concept, not only in terms of our general understanding of change relating to the person, but also specifically in connection with social work, in so far as social work situations are often closely associated with a crisis scenario of some description.

Practice focus 4.3

Peter had been working with the Dawson family for quite some time due to the multiple problems they were experiencing. Superficially they seemed to welcome his help and genuinely seemed to want to solve their problems and move on with their lives. However, when it came to taking concrete steps, they always seemed to falter. They always seemed to have one reason or another for why they had not done what they had agreed to do (or had not stopped doing what they had agreed to stop doing). Peter was beginning to wonder whether they were just making excuses and had no real commitment to improving their situation. He was beginning to become concerned that they could be trying to create a situation of dependency in which he was doing what he had agreed to, but they were not doing their side of the bargain, increasingly placing more emphasis on *his* role in resolving the family's difficulties and less on *theirs*. However, the situation changed completely when Mrs Dawson had a heart attack and was admitted to hospital. She was the domestic mainstay of the family (as is so often the case), and so what was previously a difficult situation for the family was now one that needed to change urgently. Peter found that, in the context of the crisis, everyone was highly motivated to do what needed to be done to make things work. He was amazed by the transformation that had taken place. What he had read about crisis intervention when he was at university made an awful lot more sense to him now.

Existentialism can once again be helpful in offering us some degree of understanding. In particular, what Sartre referred to as the 'progressive-regressive method' can offer major insights. The basic idea behind this is that, if we want to understand a person as they currently are, then we need to understand the past and how it has shaped their current sense of self to a certain extent (this is the *regressive* element, the looking back part) and we must also consider the future in terms of plans and aspirations (this is the *progressive* element, looking towards the future). The *present* is understood as the meeting point of *past* experiences and *future* desires. Just as individuals do not exist in a social vacuum, nor do we exist in a temporal vacuum – that is, the present does not exist in isolation; it is shaped in part by (our reaction to) the past we have experienced and the future we are anticipating experiencing. The person is a dynamic entity, not a static one (hence the emphasis on dialectical reason).

This differs from other theoretical perspectives which will generally tend to look at either of these temporal dimensions, but not both. For example, psychoanalysis has a tendency to focus on the past and how, for example, childhood influences have had a major part to play in shaping adult personality. Behaviourism, by contrast, focuses on the future in terms of how behaviour will be reinforced by a particular goal that is being pursued. Existentialism presents both of these approaches as inadequate, although neither should necessarily be rejected altogether (this is another example of the importance of not being a 'club' member and thereby having to choose between theoretical alternatives rather than seek to integrate elements to create new insights).

Existentialism recognizes that an adequate understanding of change in a person's life must take account of both past and future influences. That is, we need to understand both temporal dimensions as key contributors to the present, to who we are and where we are up to in our journey. Butt's conception of selfhood reflects the basis of this progressive-regressive method:

> what 'having a self' means is having a constructive relationship to the past and the future. It is not that past events cause anything in our action, but the way in which we make sense of them clearly informs everything we do. Similarly, nothing in the future can determine what we do. Nevertheless, we live in anticipation, and the stance we take towards things inevitably affects how we act as well as others act in relation to us.

(2004, p. 137)

Voice of experience 4.3

When I first started working with older people I concentrated solely on the present – what are their needs at the moment? What challenges do they face now? How can I help them at this present time? That's the way my thinking went. Thankfully, though, I had a team manager who helped me to understand that older people have an identity that is rooted in part in the past and that to neglect this can amount to dehumanizing them. She also taught me that older people have a future and that it is an ageist assumption to see older people as being at the end of life. None of us knows how much longer we will live but we all have a future, however long or short that may be.

Laura, a social worker in a multidisciplinary mental health team

Conclusion

One of the traditional values of social work is 'respect for persons' (N. Thompson and S. Thompson, 2008). It is to be hoped that this chapter has laid the foundations for understanding that, if we do not show respect for persons, we will be in a position where we can do more harm than good. However, what this chapter has also shown is that there is a strong need to see the person in the wider context and not to regard each individual as an isolated entity. This is a consideration that will be explored in more detail in Chapter 5.

Social work is *people* work; it involves connecting with people in a meaningful way. This cannot be done effectively and ethically if we lack an adequate understanding of the person. If we lose sight of the fact that each of us has a self, an identity that makes us unique, then the result can be a form of dehumanizing (and thus disempowering) practice that takes us far from our value base and our professional purpose. This chapter has laid the foundations for developing a fuller understanding of what it means to be a 'person' and why this is important. In this way, it should play a part in equipping us to *theorize* the practice situations we encounter.

Points to ponder

1. Why is identity an important part of the social work knowledge base?
2. Consider your own identity. What social factors have helped to shape who you are?
3. In what ways could the idea of 'narrative' be of use in social work practice?

Further reading

Craib (1998) offers a thought-provoking discussion of identity. Lawler (2008) and Pullen, Beech and Sims (2007) are also useful sources. Goffman (1990) is a classic work on the way identity can be 'spoiled' by stigma. Every social worker should read this. Parekh (2008) offers a good overview of the wider social aspects of identity, while Thompson (2002b) discusses the child development aspects of identity – see also Hunt (2005). Archer (2000) presents an interesting discussion of personal agency.

5

Interpersonal interactions

Introduction

I was fortunate enough to learn, at an early point in my social work career, that 'all action is interaction'. That is, I became aware that what we do as individuals and as groups does not take place in ways that are unconnected with the wider social world. What one person does has an impact on those around him or her. Similarly, what others do has an impact on the individual. The work of Gergen (1999) and many others has emphasized the significance of interaction as a major factor in shaping people's lives. Consistent with the view of identity presented in Chapter 4, an interactional approach is premised on the idea that our sense of who we are grows from our contact with others and their reactions to us (see the discussion of the 'looking-glass self' below). Casey captures this idea in pointing out that: 'As the philosophers Ricouer and Levinas (and Buber before them) respectively theorize, the subject-self is a relational one. It requires the other to be itself' (2002, p. 192).

There is also a long tradition in sociological thinking of recognizing the significance of interaction – for example, in the work of Mead (1967) and other symbolic interactionist thinkers (Forte, 2001) right through to current emphases on post-structuralist approaches (Petersen et al., 1999; Tew, 2002). This interactionist perspective attaches considerable importance to the role of human interactions as a basis of social life. As we shall see, this has major implications for social work theory and practice. Butt gives some important insights into how significant this can be as a foundation for understanding:

> What makes social life interesting and valuable is that the whole interaction cannot be simply assembled from the parts. It is the organising of

the parts into a meaningful gestalt that characterises interactions in the human order.

It is this formulation of the social act that Blumer (1969) and Shotter (1993) refer to as 'joint action'. The outcome of a social act cannot be traced back to the individual intentions of any of the participants.

(2004, p. 122)

This concept of 'joint action' can be seen as very relevant to social work. It captures well the fundamental role of partnership as a social work value – the need for social workers to work *with* others (clients, carers, other professionals), rather than in isolation from them.

A further important implication of an interactional approach is that, in effect, when we act, we become part of our encounters. We are not neutral observers of what goes on around us. We are part of the scenario and, in many ways, the scenarios we engage in become part of us. This is one of the reasons why reflective practice is so important: it is not simply a matter of finding understanding through personal introspection; rather, it is a case of examining both the internal, subjective factors and the external, objective ones and the interactions between the two of them, as discussed in Chapter 4. In this chapter, we build on many of the issues discussed in the previous one, but with a particular focus on the role of other people in shaping identity in particular and our life experience in general.

Intersubjectivity

Crossley is a sociologist who emphasizes the importance of understanding human experience in terms of what he calls 'intersubjectivity' (Crossley, 1999). This is a significant movement away from the traditional atomistic notion that individuals are isolated entities in their own right and can be meaningfully separated from the wider social context. Crossley's work shows due deference to the influence of one of the leading thinkers in the field of social interaction, namely George Herbert Mead (Mead, 1967) as well as to the existentialist writer, Maurice Merleau-Ponty (Merleau-Ponty, 1962; 1965). Mead's work, in particular, has proven highly influential in terms of micro-level sociology – that is, the study of how societal factors materialize at a small-scale interpersonal level. The use of the concept of 'intersubjectivity' is basically a recognition of the fact that (individual) subjectivity is necessarily *inter*subjective – that is, my sense of reality is influenced by the perceptions, actions and reactions of those people I react with. Crossley's comments illustrate this point well:

> private spaces are not inner spaces but are carved out of intersubjective space, by way of intersubjective experience; that is, we tend to keep private those matters that it is generally (intersubjectively) agreed that we ought.
>
> (1999, p. 34)

What seem to be private, personal, individual matters are therefore, in reality, shared matters – they exist in a social, intersubjective space. To see it otherwise would be to fall foul of the pitfall of atomism.

One of the other significant interactionist thinkers was Charles Horton Cooley. He introduced the notion of the 'looking-glass self' (Cooley, 1902). By this he meant that how we project ourselves to other people depends in part on how other people react to us (the metaphorical reflection in the mirror or 'looking glass'), and how people react to us will, of course, depend in large part on how we project ourselves to them:

> This describes an interactive view of the self in which the individual's self-perception owes much to the feedback he or she receives from others – that is, how I see myself will depend, to a certain extent at least, on how other people see me.
>
> (Thompson, 2002b, p. 19)

There are already, therefore, in this early theory of interaction elements of an understanding of dialectical reason, although Cooley did not express his ideas explicitly in those terms.

One important factor that social workers need to understand in relation to intersubjectivity is that people influence people. This can be deliberate or unintentional. In terms of the former, we are talking about efforts to persuade or to convince others of the value of a particular course of action. However, we are often influenced by other people (and, in turn influence, them) without there being any deliberate intention to do so (Folgheraiter, 2004). It is a fact of social interaction that people shape other people's perspectives and behaviour. As Crossley comments: 'By entering into dialogue, subjects transcend their individuation and become components in a larger whole' (1999, p. 8). We are not isolated individuals, as atomism would have us believe; we are active agents in a broader field of social interaction.

Practice focus 5.1

Jason and his parents were constantly in conflict. They did not seem to see eye to eye on anything. This was more than ordinary parent–teenager storm and stress. In fact the situation had become so problematic that his parents had approached their GP asking about having Jason 'taken into care'. The GP had referred the matter to the local children's services and, May, an experienced social worker was allocated the case. May met with the family and began a process of assessment with a view to helping the family resolve their difficulties so that it would not be necessary to receive Jason into care. One thing May noticed at an early stage in the assessment process was that there wasn't much listening going on in this family. Jason's parents constantly spoke over each other and neither of them paid much attention to what Jason had to say. She soon came to realize that a feature of this family's interactions was a strong tendency not to listen. She could see that Jason had learned this pattern of behaviour under the influence of his parents – and his tendency not to listen was being seen by his parents as a rejection of their authority (rather than a lesson they had taught him!). She could see now that, if she was going to help the family resolve their constant conflicts, she would need to help them learn how to listen to each other.

This is closely linked to the idea of the social construction of reality, as discussed in Chapter 4. This again moves us away from the idea of atomism, with each person as an isolated individual, separate from the wider social sphere. A more accurate and helpful understanding would be one which takes account of the way our interactions with each other shape our experience quite significantly. Laing (1972) wrote of the 'knots' of human experience – that is, the way we can tie each other and ourselves in knots through the complexities of interactions.

There is an important lesson here for us in relation to social work practice, as these 'knots' of complex interactions are part and parcel of the complex interweavings of social work interventions. They are not isolated incidents that will be encountered from time to time, but, rather, common aspects of practice.

Voice of experience 5.1

I must admit I came into social work with a very simplistic understanding of people and society. I knew there were individuals and that we were all part of society, but I had no conception of how complex it all is, with individuals and groups all influencing each other and, on top of that, there are all the social processes and institutions and cultural influences that play their part too. Looking back, I realize how naive and ill-informed I was in those days.

Ceri, a practice teacher in a voluntary organization

The early symbolic interactionists, such as Mead and Cooley, played a very important role in laying the foundations for our understanding. However, their work can be criticized in some respects for not taking enough account of wider social factors. Their work is predominantly at a micro-level, with little or no attention paid to larger scale macro-level phenomena (although potentially their work could be developed to incorporate those elements). For example, there are significant dynamics in terms of gender, race, age, disability, sexuality, and so on, that also play a part in shaping the way people interact and the way they develop shared meanings, which is fundamentally what the notion of intersubjectivity is all about. This brings us back, then, to the dialectic of subjectivity and objectivity, the recognition that there will be a to-ing and fro-ing between personal factors and the wider social realities.

Intersubjectivity is not only a useful theoretical concept in the abstract. It also has implications for social work practice. Indeed, it can be seen as an important part of theorizing social work: to make sense of the practice situations we encounter, we need to take account of the interactional nature of subjective experience. It involves recognizing that, while each person's reality is unique to that person, it is also part of our shared reality.

In terms of practice implications, Hamer's comments are helpful:

It has been shown time and time again that the most therapeutic part of any therapeutic relationship is the relationship itself. Not the stuff that is done, not the therapies, but the interaction between two human beings.

The gift you offer another person is just your being.
Ram Dass

You can make people feel respected, worthwhile and hopeful, you can build trust from the very moment you meet with them.

(2006, p. 12)

Also significant for practice is Jordan's concept of the 'interpersonal economy'. This refers to the way in which people interacting together create value (in the same way that financial interactions produce value or wealth in the material economy). Social interactions can enrich people's lives (or impoverish them if they are oppressive or disempowering interactions – see below). Jordan summarizes the situation as follows:

> So the value of each human being is in their membership of the interpersonal economy, and the fact that (whether we like it or not) they share in the giving and receiving of value through these interactions. In this way, they also share in the creation and exchange of emotions and cultural resources. In so far as we are all members of this interpersonal system, our fates are inextricably linked with each other's. We can enhance or damage each other, but we cannot evade our mutual influences, or escape from the web of feelings and ideas through all our encounters.
>
> (2007, p. xi)

This idea can be linked with the concept of 'social capital'. This refers to the metaphorical wealth an individual has as a result of their social connections. It describes the ways in which some people have stronger resources to fall back on in terms of relationships and connections with people. It is parallel with the notion of financial capital. Those people who are rich in social capital are likely to have lots of friends, relatives and associates, and perhaps be members of various clubs, societies, associations, and so on, while those who are low in social capital are likely to lack the benefits of such connections. Compare, for example, the differences between Mrs Moore and Miss Stout, both aged 82.

Mrs Moore

Her daughter and her family live nearby. Her son and his family live about ten miles away but visit regularly and invite her over quite frequently too.

She has neighbours on each side that she has regular contact with. She is a long-standing active member of the Women's Institute and, while she is not as actively involved as she used to be, she is still an active member and maintains contact with other members on a regular basis.

She attends the local church at least weekly.

Prior to retirement she was a teacher and still maintains telephone contact with several ex-colleagues.

Miss Stout

She lives alone, with no living relatives.

She has no contact with neighbours.

She is not a member of any club or society.

She has no church or other community connections.

Prior to reaching retirement age, she was a homemaker and part-time cleaner. She has long since lost contact with people she knew at work.

The difference between people in terms of their social capital can lead to huge differences in terms of quality of life and whether or not they are able to withstand life's pressures and challenges at times when they need help. This is a further example of the significance of interactions with other people as a set of factors that can and often do have a major bearing on how people's lives are lived, what problems (and potential solutions) they encounter and thus their overall level of well-being. We shall return to this point in Chapter 13 when we examine the significance of 'connectedness' as a dimension of spirituality.

Communication

Of course, it would be remiss to attempt to explore interpersonal interactions without considering the key topic of communication. In an earlier work (Thompson, 2003b) I made the very important point that we cannot not communicate. That is, whatever we do, individually or collectively, gives off messages to other people, whether intentionally or not. This is largely how we manage to influence one another, often unintentionally, because the messages we give off will be picked up by other people, and the messages other people give off will in turn be received by us. The upshot of these interactions tends to be that our communications play a part in shaping not only our own sense of reality, but also the reality of other people. This reinforces the point made earlier that we cannot understand individuals outside of the broader social context, including, as a key part of that context, our interactions with other people.

Communication can be divided into three main categories. These are language, paralanguage and body language. Each of these is worth considering in a little more detail:

1. *Language*. This refers to the use of speech, whether directly in terms of oral usage or in its written forms. This is clearly a very significant and powerful form of communication and we would be very remiss if we were to neglect the primary role of language in shaping social work interactions. Chapter 12, entitled 'the linguistic turn', focuses specifically on the significance of language in social work, and so we will revisit these issues at that point. However, at this juncture it is important to note that language is a fundamental feature of not only social life in general, but of professional practice in particular (Thompson, 2003b). The use of language is a highly complex subject and one that is often prone to oversimplification. It is therefore essential that the issues involved are given careful consideration, hence a chapter devoted to the subject in Part Three.

2. *Paralanguage*. This refers to the subtle signals that accompany the use of language. This would include such factors as the speech rate – that is, the speed at which somebody speaks – pitch, tone, and so on. These can be very significant and highly meaningful in terms of shaping communicative interactions. Everyday users of language will have learned how to use these accompanying features as part of the development of their repertoire of communication skills. In the vast majority of cases, the users of these skills will not even be aware that they are using them. In order to reach an advanced level of skills in these areas (as social workers can generally be expected to do), it is necessary to develop a greater awareness of what is involved in their use, so that the skills involved can be practised at a higher level of sophistication. For example, becoming more aware of the use of tone of voice can mean that it can be used to good effect to calm down someone who is agitated. Without the more advanced understanding of such matters, the result may be that our (perhaps nervous, insecure) tone of voice leads to an increased level of agitation.

3. *Body language*. Nonverbal communication is also a very powerful factor in shaping how people interact and what meanings they

attach to those interactions. Interpersonal interactions owe much to nonverbal communication, in the sense that our bodily movements play a central role in conveying meaning, establishing rapport and taking the interaction in a particular direction. As with paralanguage, the skills of nonverbal communication are generally developed as part of our repertoire of life skills and tend to be used without our being consciously aware of them or how we are utilizing them. Achieving an advanced level of skill in terms of interpersonal interactions similarly involves developing a more conscious awareness of how we are using our bodies as tools of communication and a greater ability to be able to 'read' the signals being given off by others. The highly skilled use of body language can, in certain circumstances, be even more effective as a form of communication than actual spoken (or written) language. It would therefore be a significant mistake to neglect this aspect of communication.

All three of these forms of communication involve power relations (Thompson, 2007a; Westwood, 2002). It is important to recognize at this point that communication is not something that is neutral in terms of the interplay of power. Interpersonal interactions based on communication are, in effect, power dynamics. This is a point to which we shall return below.

Practice focus 5.2

Daniel was very impressed with his colleague, Marcella. She seemed to have a great knack for putting people at their ease and establishing a really good rapport with them very quickly. One day he complimented her on this, and told her he wished he had the sort of personality she had, as he was far less successful at engaging with people. In response she thanked him for his compliment but said that it was not a matter of personality, it was one of skills. She had learned the skills of rapport building in the early stages of her career and had continued to build on them over time. She pointed out to him that seeing her ability as a personality issue rather than a set of skills was unnecessarily defeatist. He was delighted, albeit a little bit unnerved, to hear that he too could learn to be better at engaging with people by developing more advanced communication skills.

However, communication is not simply a set of skills. There is also the relationship between communication and selfhood to consider.

This is a two-way relationship, in so far as how we communicate will, to a certain extent, *reflect* who we are, but it will also play a part in *shaping* who we are. The point was made earlier that our identity will in part be shaped by our interactions with other people, and those interactions will, of course, take place through the medium of communication, reflecting all three aspects as outlined above: direct language, paralanguage and body language. Van Deurzen and Arnold-Baker argue that an existentialist understanding of selfhood is a helpful basis for making sense of this:

> The flexible view of self that comes with an existential perspective can be extremely empowering. We no longer have to think that clients are condemned to a weak ego, or perceive their personality as pathological or their character as tragically set and determined by circumstances. The existential perspective allows for a broader outlook on selfhood and identity, which shows how we are always in transformation and capable of altering the direction we take.
>
> (2005a, p. 169)

How such transformations take place will depend very much on communication in particular and interpersonal interactions in general.

We can now make links between the discussions in this chapter and the picture of 'the person', identity or self discussed in the previous chapter. What we should now be able to see is that there is a continuity between them: to understand the individual, we need to take account of the interpersonal interactions that he or she is constantly engaged in (as well as the wider cultural and structural spheres, as we shall see in Chapters 7 and 8 respectively). However, by the same token, to understand the interpersonal interactions, we also need to take account of how the person features in such interactions – for example, to ensure that we do not fall foul of the pitfall of determinism by losing sight of the individual's perceptions, choices and actions – or, to use the technical term, their 'agency' (Archer, 2000). To be able to theorize human experience (and therefore be able to respond to it in an informed and helpful way), whether specifically in a social work context or more broadly, we therefore need to understand the dialectical relationship between the individual self and the complex web of social interactions that he or she forms part of.

There is also an important relationship between communication and selfhood or identity in terms of *social* identity. As Parekh comments:

> A social identity represents the way in which individuals situate and orientate themselves in the world. It offers a point of view, a way of looking at themselves and others, and is, like all points of view, constituted by certain assumptions and categories of thought.
>
> (2008, p. 23)

Such factors will clearly influence communication, and so we need to make sure that our efforts to make sense of interpersonal interactions are firmly rooted in a *sociological* understanding that does not rely on atomistic assumptions about individual identity.

Another key sociological factor in terms of communication is the important relationship between language and discrimination. Language use can be a very significant means of reinforcing and perpetuating patterns of discrimination and thus of oppression. Unfortunately, these issues have commonly been oversimplified and dismissed as 'political correctness'. In reality, the situation is far more complex than this, as language use can be quite harmful in terms of excluding or marginalizing people, demeaning and disempowering them and stigmatizing and stereotyping them. It is something that, as social workers, we need to consider very carefully if we are to – at the very least – avoid situations in which our use of language exacerbates existing problems of discrimination and – at best – make a positive and constructive contribution to empowerment, social justice and well-being through the skilful use of language.

What is also important is the recognition of action as in itself a form of communication. That is, what people *do* can say as much as what they say. This is not simply a matter of body language which, as we noted above, is important enough in its own right. It involves going even further than this in terms of looking at how a person's actions (or inactions) may be conveying a particular message. For example, a child's use of play may give us some important clues about his or her experiences, feelings and concerns (perhaps indicating concerns about possible abuse – Corby, 2005).

This leads us to ask the important question: what are people saying through their behaviour? For example, someone not turning up for three consecutive appointments may be telling us something. As with any form of communication, we have to be careful not to jump to conclusions about what it means – missing three appointments could indicate (i) a disorganized person; (ii) a person who is not normally disorganized, but who is going through difficulties at present; (iii) a person who is trying to tell you that they do not want your help; or (iv) a person trying to establish the helping relationship on their terms, not yours; and so on. Meanings are highly context dependent and therefore not straightforward. However, they none the less need to be taken into consideration.

And, of course, this question of behaviour being in itself a form of communication applies to ourselves too – that is, we need to be clear about what we are saying through our behaviour as professional practitioners. Imagine, for example, the following scenarios and how they may be interpreted:

Scenario	Possible (adverse) interpretation
The social worker is constantly late for appointments.	The social worker is disorganized or uncommitted and therefore unreliable.
The social worker behaves in a way that gives a strong message that he or she is a very busy person (for example, rushing about a lot).	The client feels that they are not important to the worker, that he or she has other priorities.
The social worker makes decisions without fully involving the client in the process.	The social worker is a powerful person who has his or her own agenda and is not to be trusted.

If we are to be able to theorize the complexities involved in interpersonal interactions, then clearly we need to be tuned in to the role of behaviour in communicating important messages – sometimes the messages we do not want to communicate.

Patterns of communication are also very significant in terms of the potential for empowerment. In my earlier work, *Practising Social Work,* I argued that there is much to be gained from focusing on problem solving as a means of promoting well-being, as it is through the process of problem solving that people can be helped to move beyond the barriers that are holding them back. As such, this approach offers tremendous potential for empowerment. However, it has to be recognized that fundamental to this approach is communication. As we have recognized, communication is the foundation of interpersonal interactions. Clearly, then, as social workers, we need to be very well attuned to the issues of communication as they affect our work.

Voice of experience 5.2

I have worked with a wide range of social workers over the years. They have ranged from excellent to not so wonderful, but for me one of the key things that separates the good ones from the disappointing ones is *communication*. The best social workers are really skilled communicators. There's no substitute for it really.

Roy, a very experienced foster carer

Consensus, conflict and power

It is commonly assumed that harmony and consensus form the fundamental basis of human experience and, as such, they are perceived as the building blocks of our reality. However, when we look at this assumption more closely, we very quickly see that conflict is a key issue too. A more accurate portrayal of the basis of reality, then, is a mixture of harmony and conflict. It is therefore a mistake to see conflict as the breakdown of normality, the end of a previous basis of consensus. That would be too simplistic an understanding of a very complex set of issues. Existentialism recognizes that conflict is a basic feature of human existence, in so far as people's plans and projects will inevitably become crossed – it would be naive in the extreme to assume that people are not going to get in each other's way from time to time. However, the matter is often greatly oversimplified. For example, many people equate conflict with fighting and therefore see it as something to be frightened of. Fighting is, in effect, what occurs when our conflict management approaches have not been successful. Fighting is not in itself a form of conflict management.

Conflict is something that we are generally skilled in managing up to a point. For example, as part of our everyday life skills is the ability to deal with low-level conflicts and to prevent them from escalating into something more serious and potentially destructive. Those who are involved in dealing with conflict management at a more taxing and serious level (social workers, for example) are, in effect, called upon to use more advanced interpersonal skills.

One of the implications of this is that, when it comes to interpersonal interactions, some of the most important skills that social workers need are around assertiveness and negotiation and these are, of course, primarily communication skills.

Practice focus 5.3

Julie was a social worker in a 'looked after' children team. She enjoyed her work for the most part, but found some parts of the job quite a strain. This was when she felt she was getting nowhere, where she felt stuck in certain situations. However, this changed when she attended an in-service training course on conflict management. On the course, the nature of conflict was explored and, as a result of the interesting discussion that ensued, it all fell into place for her. She came to realize that those situations she had been finding difficult and potentially stressful all had one thing in common – they were all characterized by conflict. She had not made the connection before, but she could now see that what led to the sense of 'stuckness' was generally some form of unacknowledged conflict. She could see now that by making the basis of such conflicts explicit, she would be in a much stronger position to develop the confidence and skills needed to deal with them.

Conflict will of course reflect power relations and, as I have argued elsewhere (Thompson, 2007a), such power relations can be understood to operate at personal, cultural and structural levels. The work of Foucault has taught us that power is ever-present, in so far as it occurs in all human situations. To put it another way, where there are people, there is power. This leads to a further important set of concerns that merit our attention, namely the four types of power. These can be characterized as follows:

- *Power to*. This refers to the capacity individuals and groups have for bringing about their wishes and fulfilling their goals. It is clearly a very positive form of power. When we talk about empowerment, it is often this type of power that we are trying to promote.
- *Power over*. This refers to, on the one hand, the legitimate use of power in terms of the exercise of authority, but can also refer to power being used oppressively to make people subordinate. Processes of empowerment often involve helping people to break free from this type of power relationship, especially where that

relationship is being very restrictive, where the power is being abused or misused.

- *Power with.* This refers to the potential for people to exercise greater power by coming together and supporting one another collaboratively. This can be an excellent basis for empowerment. People pulling together to achieve agreed goals can be a very liberating and supportive experience. This is one of the reasons why partnership is such an important part of the social work value base.
- *Power from within.* This is a spiritual aspect of power. It refers to how, in certain circumstances, individuals can draw on inner strengths that they often did not know they had. This often occurs when someone is plunged into a crisis or experiences a significant loss or trauma. Being faced with major challenges can bring the best out of people and give them great strength. This type of power is also associated with resilience – the ability to 'bounce back' from adverse circumstances (Liebenberg and Ungar, 2008).

Each of these four types of power is very relevant to social work, and is therefore worthy of fuller attention (see the 'Further reading' section at the end of the chapter). However, for present purposes, we must limit ourselves to noting that power in all its forms is an important ingredient of interpersonal interactions and we leave ourselves in a seriously weakened position if we attempt to develop our understanding without including such factors in our thinking.

Voice of experience 5.3

When I was at university one of the tutors was always going on about power. I just thought it was one of her hobby horses and didn't take what she said too seriously. But it's different now. Boy, can I see just how significant power is in what we do in social work. Once you tune in to the workings of power, you can't help but see how significant it is. It's major stuff really.

Glen, a social worker in a community care team

There is also an ethical dimension to how professionals use power in relating to the people we serve. This is because there is always the potential for power to be (deliberately) abused or (unintentionally) misused (Thompson, 2003a). This places a responsibility on us as professionals to ensure that our interactions are not characterized by the inappropriate use of power. One aspect of this is the basis of our relationships with others, especially with clients. The work of Buber has been an important consideration in this regard for several decades. In his classic work (Buber, 2004) he distinguishes between two types of relationship:

1. *I-Thou.* This describes relationships based on respect. The worker treats the client as a human being and therefore attends to him or her appropriately, with due attention to safeguarding dignity.
2. *I-it.* This is an instrumental relationship, with little attention given to respect or dignity. In such a relationship, the client is just another case, a statistic to be registered or a set of boxes to be ticked and barely features as a human being.

In unpressurized circumstances it is clear to see that the former is a more solid ethical basis for social work practice and the latter is far from acceptable. However, when workers are under a high level of pressure and are perhaps also operating in a managerialistic culture (see Chapter 2), the second type of interaction can easily creep into their practice. This is another reason why it is essential for our theorizing – our efforts to make sense of what we are doing by drawing on a professional knowledge base – to incorporate an understanding of interpersonal interactions in general and the workings of power in particular. Without such an understanding – and the awareness it brings – we run the risk of allowing I-Thou to become I-it. As Buber explains, if we relate to people on an I-it basis, not only are we dehumanizing them, we are also dehumanizing ourselves.

Conclusion

It is necessary, if we are to do justice to the complexities of social work, to recognize the practice world we engage with as a dynamic and ever-moving one. We therefore need a *dialectical* understanding – one premised on interaction, mutual influence, conflict and change, rather than one based on a static model. This is why interpersonal interactions need to be acknowledged as such an important part of social work: because the very concept of interpersonal interaction characterizes the dynamic nature of human experience.

This chapter has also emphasized the significance of communication, establishing it as a central feature of our work. We neglect it at our peril. We have seen that it is not only what we say (or write), how we say it and what our body is also saying that are important, but also what our behaviour is saying. Failing to give adequate attention to communication issues can therefore be seen as a significant error, and one that we should work hard to avoid.

What our understandings also show us in relation to such matters is that conflict and the operation of power are ever-present features. If we are to maximize the potential for positive outcomes from our work, then we need to look very carefully at the idea of working in partnership. A key part of this is recognizing the significance of group dynamics and intergroup relations – that is, understanding not only how individuals interact, but also how groups of people interact. These will be the subject matter of Chapter 6.

Points to ponder

1. How does the idea of 'intersubjectivity' highlight the dangers of 'atomism'?
2. In what ways is communication a central part of social work?
3. How is conflict a significant part of social life in general and social work in particular?

Further reading

Crossley's (1999) work on intersubjectivity is a helpful introduction to the subject. The classic works of Mead (1965) and Buber (2004) are also well worth reading. Butt (2004) is a very well-written text that offers important insights in general, while Folgheraiter (2004) has important things to say about social work. Forte (2001) is also an important social work text in this regard. Guirdham (2005) helps us to understand the intercultural aspects of human interaction. Jordan (2007) is an excellent book that emphasizes the interpersonal nature of social work, and Moss (2008) is an equally excellent work on communication. Thompson (2003b) also explores the complexities of communication.

6

Group dynamics and intergroup relations

Introduction

Almost everybody is a member of one or more groups, whether they are formal, such as teams, clubs or societies, or informal, such as gatherings of friends and other associates. Such groups tend to serve as a powerful influence on us, both directly and indirectly. They can be a source of significant problems for us in terms of conflicts and tensions, but they can also be a significant source of solutions in terms of support, camaraderie and important resources to fall back on (see the discussion of social capital in Chapter 5). A well-informed social worker therefore needs to have a good understanding of groups, partly because the vast majority of social workers will be members of teams – as teams are, of course, also groups – and partly because group membership and dynamics will often be part of a client's problems and potentially a source of solutions.

This chapter therefore explores how group processes tend to operate (the common patterns that tend to emerge in groups) and what implications these have for practice – what issues we need to bear in mind when considering the group dimension of people's lives and, indeed of the organizations we work for. In addition, I provide an overview of the significance of the distinction between 'in groups' and 'out groups', an important issue that links the topic of groups with the need for anti-discriminatory practice. Finally, we focus on the significance of partnership and teamwork as fundamental underpinnings of social work practice.

Chapter 5 built on the discussions in Chapter 4 of 'the person' by showing how individuals cannot be understood in isolation and need to be seen in the context of interpersonal interactions. This chapter, in turn, builds on those discussions by showing how interpersonal interactions can helpfully be understood in the context of groups – when people are interacting, for the most part, they are doing so as members of groups, and so the group aspects are relevant too; they add a further dimension to our understanding. But that is not all. There is also *intergroup* interaction to consider – that is, not only how individuals interact in the context of group membership, but how groups themselves relate to one another as collective entities. To use the technical terminology, we are concerned with both *intra*group and *inter*group dynamics.

Hamer makes the vitally important point that: 'For a social worker being able to perceive interconnectedness is a vital skill' (2006, p. 62). This chapter builds on this idea by showing how the group as a social phenomenon is a prime example of the importance of 'interconnectedness'. It is a key element of what links individuals together as part of society.

Before going too much further, it would be wise to point out that an understanding of groups is essential for *all* social workers, not just those who practise groupwork as a particular method of intervention. So, readers thinking of skipping this chapter because they have no intention of undertaking groupwork should think again, as the issues covered here apply to all forms of social work – for the simple reason that more or less all the people we deal with in social work will be members of groups, and that, in turn, will have implications for the problems people encounter and the potential solutions available to them.

Groups in context

The term 'group' is used very loosely in everyday conversation to refer to any gathering or combination of people. An important distinction to draw is between two types of groups. First, there are groups of people that have the capacity to develop collective agency – that is, people who can pull together to act in concert, rather than simply be assigned to a category. In this sense, the term 'group' refers to people coming together in *meaningful* ways – that is, in ways that connect the people together in more than a technical sense. Second, 'group' can be used to refer to what Sibeon (2004) describes as 'taxonomic collectivities' – men, women, the working class, and so on – who do not have collective agency (this relates back to the discussion of reification and agency in Chapter 1). My interest in groups in this chapter therefore revolves primarily around groups used in the first sense – that is, groups that have agency, the potential to act *as a group*, rather than simply a collection of disparate individuals who may or may not have certain characteristics in common. The significance of this distinction should become clearer in the pages that follow.

Groups are important from an existentialist perspective because human existence is recognized within that philosophy as inherently social. Groups are a basic feature of that sociality and are therefore a necessary dimension for us to consider in developing an understanding of what it means to be human in general, and what it means to be a human in difficulties in particular. We shall return to the existentialist conception of groups below. For now, however, one existentialist concept in particular is worth examining, that of *Mitwelt* (literally 'with world' or 'world with'). Van Deurzen and Arnold-Baker offer helpful comment:

> The *Mitwelt* represents the social dimension of existence; it is the world of relationships with other human beings. This world is not just about relationships with others, it is also about relationships to culture, society and language. This is the public realm of experience, which includes people's relationship to their race, their social class or other reference groups. It also covers a person's attitude to their country, language and cultural history, to their family and work environment and their general attitude towards authority. The *Mitwelt* is categorized by relationship and is regulated by feelings.
>
> (2005b, p. xix)

While this goes beyond our conception of groups as used in this chapter, it none the less paints a helpful picture of how groups fit into this broader picture of social life. It is very easy, when immersed in the concerns of one individual, to lose sight of the fact that the unique individual you are dealing with is part of a much broader and more complex social configuration – and that configuration is also part of him or her, in the sense that the social context is part of identity, as discussed in Chapter 4.

Group processes

A group by its very nature is a dynamic, evolving entity, rather than a static one. In looking at groups we are therefore dealing with a moving picture, a set of processes and interactions – hence the term: 'group

dynamics'. This is what makes understanding groups such a complicated matter, but also such a fascinating one.

A common understanding of groups is that, in becoming established, they go through a process in terms of forming, storming,
norming and performing (Tuckman, 1965). It is worth considering
each of these aspects a little more fully:

- *Forming*. This refers to the work that goes into groups finding their
  feet, as it were, getting to know one another, deciding on a direction, and so on and so forth. It is a fundamental part of the group
  establishing itself as a group, rather than just a random collection
  of individuals. In some ways it can be an exciting time, but it can
  also lead to a great deal of anxiety and feelings of insecurity. In a
  sense, this stage in the process is beginning to map out the foundations for the group, and so it can be quite influential in shaping
  its future direction, tone and ethos.
- *Storming*. This is the process whereby differences and conflicts are,
  to a certain extent at least, ironed out to try and work through to a
  position where there is some degree of consensus in terms of how to
  move forward. In some groups, this can be a simple and straightforward process. In others it can be a long, difficult and even
  painful process. This stage also has an important part to play in
  shaping the future make up of the group. On the positive side, it
  can clear up conflicts and allow people to come together in a
  genuine spirit of collaboration. However, on the negative side,
  tensions and disagreements arising at this point in the process can
  become embedded and have a longer-term negative effect on how
  the group works.
- *Norming*. This is where the group starts to settle down and
  members begin to feel comfortable with one another. At this point
  group norms are formed – that is, patterns of behaviour and interaction are established; they become 'institutionalized'. A culture is
  in effect forming within the group, in the sense that the habits,
  unwritten rules and 'taken-for-granted' assumptions that characterize a culture are being firmed up. The group will now have a
  much stronger sense of identity. This is a crucial stage in the
  process, as the norms established may help the group a great deal,
  but may also be a significant hindrance, in so far as they serve to
  inhibit in some way the optimal functioning of the group.
- *Performing*. This is where the group has now settled well enough to
  be doing its job (whatever that may be) to good effect. By this stage,

the group is well established and, all being well, will go from strength to strength. The group has, in effect, 'arrived'.

I am always suspicious of any schema that tries to fit complex processes into simple, neat stages, but, provided that it is not used in a reductionist way, it is a model that can offer a helpful basis for developing our understanding. For example, it can be informative at times to identify where a particular group is up to in its development, to be able to gauge what issues it is wrestling with or what processes it is going through.

A further process or stage in the process has been added to this basic model in terms of the significance of mourning. This refers to what happens when groups break up and how it can produce a painful experience very similar to grief – indeed, it can be seen as an actual experience of grief, an aspect of organizational life that is often given far less attention than it deserves (Stein, 2007; Thompson, 2009d).

Practice focus 6.1

Karen was a member of the service planning group that was set up to implement the new policy on personalization. She was excited and daunted in equal measure by the tasks they faced. She was very committed to the personalization agenda but realized it would be a difficult policy to implement, as it presented quite a few challenges. The group found it difficult to begin with and there was a lot of uncertainty about what was happening and what needed to happen. There were clearly some tensions, but these seemed to resolve themselves fairly quickly. After a while, things started to settle down and, before long, it was a much more comfortable experience and the group members all seemed at ease with one another. Once they got into the swing of things, they made excellent progress and were very pleased with how things were working out. It was a very satisfying experience for Karen until she got to the point where the group had finished its task and produced the document and guidance required. What she had not anticipated was how much she would miss the group after it had disbanded on completion of the work. She felt a strong sense of loss. It seemed quite bizarre to her that she seemed to be grieving even though no one had died. When she bumped into Matt, another member of the former group and talked to him about this, she was surprised to find that he felt exactly the same.

Groups can also 'revisit' this process (or set of processes), in the sense that, where a significant change in the group's circumstances occurs, the group can find itself going through a new process of forming, storming, norming and performing all over again. For example, imagine a team being relocated to new offices and having two new members of staff join at the same time.

As we have already noted, groups have a tendency to establish norms and therefore to create a group culture. Original members of the group will internalize those norms, but what will also happen is that, as new members join the group over time, they will become socialized into those norms, with the result that, as they become part of the group, the group becomes part of them in terms of the process by which they internalize the expectations of how they should behave, communicate, and so on within the group context.

Group processes are also involved in developing group myths. Here I am using the term 'myth' in its anthropological sense, by which I mean a widely held assumption which may or may not be true, but is none the less a powerful influence. So, what happens in groups very often is that certain assumptions become established, and these subsequently tend to be taken for granted as 'the truth' of the situation, even though in reality they may be based on a fallacy. An example of this would be the process by which certain things appear to be taboo – that is, unacceptable – to the group. It may well be that, at some point somebody challenges this taboo by mentioning the allegedly forbidden subject, only to find that there is no negative reaction, that the notion of taboo has been based on a myth.

Voice of experience 6.1

When I first started working here everyone told me that you should never take out a grievance. If you are not happy about something, they said, just say so, but if you take out a grievance, your card will be marked, you will never get promotion and things will not go your way. It was clearly seen as 'not the done thing' to take out a grievance so I asked for examples of people who had done so to find out what terrible things had befallen them, but no one could give me an example of somebody who had taken out a grievance. 'See', they said 'you just don't do it here.' For me this was a wonderful example of an organizational myth – it had become an established part of the culture, but no one had any evidence to back it up at all. Amazing really.

Sally, a social worker in an access team

Group processes can be positive in terms of boosting confidence, giving a sense of connectedness and camaraderie, but they can also be negative and destructive. An example of this would be scapegoating. This refers to the process by which usually the weakest member of the group can be blamed for what happens to the group as a whole. This is a very unfair and damaging process, but it is none the less a very common one. It happens in formal and informal groups, as well as in families. It involves harmful processes of exclusion and marginalization which lead to certain people feeling they do not belong. Scapegoating can apply at a group–individual level or group–subgroup. By the former, I mean situations in which particular individuals are scapegoated by the group, while the latter refers to situations in which it is not just particular individuals who are scapegoated, but a whole subgroup within the main group – for example, members of minority ethnic groups, gay or lesbian people or a subset of workers within an organization, such as the cleaners or administrative staff. Scapegoating can range from minor teasing to strong intimidation, humiliation and abuse.

Another negative and unhelpful process is what is referred to in the literature as 'groupthink' (Janis, 1982). This relates to situations where a pleasant atmosphere develops within the group and, as a result of this, no-one is prepared to disagree or offer a different perspective for fear of spoiling the pleasant atmosphere. The result of this can be quite dangerous, in so far as somebody may propose a very unwise course of action and many of the members of the group may think it is unwise, but will not actually say so. They will keep their own counsel for fear of 'rocking the boat'. The consequences of this can often be quite disastrous.

A similar factor that involves risk is what is referred to as the 'risky shift phenomenon' (Collins and Guetzkow, 1964). This describes the process whereby groups of people will tend to be more willing to take risks than individuals would if they were not part of a group. It is based on experiments that were carried out in which individuals were asked to rate how much of a risk they were prepared to take. They were then asked similar questions when part of a group and the experiments showed that, when people were in groups, they were willing to take much greater risks. This is not necessarily a problem, as the confidence gained by being a member of a group to take a higher level of risk can mean that much more positive outcomes are achieved by what could otherwise have been a group of individuals who lack the confidence to take matters forward. However, there is also a significant danger that the risky shift phenomenon can produce complacency; it can lead to groups being insufficiently cautious about the course of action they are embarking on.

Within any group there will be a mixture of positives and negatives and one of the key factors that will affect the success or otherwise of a group project is the success or otherwise the group has in handling negativity. If, for example, there is a tendency to ignore negative factors, to sweep them under the carpet, as it were, then that can be quite dangerous. If, however, there is an open and supportive approach to dealing with any problems or concerns within the group, this is likely to produce a much better result and a much 'healthier' form of group process.

The opposite situation can also apply – that is, where negatives are emphasized and pored over, creating a pessimistic atmosphere characterized by defeatism and cynicism. Where this becomes a norm for a group, the result can be a significant stifling of initiative and creativity and a dampening down of morale and energy. Clearly, groups that develop such a dynamic will be operating far below their level of potential, and it can also be a very unpleasant and soul-destroying experience for the individuals involved.

Practice focus 6.2

Bryn had worked for almost three years in the same team, and was very happy there. However, he realized that it was time for him to have a new challenge. He therefore applied for a senior practitioner post in a neighbouring authority and was delighted when he was successful. His first day, however, was quite a nightmare. He found that his team was at rock bottom in terms of morale and the atmosphere was dreadful. He was not made to feel the slightest bit welcome. The team members seemed to be more interested in moaning about how long the recruitment process had been and how they had been doing extra work while the team was carrying a vacancy. On the second day he spoke to the team manager about his concerns and was met with a wave of cynicism and negativity. That evening he phoned his former boss at home and asked whether his old job was still available. He was told that it had already gone through the system to be advertised. This did not deter him, however, and, in the end, he applied for and got his old job. He felt so glad he would be returning to a team that was much more positive about the challenges it faced. He knew that he could never have flourished as a member of such a negative group.

Groups can be understood by reference to the rituals that they develop. This refers to patterns of behaviour that become institutionalized within a group's practice. This may be a matter of having rites of initiation, which is quite a common occurrence in certain groups – for example, in the military. Rituals can be a very helpful way of giving a group a sense of identity and thus strengthening the group's sense of common purpose. However, there is also the risk that rituals can become problematic and harmful in some ways if taken to extremes, or if the rituals are maintained in a rigid and dogmatic way that does not allow for the flexibility and variability of human situations.

Sartre, the leading existentialist thinker, wrote extensively about groups (Sartre, 1982). He talked about the difference between a 'series' and a 'group in fusion'. A series is a group which has no common purpose. For example, people waiting at a bus queue may at one level form some sort of group, but there will be no sense of common identity and, in fact, there will be considerable potential conflict. Imagine, for example, the bus arriving with room for only six passengers, but with ten people in the queue. This can cause considerable bad feeling and resentment among the people left behind. There is therefore no sense of solidarity or group identity within a series. A group in fusion by contrast is where people come together to establish common goals and agreement about meeting them.

Sartre also describes the way in which groups can become institutionalized and this can lead to the loss of their vibrancy and their potency. They become mired in habits and rituals that detract from the overall purpose or interests of the group. In this way, being a member of such a group can sap morale, reduce motivation and produce very negative results. This contrasts strongly with a positive group experience that can be stimulating, rewarding, enriching and empowering. The subject of group processes is therefore a very complex one that merits close attention. This is important not only in terms of developing our theoretical understanding of people and their problems, but also in relation to our ability to relate such matters to practice – that is, to theorize our work. Negative group dynamics may be a significant part of an individual's (or family's) problems, while positive group dynamics may make the difference between someone finding the strength to cope with highly demanding problems they face or 'going under'. Similarly, positive group dynamics can offer great strength and support ('power with', as discussed in Chapter 4) which can form the basis of developing solutions.

The positive or negative nature of group dynamics is very relevant to understanding families. It would be a serious mistake not to recognize the significance of families as groups. Family dynamics – that is, the interactions between family members that can be highly significant – form a phenomenon that social workers need to take seriously. As we have noted in our discussions of atomism, it is a common mistake to see individuals in isolation, without taking account of the influence of the wider social context. The role individuals play in their family and how their family plays a part in the development of their problems (and, as we shall see, their potential solutions) is a key part of that social context.

Developing an understanding of group processes therefore has to incorporate a detailed understanding of family dynamics. Indeed, this is the basis of family therapy, a well-established practice modality in social work (Carr, 2000). An important concept here is the notion of family scripts (Byng-Hall, 1995). Families can be seen to develop their own narratives, their own stories of reality that shape understanding. If we try to engage with people without having some understanding of what their family script is telling them, then we are scratching at the surface and not really getting to grips with the complex factors that lie underneath. We are highly unlikely in such circumstances to have any considerable success.

Finally, in terms of group processes, a further issue to put on the agenda is that of alienation. Reference was made earlier to the significance of people being estranged from their experiences. This can be a common occurrence when group dynamics, whether in families or other such groupings, have the effect of undermining confidence by making people feel that they do not belong or that they are not worthy. Practice focus 6.2 presents a good example of how group dynamics that produce and sustain negativity and cynicism will generally result in feelings of alienation. Other examples would include members of minority groups being made to feel that they do not belong, that they are 'other'; and a macho, competitive ethos which can undermine the self-esteem of some members of the group who are made to feel that they are 'losers' in some sort of battle, rather than partners in a shared endeavour. A well-informed social worker will be attuned to the significance of alienation in such circumstances. This is necessary because if, in theorizing the practice situations we are engaged with, we are not aware of how group dynamics can either empower and enrich or disempower and alienate, we could be missing vitally important parts of the situation or, perhaps worse still, misinterpreting these group factors as indicators of some sort of personal inadequacy or pathology (for example, someone's angry reaction to being alienated within a group being seen as a sign of 'having a short fuse' or 'being volatile' for 'no apparent reason').

Voice of experience 6.2

I had not realized how significant group issues were until I went on a course on groupwork. I learned a lot about actually doing groupwork, as I expected to, but what I hadn't bargained for was how much I would learn about working with individuals. It taught me that so many things that I had previously seen as characteristics of individuals were actually more to do with group dynamics. Like someone being secretive, for example, may actually be showing loyalty to the group, rather than reflecting a personal characteristic.

Katy, a social worker in a family support team

In groups and out groups

One thing we have learned about groups over the years is that they tend to become ranked in some sort of hierarchy, awarded high or low status. This can lead to many people being stigmatized because they are members of certain groups, especially those deemed to be low status. For example, families from travelling communities are often stereotyped as being 'bad people' by members of the wider community, who may never have met them and therefore have no direct evidence on which to form such a judgement. Indeed, the process of stereotyping is a key factor in determining which groups are seen as positive (the 'in groups') and which are seen as 'out groups' – the groups that are socially disapproved of for one reason or another, whether such disapproval is justified or not (Tajfel, 1981). In social work, we will often be involved in working with people who are predominantly from 'out groups'. This is something we need to bear in mind, as it can be a key factor in shaping the situations we are dealing with.

Groups also have a degree of status in terms of how they may be seen as 'reference groups' (Hyman and Singer, 1968). A reference group is a group with which particular individuals associate themselves. We can identify two types of reference group: a *membership* reference group, which applies in situations where the individual concerned is an actual member of that group. For example, as a social worker I am a member of a social work reference group – that is, I identify with other social work professionals; I feel that I am part of that group. The other type of reference group is a group characterized by aspiration, rather than actual membership. For example, a social work student working towards becoming a qualified and registered social worker would have social work as an *aspiration* reference group – they are not yet a full member of that group, but aspire to be so. Aspiration groups can further be subdivided into two types, depending on how realistic the aspiration is. For example, a social work student aspiring to be a social worker is reflecting a reasonable degree of realism. That is, while not all social work students will succeed in achieving their aspiration, the majority will, and so such an aspiration is fairly reasonable and realistic. However, for the child who is learning to play the guitar who aspires to be a world-famous rock star, this is a less realistic and reasonable reference group to aspire to (even though some, of course, will achieve that aim)

Whether the reference group is directly one of membership or indirectly one of aspiration, either way the result is that reference group factors can be very influential in shaping individual and group behaviour. The existence of reference groups can lead to conflicts between groups where some become valued and others devalued or even stigmatized. Effective multiprofessional collaboration depends on being able to avoid this process taking place, or at least to avoid it having a detrimental effect on working relationships.

Unfortunately, it has commonly come to be seen that different groups are necessarily in competition and are not necessarily complementary. For example, it is not uncommon for supporters of rival football teams to regard the other group as 'the enemy', as if it were a war situation, rather than as the opposition in a sporting sense. This can be quite significant, as the attitude of one group towards another can dictate whether those two groups are able to operate side by side in relative harmony or whether there is exacerbated conflict between the two that can lead to aggression and violence (as in the case of football hooliganism). While professionals working alongside one another cannot realistically be compared with football hooligans, very real tensions that can get in the way of effective multidisciplinary practice can arise where a spirit of competition displaces an emphasis on partnership and cooperation.

Practice focus 6.3

Ken was a social worker in a multidisciplinary mental health team. He worked closely with, Paula, a community psychiatric nurse who was a trained counsellor. At a personal level, the two got on very well, but professionally things were very different. They had very different perceptions of their respective roles. Paula understood the social work role to be primarily about welfare benefits and housing issues, and saw her own role as primarily a 'therapeutic' one. Ken, for his part, saw himself as being more concerned with addressing clients' social needs and problems more broadly than just the practicalities of bene-fits and housing, and saw himself as a legitimate person to be using a range of therapeutic methods, especially solution-focused work which he particularly favoured. He saw Paula's role as mainly a nursing one and felt she should restrict herself to such concerns and not get involved in the therapeutic side of things. This mismatch of perspec-tives about the respective professional groups led to a great deal of tension and ill feeling and therefore a level of practice far below the optimal. Both Ken and Paula seemed to have failed to appreciate the nature of multiprofessional collaboration. They were allowing group rivalries to stand in the way of effective practice.

Groupwork

Existentialism, with its roots in phenomenology and hermeneutics (and thus an emphasis on perception and meaning), has shown us that people will inevitably have some degree of conflicting understandings and defi-nitions of the world (Merleau-Ponty, 2002). Existentialism shows us that the idea that we are all on the same wavelength in terms of under-standing the world is naive in the extreme. This means that conflict is a key part of group dynamics (that is, what happens within specific groups) and intergroup relations (that is, what happens between two or more groups). This therefore emphasizes the importance for the social worker of understanding conflict as a central feature of human exis-tence. Groupwork as a practice modality starts from the premise that groups contain a degree of both consensus and conflict. The aim, then, is to minimize the conflict and, where possible, use it constructively as a way forward and thus maximize harmony and cooperation.

Groups can give a sense of solidarity, belonging and connectedness and can therefore be a huge help to people as they face life's difficulties. However, groups can also create divisions, both within the group itself and between one group and another. An 'us them' mentality can very easily develop as a result of group membership and interactions between groups. Parekh (2008) writes about the significance of identity politics in these terms. By this he means the tendency to see individuals as members of particular sets of people, such as men or women, black people or white people, and so on. However, as mentioned earlier, the work of Sibeon (2004) has shown us that there is a danger in confusing broad social categories ('taxonomic collectivities') with groups that can have agency – that is, can make decisions and act in concert. Consider, for example, the discussion above of series, as used in the work of Sartre. A 'collectivity' has the *potential* for a group to develop from a series, but this is a process that needs to be followed through. The fact that people have certain things in common (working-class people, for example, or children who have been abused) does not in itself form a basis for action. This is where groupwork can come into its own. It offers the potential for 'fusing together' (in Sartre's sense) disparate people by helping them to develop a common identity and a recognition of their common interests. Groupwork, then, can be seen as the process of trying to convert that potential for mutual support, solidarity, empowerment and progress into reality.

Groupwork can be a specialist approach used in specific therapeutic settings and it can be used in a community development context to cultivate a sense of solidarity. However, it can also potentially be used in any social work setting where there is enough imagination and creativity to break out of the tramlines of routinized practice.

Partnership and teamwork

In Chapter 5, the point was made that interpersonal interactions mean that partnership is a key part of social work practice. Such partnership can be understood at two different levels, that between worker and client on the one hand and that between worker and fellow worker, or even agency and partner agency, on the other. The latter is the basis of multiprofessional collaboration, a key dimension of current social work practice. If efforts to achieve successful partnership working are to be a success, then what is needed is not simply professionals being nice or polite to each other. There is also a need to address the conflicts of perspective that are likely to be underpinning their approaches to practice – conflicts around values, priorities, the nature of their respective roles, and so on (see Practice focus 6.3 above). This reinforces the significance of understanding conflict in particular and group dynamics and intergroup relations in general. Without that understanding, social workers will struggle to work effectively in partnership with others.

Parallel with the notion of partnership is that of teamwork. A small minority of social workers will work in relative isolation, but the vast majority will, of course, be members of teams, whether specifically social work teams (that is, comprising entirely or almost entirely of social workers) or multidisciplinary teams alongside members of other professions. In either case, the important question to ask is what makes for good teamwork. What understandings do we need to have of group dynamics and intergroup relations that will equip us to make the most of the teams that we are part of? This is because, at the end of the day, teams are, in effect, groups, and so the same considerations apply. That is, a team can be extremely helpful in providing a sound basis for high-quality practice, but teams that are having difficulties in terms of creating positive dynamics can do considerable harm, both to the individuals within that team and to the overall organization and its stakeholders.

Voice of experience 6.3

I have been lucky in my career, because I have been a member of some excellent teams that worked really well, but I have also been part of awful teams too. It was no fun at the time, but it meant that I learned a great deal about what is good and what is not so good when it comes to pulling together as a team. As a manager, I now have a very clear picture of what I need to do (and not do) to promote good teamwork.

Denise, team manager of a child protection team

Conclusion

A very important conclusion for us to draw from this chapter is that it is very easy to focus narrowly on the task at hand and to lose sight of the group factors that can be so crucial in promoting positive moves forward or preventing such helpful developments. If we are to have a holistic foundation on which to base our theorizing of practice, then we need to make sure that we incorporate an understanding of the group dimension of people's lives. This should not be to the exclusion to other factors, such as the person, interpersonal interactions or the wider social context: people are highly complex and need to be understood in their complexity if we are to do justice to our mission to engage with human problems and challenges sensitively and constructively.

This chapter has shown that groups are not only an important part of people's lives, our sense of who we are and how we fit into the wider world, but also potential sources of both problems and solutions. A social worker with a good understanding of group dynamics and inter-group relations will be far better equipped to carry out their duties than someone who lacks such knowledge and appreciation.

Groups have a tendency to develop their own culture – the unwritten rules and taken-for-granted assumptions that become part of everyday reality. Groups will also interact with other cultural factors – ethnicity, for example – and so culture can be seen as another important factor that merits our attention. Chapter 7, with its focus on the cultural context of people's lives, should therefore cast further light on how human experience, however personal, unique and intimate it may be, is none the less deeply social in its nature. It is therefore to the question of the cultural context that we now turn.

Points to ponder

1. Consider what groups you are a member of. In what ways do they play an important part in your life?
2. Can you identify an example of someone being treated as a scapegoat? What harm might this process do (i) for the individual concerned; and (ii) for the group who are doing the scapegoating?
3. In what circumstances do you think a groupwork approach might be helpful?

Further reading

Tajfel (1981) is a classic work on group dynamics. Doel (2005), Doel and Sawdon (1999) and Preston-Shoot (2007) are all helpful groupwork texts that also offer insights into how groups operate in general. Sartre (1982) is a very difficult text to read, but offers a helpful basis for understanding the complexities of group processes. Family dynamics are explored in Carr (2000) and Scott, Treas and Richards (2007).

7

Cultural contexts

Introduction

Just as people are commonly members of a range of groups, as we noted in the previous chapter, each of us is also part of at least one culture and often a range of them. A culture is a very strong influence on every one of us. It acts as a lens through which we see the world, colouring and shaping our perceptions and thus our understandings. A culture is, in a sense, an accumulated collective knowledge base, bringing understanding and sets of meanings that are passed on to its members. This can be linked to Foucault's work on discourses (Foucault, 1991; 1998; 2001) and how they shape social encounters and also the work of Gadamer (2004) on how traditions develop and create a sense of normality. In trying to understand people and the problems they face in a social work context, it is necessary to take account of how cultures tend to have profound and far-reaching effects on people. It is significant that I am using the term 'culture' in the plural. This is because most people will be exposed to the influences of a number of cultures, including workplace cultures. For example, some of us will be brought up in one culture, but then live our adult life in another cultural setting, in which case both sets of cultural norms will be influential factors in shaping our sense of who we are and how we fit into the world.

I shall therefore be using the word 'culture' as a shorthand for 'cultural contexts'. This is because there will be multiple influences on people from the different cultures to which they will be exposed during their lifetime. It is not a simple matter of each individual neatly being part of a single culture in a direct way – that would be a reductionist understanding of culture. The reality is far more complex, involving the multi-level interactions of different sets of cultural influences, some of which will overlap and thus reinforce each other, while others will be in tension and thus lead to conflict and potential strife.

The chapter explores the nature of culture before moving on to consider the benefits to us of our cultural contexts as well as the drawbacks of culture – the problems that can arise from being a member of a culture. Finally, we explore, albeit briefly, some aspects of the relationship between diversity and equality.

An important theme of the book that continues to feature in this chapter is the *dynamic* nature of human experience. Selfhood is not a static, fixed entity; interpersonal interactions are, by their very nature, dynamic, as are group processes. We shall see in this chapter too that culture is not a static entity – it is a set of forces which interact with one another and with other social forces and which are therefore constantly changing and developing. Our theorizing of practice therefore needs to incorporate this dynamic conception of culture as a set of complex issues, rather than simply a straightforward backdrop to people's lives.

What is culture?

Although, as we have already noted, culture is a highly complex phenomenon, at its simplest it can be defined as shared ways of seeing, thinking and doing. This refers to the ways in which groups of people in close contact develop shared ideas about the nature of the world, how it should be managed, their (and everyone else's) place within it, and so on. As a result, cultures develop, each of which provides a set of unwritten rules, taken-for-granted assumptions and expected ways of behaving – in effect, frameworks of meaning. Culture can be seen as a source and basis of the following:

- *Values*. A value reflects what we regard as important and worthy of an investment of our time and resources. Values are also significant in terms of morality, our sense of right and wrong, and related matters. Much of this is on an individual basis but, of course, each individual will, to a large extent, draw their values from their cultural context, or, as we noted earlier, in opposition to their cultural context if they choose to reject all or some aspects of that culture.
- *Norms*. Everyday patterns of behaviour are very strongly linked to the cultural context. This is why, when people find themselves in a cultural context different from what they are used to, they can experience what is known as 'culture shock' – they feel as though so many of the norms and taken-for-granted assumptions that they rely on to get through the day no longer seem to apply in this new context.

- *Communication.* Cultures develop scripts or discourses that are characteristic of the particular culture in question. For example, certain cultures develop a particular dialect or form of language use. There will also be particular patterns of communication that are culturally specific – for example, the 'rules' around courtship (what is considered permissible in terms of attempting to form a relationship and what is 'improper') will differ from culture to culture.

- *Identity.* Our sense of self and belonging are also culturally linked. Much of our sense of who we are and where we fit into the world comes from the cultural norms and values to which we have been exposed over time. The extent to which a person's sense of self matches or deviates from their cultural roots will vary from individual to individual, but everyone's identity will be influenced by their cultural background in significant ways.

- *Rituals.* Cultures can be characterized by particular rites or rituals – established, institutionalized practices associated with particular processes or events. They can be formal and 'official' or informal. These can be very significant in terms of keeping a culture going over time, but also in helping people to feel they are part of the culture, so that it reinforces their sense of belonging and identity. These add to the cohesiveness of the culture.

- *Art, craft, music, and so on.* This is culture in its everyday sense, and is very much a part of culture in the sense that we are using it here. Different cultures develop different forms of artistic expression. Consider, for example, differences between western and eastern forms of music.

- *Pride.* By being a member of a culture, a sense of connection and belonging develop which can make people feel proud to be associated with a particular cultural context.

What tends to happen is that, as people grow up, they are 'taught' their culture, albeit not in a direct, didactic way. It is more of a process of gradual but constant exposure to the fundamental elements of that particular culture. This is a process that is referred to as 'cultural transmission' – the norms and so on are transmitted from one generation to the next as part of the upbringing of the individuals concerned. It also leads to a process of socialization – that is, the individual internalizes the cultural norms, values, rules, and so on. In effect, what happens is that there is a very subtle process, or set of processes, through which the culture becomes part of the person and the person becomes part of the culture. It is from this that ethnicity develops, a strong sense of cultural identity. Parekh emphasizes just how important this cultural identity is to the individual:

> Thanks further to the developments in the sociology of knowledge, psychoanalysis and cultural psychology, we appreciate better than before that culture deeply matters to people, that their self-esteem depends on others' recognition and respect, and that our tendency to mistake the cultural for the natural and to unwittingly universalize our beliefs and practices causes much harm and injustice to others.
>
> (2006, p. 8)

Given the importance of culture for people's lives in general and their identity in particular, there is a very clear message here for social work practice. If we are to ensure that our understanding of the situations we encounter is to be adequate for the task, then we need to incorporate at least a basic knowledge of how cultural factors shape people's lives in general and how each culture will have its own particular set of influences. This is often referred to these days as 'cultural competence' (Constantine and Sue, 2005). No one can realistically be expected to know about all cultures, but there is a need for an understanding of the significance of culture and a willingness to find out more about specific cultures as and when the need arises.

Practice focus 7.1

Kelly was brought up in a strongly multi-ethnic area. Her family was one of the few white families in her particular street. When she became a social worker and was introduced to the idea of cultural competence as part of a broader commitment to anti-discriminatory practice, she felt quite comfortable with it. She had mixed with people from a wide range of ethnic backgrounds and, while some of the other white social workers she worked alongside had shown some degree of nervousness about practising in ethnically sensitive ways, she had no such qualms. However, one day Kelly was allocated a case that involved working with a family of Arab origin. When she went to meet them, she was completely thrown by the encounter, as she had never even met somebody of Arab background and felt very ill-equipped to respond to the family's needs. She realized that she had become complacent, relying too heavily on her experiences of growing up in a multi-ethnic area and had not taken seriously enough the professional challenge of developing cultural competence, knowledge and understanding more broadly. She recognized that she still had a lot of learning to do.

A person's cultural context is shaped by a wide range of factors, but the following can be seen to be particularly important:

- *Nationality.* There are strong national cultures that can be discerned – for example, Australian, Japanese or Canadian cultures. Within the UK we have a very interesting, complex and contentious mix, as there is British culture, but also, alongside a generalized notion of British culture, we have Scottish, Northern Irish and Welsh national cultures as well. To complicate (and enrich) the mixture even more, we have a wide range of other cultural factors, Asian especially, that contribute to the overall sense of 'British culture'.
- *Religion.* This refers to a highly complex set of factors stemming from different religions, such as Christianity, Islam, Judaism, Sikhism and Hinduism, but also from particular sects within a particular religion – for example, Protestantism and Catholicism within Christianity. All these factors tend to be highly significant in shaping cultural practices and expectations.
- *Politics.* This is partly a reflection of class and socioeconomic position, but in general there will also be cultural factors associated with a particular political leaning or tradition.
- *Class.* Regardless of politics, class in itself can be significant in terms of shaping the way we understand the world. People brought up in different class groups may have very different understandings of the world, depending on the characteristic perceptions of the world associated with that particular class-based culture. Meal times and what terms are used to refer to meals (Is it 'tea' at 5.30 or 'dinner' or even 'supper' at 7.30?) are a good example of different cultural practices and understandings linked to class.
- *Workplace cultures.* These can be specific to particular organizations or sections of an organization or they can relate to a professional or vocational grouping. For example, a social worker's cultural context will owe much to the organization in which he or she is employed (its norms, values, unwritten rules and so on) as well as to the cultural influences that stem from being a member of the social work profession. I shall have more to say about workplace cultures in Chapter 9.

Voice of experience 7.1

As a Northern Irish Protestant married to a Scottish Catholic, now living in Wales and working for an English company, I know just how complex cultural issues can be! And, don't even mention class; that makes it even more tricky. I was on a course once and we were talking about the importance of culture and ethnicity. One woman said it didn't have much to do with her because she worked in a white area. I couldn't believe how naive she was and how little she understood about how significant culture and ethnicity are, whether you are black or white.

Heather, a social worker in an adoption agency

There is also much to be gained from taking account of the significance of cultural change. This is because, while cultures rely on a degree of stability, they none the less evolve over time and, of course, individuals over time become exposed to different cultures. It would therefore be a significant mistake to see culture as a fixed phenomenon. Although there is a strong degree of continuity within cultures by their very nature, there is also a degree of change and movement over time. That is, cultures are *dynamic*.

As social workers, we would clearly be very wise to give careful consideration to the cultural context of the situations we encounter, including how our own cultural upbringing and subsequent exposure to other cultural forms may be influencing the way we see the world in general and the specific situation we are encountering in particular. It is important that we do not allow our own cultural assumptions to place clients and carers at a disadvantage (for example, by relying on stereotypes). It is also important that we have at least some understanding of people's cultural context if we are going to be able to 'tune in' to their needs, their problems and challenges and their strengths and potential for resilience.

One further aspect of our understanding that needs to feature is the recognition that cultures do not exist in a vacuum. They are part of – and contribute to – wider structural formations (Rubinstein, 2001; Thompson, 2003a). Parekh reflects this point when commenting on the need to adopt a broad perspective on cultural conflicts:

Since culture is a site where major social and economic conflicts are played out, no cultural conflicts are exclusively cultural, even as few social conflicts are without a cultural dimension. We fail to understand the nature and causes of cultural conflict if we concentrate on culture alone.

(2008, p. 156)

This can be seen to be part of a dialectic in which cultural and structural factors interact, with their interweavings creating a complex set of social factors. We shall be exploring issues relating to the wider structural context in Chapter 8, and so we shall see at that point that cultural factors need to be understood as part of – and in dialectical interaction with – the social structure.

In order to develop a fuller understanding of the importance of culture for social work, we shall now explore the benefits and drawbacks of culture, beginning with the positive aspects.

The benefits of culture

When we look closely at the individual in society, we can see that there are many benefits to be gained from being a member of a culture. This includes a strong sense of identity as well as a degree of solidarity and belonging. Cultures play an important part in shaping the narratives of identity that give us a coherent sense of self and a feeling of security in the world. Ontological security, to use the existentialist term, is an important underpinning to our engagement with the world, and culture can, to a large extent, be a major source of ontological security. Feeling that we belong to a group of people who have much in common with us can give us a strong sense of reassurance. Also, the factors that are meaningful to us in terms of what we feel comfortable with, the norms, the rituals and so on, are all likely to have at least some connection with our cultural background.

A good example of this would be at a time when someone is grieving. The rituals associated with mourning and the sense of the community 'paying its respects' to the deceased can be a considerable source of comfort at a most difficult and vulnerable time. Doka's (1989) notion of 'disenfranchised grief' (grief that is not socially sanctioned and supported – for example, grief arising from a suicide) reinforces this point, as the absence of recognition within one's own culture at the time of a significant loss can be sorely felt. People dealing with disenfranchised grief are likely to feel that their task is much harder because they will tend to lack the social recognition and support that generally accompanies a major loss.

There is also the benefit of multiculturalism, in the sense that it is increasingly being recognized now that diversity is something to be valued and even celebrated (Parekh, 2006). The variety of cultures that we encounter in modern societies offers the potential for immense enrichment. By having a variety of cultures with different perspectives, different forms of art, cuisine, and so on, we are exposed to a wide array of influences and opportunities. As we shall see below, this can be an important plank in our efforts to promote social justice by recognizing that differences can be seen as assets and benefits for society and not problems to be solved or reasons to justify discrimination.

Practice focus 7.2

Michelle was a very experienced practice teacher who took a lot of pride in this aspect of her work. She had never faced the prospect of having to fail a student until she worked with Tracey on her initial placement. Tracey's work showed a lot of promise in many ways, but she was struggling in relation to anti-discriminatory practice. She had had a very traditional working-class upbringing and had little experience of the world beyond her local, predominantly white neighbourhood. She therefore had little knowledge or experience of the complexities of difference, diversity and discrimination. She listened carefully to what Michelle had to say on the matter, but then went away and carried out her work without showing any signs that she had taken on board any of the important messages Michelle had been giving her. One day, Michelle received a notification from the Workforce Development Unit in her organization about a one-day course on Valuing Diversity. She booked two places on the course, one for herself and one for Tracey. This did the trick nicely. The discussions of the importance of valuing diversity and the dangers of discrimination that can arise if we do not really hit home to Tracey. Michelle learned quite a lot too. In the next supervision session Michelle was keen to find out what had made the difference in terms of Tracey's learning. Tracey found it difficult to articulate precisely, but it seemed to have a lot to do with her taking on board the idea of *valuing* diversity – seeing the issues as positive ideas to pursue, rather than thinking negatively about things to avoid.

Culture is therefore something to be valued for contributing to the enrichment that diversity brings. By embracing our own culture, but also being open to what other cultures can offer and what they can teach us about the wider world and indeed of the human experience, we have much to gain. If we did not have cultures, we would not have the benefits of cultural diversity. Kallen's comments capture the picture nicely:

> International human rights principles provide an overarching paradigm for social equality and social justice for all of humanity, rooted in the twin foundations of human unity and cultural diversity. The principle of biological unity of humankind emphasizes the oneness of all human beings as members of the same human species and recognizes the close affinities between members of all human populations. The principle of cultural diversity respects the unique contributions to all of humankind made by each ethnocultural community throughout the globe. Embraced together, these cardinal principles underscore the theme of *unity in diversity*, recognizing and embracing the essential oneness of humanity, while at the same time celebrating the uniqueness of each human being and of each human group.
>
> (2004, p. 30)

This is a point to which we will return below under the heading 'Equality and diversity'.

From a professional point of view, an understanding of culture offers us a degree of the sensitivity we need to understand, and respond to, people's needs and to work out how best to help them in culturally appropriate ways. If we are not attuned to the role culture plays in shaping people's life experience, then we are missing significant elements of the picture we need to form as part of our assessment in order to plan how to help people as effectively as possible within our limited resources.

The drawbacks of culture

While there are clearly considerable benefits to be gained from culture, closer inspection shows that the picture is not an entirely positive one. There is also a price to be paid for culture in the form of a number of potential or actual drawbacks. I shall comment briefly on some of the main ones by way of illustration.

Some cultures at some times can be stifling. They can impose rigid expectations on people that can become counterproductive. For example, in many cultures there are fairly rigid expectations of men and women in terms of their respective gender roles that can lead to members of either gender feeling frustrated because they are, in effect, being blocked from following paths that they would otherwise like to. Or, if they choose to follow such alternative paths, they may find that they face sanctions, discouragements, ridicule and even outright hostility for what is seen as going against the appropriate cultural norms.

Similarly, there is the drawback associated with 'ethnocentricity'. This refers to the tendency for people to see the world through the lens of their particular culture, without acknowledging that different cultures have the legitimate right to have different perspectives. An ethnocentric approach can potentially lead people to develop negative or dismissive attitudes towards members of other cultures: 'different' becomes defined as 'other' and therefore tends to be seen as either inferior or a threat to us or both. This form of cultural 'blindness' is often part of the foundation of racism, in so far as the assumption is made that ethnic groups different from one's own are worthy of less respect and that it is therefore legitimate and appropriate to discriminate against them. People becoming overly attached to their culture can therefore lead to difficulties without an appreciation that it is one legitimate perspective among many. Clarke cites Eagleton (2000, p. 26) who captures an ethnocentric point of view in the following terms: 'One's own way of life is simply human; it is other people who are ethnic, idiosyncratic, culturally peculiar' (2004, p. 32). While it is helpful to see one's own culture as a reassuring basis of our normality, it is not helpful to draw the false conclusion that any other culture is therefore 'abnormal' or 'deviant'.

Voice of experience 7.2

Before I came to work in Wales, I had not realized how many assumptions I had been making about the place and the people. I had fallen in love with the place when I came here on holiday as a child. To me, seeing bilingual signs and hearing Welsh spoken seemed just a slightly eccentric part of the local way of life. But now that I have lived here for two years and have learned to speak Welsh, I can see just how significant these issues are and how they are signs of Wales having a very different cultural system from England. I suppose as a child I just saw it as England with a few quirks, but now accept how inaccurate and disrespectful that assumption was.

Gaynor, a social worker in a child care team

A related problem is that of insularity. Where this occurs, some people become so firmly attached to their culture that they do not allow themselves to be open to the influences and opportunities of other cultures. Unlike ethnocentricity, they do not deny the validity of other cultural perspectives; they are just not prepared to engage with what they have to offer. A simple example of this would be in terms of cuisine. Some people will not experiment with any form of food that they do not associate with their own culture. Similarly, some people may be reluctant to travel to particular areas because it would bring them into contact with people of a different culture and, rather than seeing this as an opportunity for growth, development, learning and expansion of horizons, it is seen as a threatening experience and therefore one to be resisted.

Just as ethnocentricity can be the basis of racism, there can also be cultural assumptions that are profoundly discriminatory in other ways – for example, attitudes towards older people or children which can be quite restrictive and harmful, but which are part and parcel of a particular culture. Similarly, attitudes towards other minority groups can be very negative on the basis of cultural assumptions and stereotypes. Given that most of the people we seek to help in social work are in a minority category of some description (older people; people with physical or learning disabilities or mental health problems; children in the care system; young offenders; and chronically sick or terminally ill people), this tendency for cultures to devalue, stigmatize and discriminate against certain groups is clearly a major issue for us. We shall return to these themes in Chapter 14.

A further potential problem in terms of the cultural context is that there can be tensions and conflicts arising because of cultural differences. A clear example of this would be sectarianism. It is unfortunately the case that there have been many examples of sectarianism over the years in which members of different religious groups have inflicted violence on each other because of a clash over their beliefs and the political consequences of those beliefs. In Northern Ireland, the era of the 'troubles' was characterized not only by religious differences and thus conflicts, but also opposing views about nationality (the six counties as part of Ireland vs. Northern Ireland as part of the United Kingdom and therefore British) – see Ross (2005); Welsh (2003).

Practice focus 7.3

Colin was a very experienced mental heath social worker in the North West of England. After marrying Kathleen, a nurse originally from Northern Ireland, the question they wrestled with was whether to remain in England or move to Northern Ireland. When Kathleen became pregnant, they decided the time was right to move so that she could have the support of her family. Colin was appointed to a post very similar to the one he left, so he was confident he would do well. However, what he had not bargained for was how big a role sectarianism played in people's lives and how different the two sets of communities were. Even though the situation had improved significantly since the worst days of the conflict, he had not realized how embedded the issues were and how careful he had to be not to offend anyone or unwittingly give the impression that he was in favour of one perspective or the other. He found the whole situation quite challenging and, for a while, it affected his confidence. He was just glad that he had the support of his wife and her family to help him make sense of what to him was a totally novel situation.

Finally, one further potential drawback of culture is the other side of the coin from one of the advantages mentioned earlier, namely the benefits of solidarity and belonging. Unfortunately, cultures can also have the effect of alienating a proportion of their membership, making them feel that they are in some way 'other' to the mainstream culture. The caste system in India is a good example of this. Similarly, gay, lesbian, bisexual and transgender people can be ostracized in many cultures, treated as pariahs because they do not fit the cultural norm. These examples illustrate how cultures can be inclusive and welcoming for many members, but can also be cruelly exclusive and rejecting for certain minority elements.

Having reviewed the benefits and drawbacks of culture, we can now see that membership of a culture can be a mixed blessing. We can also see that certain groups (that is, relatively powerless minority groups) are likely to experience the drawbacks more often and more intensely than other sectors of the community. All this adds up to two important conclusions: (i) culture is a complex matter, and so there are dangers in oversimplifying it or neglecting its significance; (ii) an understanding of culture's positive and negative aspects can put us in a better position to help people by being able to seek to minimize the negatives and maximize the positives.

Equality and diversity

The emphasis in recent years on cultural and other forms of diversity has caused a lot of confusion in some quarters. Many people (correctly) associate diversity with difference, but (incorrectly) associate equality with sameness. They therefore see the linking together of equality and diversity as a contradiction, a juxtaposing of incompatible elements. However, this is a gross oversimplification based on a misunderstanding of the term 'equality'. While equality literally means 'sameness', it is not intended to be taken literally when used in its legal, moral or political sense. It can better be understood to refer to treating people with 'equal fairness', rather than simply treating everybody the same (and thereby reinforcing existing inequalities – see Thompson, 2009e). Parekh provides a very helpful summary of this complex situation when he explains that:

> Human beings do share several capacities and needs in common, but different cultures define and structure these differently and develop new ones of their own. Since human beings are at once both similar and different, they should be treated equally because of both. Such a view, grounds equality not in human uniformity but in the interplay of uniformity and difference, builds difference into the very concept of equality, breaks the traditional equation of equality with similarity, and is immune to monist distortion. Once the basis of equality changes so does its content. Equality involves equal freedom or opportunity to be different, and treating human beings equally requires us to take into account both their similarities and differences. When the latter are not relevant, equality entails uniform or identical treatment; when they are, it requires differential treatment.
>
> (2006, p. 240)

So, whether we are talking about cultural diversity or other forms of human variability (gender, age, disability, sexuality, language, class, religion, and so on), there is no contradiction with the idea of promoting equality. Indeed, recognizing and valuing diversity can be seen as important elements of promoting social justice.

Social justice involves attempting to prevent unfair discrimination, making sure that people are not 'punished' in some way or allowed to lose out because of legitimate differences. Culture is a crucial part of this, not only because culture can be a basis for discrimination (that is, people can be discriminated against because of their culture), but also because culture is a vehicle for discrimination (in the sense that cultures commonly contain well-established, deeply rooted discrimi-natory assumptions and stereotypes – for example, the idea that people with mental health problems are likely to become frenzied killers). This is the C level of PCS analysis (see Thompson, 2003a; 2006a; 2007a).

Voice of experience 7.3

I had always seen discrimination as a matter of personal prejudice, but reading about PCS analysis helped me to see that there is much more to it than that. It made me realize that the cultural and structural levels were really important too. I find the cultural level particularly significant in my work, as I can see how so many of the ageist assumptions I encounter come from people's upbringing. Most people don't realize how disrespectful and patronizing they are being when they talk about older people. It's not personal prejudice as such; it's just that's the way their culture has taught them to talk and think about the older gener-ation.

Megan, a social worker in an older people team

Conclusion

As noted earlier, what has been established in social work in recent decades is the need for what has come to be known as 'cultural compe-tence'. This means being able to recognize the significance of cultural factors in shaping people's life experiences – including their problems and their potential solutions – as part of a broader sociological under-standing of social work. As we shall see in subsequent chapters, this basic cultural competence is a necessary underpinning for emancipa-tory forms of practice – that is, approaches to social work which are committed to tackling discrimination and oppression.

This chapter has shown that culture, as an important aspect of social life, brings a range of benefits, but also a number of drawbacks or disadvantages. An ill-informed social worker in matters relating to culture may well be unwittingly reinforcing the negatives and missing out on the opportunities offered by the positives, while a social worker who is clued into such issues is in a much stronger position to guard against the drawbacks and capitalize on the positive potential.

Also important has been the linking together of equality and diver-sity. Not only have we seen that there are benefits to be gained from valuing diversity (cultural or otherwise), we have also been able to note that diversity and equality are concepts that can usefully be used in tandem as part of a commitment to social justice.

We have also introduced the notion that culture is important within organizations, in so far as whole organizations or subdivisions within them tend to develop cultures in the same way that societies and communities do. We shall return to this issue and explore it in more depth in Chapter 9 when we explore the organizational context. However, for present purposes, it is important to note that, as social workers, we need to have a good theoretical understanding of the significance of culture if we are to ensure that our practice is sufficiently well informed to do justice to the challenges we face.

An understanding of culture throws further light on our earlier discussions of identity (the 'person'), interpersonal interactions and group dynamics, as all of these will interact in significant ways with culture. In this way, our discussions of culture can be seen as a development of the picture the earlier chapters in Part Two have been painting about the person as part of a complex social context (rather than an isolated, 'atomistic' individual). In turn, these discussions set the scene nicely for our explorations in Chapter 8 of wider sociopolitical structures and processes and their influence on people's lives in general and on social work practice in particular.

Points to ponder

1. How would you describe your own cultural context? How has this helped to shape who you are?
2. What dangers are there in failing to consider an individual's cultural context?
3. What is your understanding of 'valuing diversity'? How can this help to prevent discrimination?

Further reading

Parekh (2006) and (2008) provide a helpful overview of the significance of culture. Guirdham (2005) helps us to understand the significance of intercultural communication, as do Holliday, Hyde and Kullman (2004) and Jandt (2006). Seale (2004) and During (2006) are also interesting sources.

8

Sociopolitical structures and processes

Introduction

Chapter 7, with its emphasis on culture, helped us to appreciate the importance of bringing a sociological perspective to bear in considering the social work world. While there are clearly important psychological issues to consider, we also have to give due attention to the wider sociological picture, with its focus on social processes, structures and institutions. This chapter builds on this idea of recognizing social work as a broad psychosocial undertaking, rather than simply an individualistic one-to-one process of helping. To understand the significance of sociology, this chapter explores how sociopolitical structures and processes are often crucial factors in shaping the situations that we encounter in social work.

We have already noted in earlier chapters the dangers of atomism and the way in which an unduly narrow focus on the individual that fails to take due cognizance of the wider social factors can lead to a process of blaming the victim (Ryan, 1988), of making people who are in difficult social circumstances appear to be the villains of the piece. If we fall into this trap, our practice can be seen as oppressive, rather than emancipatory – in other words, part of the problem rather than part of the solution. This chapter is therefore an important foundation for understanding emancipatory practice, a topic to which we shall return in later chapters, especially Chapter 14.

This chapter begins by exploring the nature of social work as a psychosocial matter, drawing on both psychological and sociological insights and understandings. This is followed by a discussion of the significance of social divisions, before we then move on to explore how social and political processes interact with social divisions. Finally we consider once again the crucial role of power in social work.

Social work as a psychosocial enterprise

The term 'psychosocial' was previously used in social work to refer to a specific approach associated with Florence Hollis, one of the early social work authors (Hollis, 1966). However, more recently, the term has come to be used more broadly to denote an acknowledgement that social work practice takes place where the personal/psychological and the social/political meet. The basic idea underpinning the use of this term is the recognition that approaches to practice based purely on psychological understandings will be far from adequate and need to be supplemented by sociological concepts and insights.

Without an understanding of sociology and related political matters we would have a very narrow perspective that would leave us far from the level of sophistication we need in order to make sense of the complexities we encounter in social work. As Bauman and May comment:

> To think sociologically can render us more sensitive and tolerant of diversity. It can sharpen our senses and open our eyes to new horizons beyond our immediate experiences in order that we can explore human conditions which, hitherto, have remained relatively invisible. Once we understand better how the apparently natural, inevitable, immutable, eternal aspects of our lives have been brought into being through the exercise of human power and resources, we shall find it much harder to accept that they are immune and impenetrable to subsequent actions, including our own. Sociological thinking, as an antifixating power is therefore a power in its own right. It renders flexible what may have been the oppressive fixity of social relations and in so doing opens up a world of possibilities. The art of sociological thinking is to widen the scope and the practical effectiveness of freedom. When more of it has been learnt, the individual may well become just a little less subject to manipulation and more resilient to oppression and control. They are also likely to be more effective as social actors, for they can see the connections between their actions and social conditions and how those things which , by their fixity, claim to be irresistible to change, are open to transformation ... Sociology thus stands in praise of the individual, but not individualism.

> (2001, p. 11)

This is an important passage that raises a number of key issues that are worth exploring in a little more detail:

- *Thinking sociologically renders us more sensitive to, and tolerant of, diversity.* This point connects well with our discussions in Chapter 7. The breadth of vision that sociology offers provides a better platform for being open to the enrichment afforded by cultural and other forms of diversity. A narrow, individualistic focus gives us no such scope.
- *Seeing what was previously invisible.* As we shall see in Chapter 10, ideology brings certain dominant ideas into focus and de-emphasizes other aspects of social reality (those aspects that could undermine existing power relations, for example). Sociology helps to cut through the fog that ideology creates in order to be able to see social issues in a much broader view, trying to see the full picture rather than just the aspects of the picture that serve vested interests.
- *The potential for change.* What has been made by human action can be made differently by human action. Presenting the way society works as 'natural' gives the impression that this is the way it must be, that there is no possible alternative. According to this view, people in disadvantaged social positions need to learn to accept their lot, as this is the 'way of the world'. However, recognizing that the current way society is organized is the outcome of historical processes and thus human action introduces the potential for society being organized in different ways. In this way, sociological understanding gives us the potential for transformation and thus for hope.
- *A basis for challenging oppression.* The potential for transformation and hope in turns gives us a basis for challenging oppression by identifying, and seeking to change or remove, the processes of discrimination that give rise to it. The social element of the psychosocial is therefore an essential underpinning of emancipatory forms of practice.
- *More effective as social actors.* This is particularly important for social workers. If we seek to change aspects of the social world through our practice (for example, through attempting to alleviate the effects of poverty), then we will be much better equipped to do so if we have an understanding of how society works in terms of the processes, structures and institutions that drive it.
- *The individual but not individualism.* This is entirely consistent with the approach taken in this book: recognizing the importance

of the individual so that we do not fall into the trap of determinism, but without falling foul of atomism. Bauman (2001) refers to Beck's (1992) distinction between 'individuation' (the process of becoming and remaining a unique individual, an active social actor with agency) and 'individualization' (the social process by which social factors are translated into individual terms – in effect, a process of 'atomization'). Sociology helps us to appreciate the value of the former and the dangerous distortions of the latter.

For decades social work operated within predominantly, if not exclusively, psychological parameters (and still does in some quarters) and paid only minimal attention to the social context. When it later developed a greater degree of social awareness, this was in the form of systems theory which had the benefit of some degree of sociological understanding but lacked a critical edge – that is, it failed to look beneath the surface of society in terms of power relations, conflict, ideology, discrimination and oppression (Thompson, 1992). More recently this psychological focus has been supplemented by a broader (and more critical) sociological perspective in an effort to make social work truly a *psychosocial* enterprise.

In order to attempt to do justice to the sociological aspects of the issues social workers need to engage with, we need to look at some of the key elements of sociological thought. Identity, interpersonal inter-actions, group dynamics and culture, as covered in the preceding chap-ters, are all sociological concerns, but they are not the only ones. This chapter extends the analysis presented so far by filling in some (but, realistically, not all) of the gaps that relate to a macro-level under-standing of society. We begin with the key concept of 'social divisions' – the way in which society being divided up in various ways creates a social structure, a hierarchy with various dimensions, each of which has implications for power in particular, as well as for people's life experiences as a whole.

Social divisions

Perhaps the most important point we need to make about social divi-sions is that society is not a level playing field – that is, people are born into a particular social position which may, on the one hand, enhance their life chances and position within society or may, on the other, act as a barrier. This is what is referred to as a person's 'social location'. This can apply in terms of a wide range of social divisions, such as class, race, gender, age, disability, sexuality, language group, religion, and so on. In effect, social divisions both create and reflect a social structure, and where a person fits into that complex web of social divisions will determine his or her location within that structure. There will be different sets of benefits and costs, advantages and disadvantages, depending on what that location is. It is not therefore a matter of categorizing people for the sake of it. Our social location (that is, our position in this complex web of hierarchies that make up the social structure) will have major consequences – positive or negative – for the individual concerned.

Historically, in terms of the development of interest in social structural factors in social work, the initial emphasis in relation to social divisions was on class. Earlier forms of social work were criticized by the emergence of radical social work in the late 1960s and early 1970s for lacking a sociological dimension – in particular, this revolved around the failure to take account of such class-related factors as poverty and deprivation (Corrigan and Leonard, 1978). Subsequently, attention began to focus also on race and gender as key social divisions. From this, there developed a broader perspective on social divisions which recognized that, not only are class, race and gender (for many years the mainstay of sociological theory) significant underpinnings of social work, but so too are other social divisions, such as those mentioned above.

What has also come to be recognized through the development of our understanding of the complexities involved here is that the effects of such social divisions are interactive and thereby cumulative – that is, what is needed is a *multiplicative* approach, rather than an *additive* one. What I mean by this is that being, for example, a black woman involves the interaction of racism and sexism in ways that can combine quite significantly to disadvantage the person concerned. However, it is important to note that these factors interact in complex ways, rather than simply being 'lumped' one on top of the other. To understand the significance of a person's life experience, we must therefore understand how social disadvantages multiply and influence each other, rather than simply stack up in a straightforward, additive way. Social divisions and the disadvantages they can bring are best seen as dimensions of lived experience (*le vécu*, to use the existentialist term). To give due credit to their significance, we need a dynamic, dialectical understanding and not an essentialist oversimplification that sees these factors in reductionist terms.

Practice focus 8.1

Jill was a white social worker in a mental health team. She was asked to see Carla, a black woman who had been struggling with depression. Conscious of the need to ensure that her practice took account of Carla's ethnicity and the potential or actual role of racism in her life, she was very tuned in to making sure that her practice was anti-racist. When she met Carla and began her assessment, she soon realized that she had been right to incorporate an anti-racist dimension into her work, as racism had clearly featured a great deal in Carla's life and problems. However, what she had not anticipated was that sexism was also a major feature, as gender stereotypes had contributed a great deal to undermining her self-esteem (something that was 'feeding' her depression). She also became aware that, as someone who was labelled 'mentally ill', she had also experienced a great deal of discrimination. As Jill built up her picture of Carla's life she could see how the different types of discrimination interacted and reinforced each other. Working with Carla was proving to be an important lesson in anti-discriminatory practice for Jill.

As mentioned above, there is a significant danger of 'blaming the victim' if wider sociopolitical factors are not taken into consideration. This can lead into ethical problems around being judgemental. For example, it is an easy mistake to make to assume that somebody who is unemployed is lazy and feckless and not sufficiently motivated to find work. However, on closer examination, it will be found that, in the vast majority of such cases, people are disadvantaged by their social position in terms of, for example, access to educational facilities and/or prejudice within the educational system which prevents many people from working-class backgrounds fulfilling their potential. This is evidenced by current debates and campaigns relating to 'widening participation' in higher education in the UK, with universities under pressure to make sure that, as far as reasonably possible, potential students are not held back by their class background.

In considering social divisions it can be helpful to break the term down into its component parts, 'social' and 'divisions':

- *Social.* This emphasizes that we are dealing with the way society is organized – that is, with a fundamental part of human experience. This underlines how important these issues are. Traditional social work approaches that remain at an individualistic level are therefore missing out a key part of the picture.

- *Divisions.* As the term implies, social divisions are *divisive.* They can cause tensions and conflicts that are socially unhelpful. Consider, for example, people looking down on members of working-class communities because they see them as inferior in various ways. In other words, social divisions create the 'fault lines' that act as the basis for systematic discrimination.

It would be unrealistic to expect social work to change the structure of society (although everyone can contribute in a small way over time – social structures are created and recreated through human action; see Thompson, 2003a), but we do, none the less, need to be aware of how social structures have shaped people's lives to date, how they are shaping their current circumstances, and how they may be significant in terms of our interactions with clients and carers (for example, where differences of background exist between worker and client, there will be scope for misunderstanding based on each party interpreting the situation in different ways).

Voice of experience 8.1

Until I became a social worker I had not realized how much of a difference social structure makes to people's lives. It's not just about what area you live in and how much disposable income you have (or don't have), it's much more complex than that. There are just so many ways in which social differences can affect the way you see the world. It makes my work more complicated, of course, but it's fascinating to see how these things work.

Angie, a social worker in a community development project

The question of interpretation is an important one, as it shows that social structures do not exist in isolation. They are connected to frameworks of meaning established at the cultural level. That is, while structures have objective consequences for people, there is also a subjective dimension, in terms of what the social divisions *mean* to the people who live and work within them. This illustrates how the personal, cultural and structural levels interact (Thompson, 2006a) – see Chapter 14. This can be seen to apply, for example, in terms of race and racism. Malik makes apt comment when he argues that:

As in many controversies about the human condition, the debate about race is less about the facts of human differences than about the *meaning* of these facts. It is only through open debate that we are able to decide which interpretation of the facts is the most meaningful. A scientific debate that is policed to ensure that opinions do not wander beyond acceptable moral and political boundaries is no debate at all and itself loses any meaning.

(2008, p. 4)

One of the implications of what Malik is saying is that there is no room for dogmatism in relation to tackling racism (see my comments on this below and the further discussion in Chapter 14) and there can be no definitive scientific 'answer' – see the discussion of positivism in Chapter 2. Race and ethnicity are highly complex matters as, indeed, are all social divisions. We therefore have to wrestle with these complexities – that is, we have to theorize them as they arise in the context of our work, rather than look for easy answers, whether 'scientific' or not.

Social and political processes

Social work is a political entity in two senses. Politics as an academic discipline is, in effect, the study of power, and power is a recurring theme within social work, as we have already noted. However, more specifically, social work can be seen as political in terms of being:

1. A phenomenon that is shaped by political processes, such as the workings of government which result in the development of Acts of Parliament which, in turn, produce social policies which then, in their turn, create the working context for social work practice. The social work world is therefore a *political* world, in the sense that it is shaped in part by political processes, locally, regionally, nationally and internationally.
2. A professional activity (or set of activities) that involves the operation of power – in terms of the exercise of care and control, for example. This is quite a complex situation, with power operating at multiple levels (see Thompson, 2007a). Whether we are using power formally (through court proceedings, for example) or informally (through efforts to persuade or otherwise influence the course of events, perhaps), the situation is the same: we are professionals accountable for our actions and therefore have to use such

power ethically and responsibly. The social work world is therefore a political world for this reason too – the fact that it involves the (ethical and responsible) use of power on behalf of society.

The law – a fundamental basis of social work – is, in essence, an exercise of power and therefore a political process. Social work, being closely associated with the legal context which gives it its mandate, is therefore also a *political* process. Recognizing this takes us a step further in our process of broadening out our understanding of social work and, in so doing, moving away from an atomistic approach.

Practice focus 8.2

Martin was nervous about going on his first placement as a social work student, but was looking forward to it none the less. His practice teacher, Bal, was strongly committed to anti-discriminatory practice in general and anti-racism in particular. As a result of Bal's interests, Martin had the opportunity to learn a great deal about how powerful processes operated in society and conspired to place minority groups at a significant disadvantage. He was particularly fascinated by the way in which power could sometimes be exercised very openly (for example, when he saw young offenders being sentenced by the courts) and sometimes much more subtly (for example, when experienced team members were trying to influence the courts through their reports or their comments when called upon to speak in court). Bal helped him to realize just how complex power was – and also just how fundamental it was in social work. The placement proved to be an excellent learning experience for him all round, but the power aspect was particularly informative for him, because he had never given any thought to such matters before. He was very grateful to Bal for the support he had received in helping him to learn about issues that he could have found difficult to deal with if the situation had been approached in a confrontational or heavy-handed way.

It is also crucial to recognize that there are negative social processes that are so often key features of the social work world, aspects of how society works that produce problematic outcomes. These include, but are not limited to, the following:

- *Exclusion and marginalization.* Certain groups become seen as 'less than' the majority. People from certain groups are therefore subject to social exclusion and are marginalized – that is, pushed to the margins of society. Examples of such groups would be people with mental health problems, ex-offenders and people who have addiction problems. Such processes tend to work very subtly to exclude people – for example, through the way some groups are portrayed by the media as 'undesirables'.

- *Stigmatization and scapegoating.* These are processes that have already been mentioned earlier, but it is worth re-emphasizing their significance in the broader context of social and political processes. Stigma is something that can exist at an individual level in the sense that, for specific local reasons, a particular person may become stigmatized. However, it would be problematic to adopt too narrow and individualistic a perspective on stigma. What has to be recognized is that stigmatization is a broad social process. It is no coincidence that certain groups of people will characteristically become stigmatized in some way – for example, children who, for no fault of their own, have been brought up in care. Scapegoating is a common result of stigmatization and also, in turn, commonly a cause of it. Where somebody is scapegoated on an individual level, this is because they are seen in some way as the weak link in the chain, in the sense of being the least powerful person. For example, in a family system, with the result that a particular individual will often be seen as the source of a family's problem. However, scape-goating is also a process that can be seen to happen at a much broader social and political level. Consider, for example, the way in which people with mental health problems are often depicted stereotypically as potential killers. The reality of the situation is that, if somebody is murdered, it is highly unlikely that the perpe-trator of that homicidal act will have mental health problems. People with mental health needs face this form of stigmatization and scapegoating because of the way in which they have become a group demonized by society.
- *Alterity.* Alienation has already been recognized in earlier chapters as a significant factor. Alterity is one of the processes through which alienation arises. 'Alter' is the Latin word for 'other', and so alterity refers to the process by which particular individuals and groups are identified as 'other' – in other words, as not belonging, as being alien. De Beauvoir's (1972) work on gender equality, which has proven to be very influential in shaping feminist thought over the decades, uses the concept of alterity to explain how women are placed in a subordinate position because they are portrayed as 'other'. The masculine is presented as the norm and the feminine

as a deviation from it. Consider, for example, the tendency to use 'he' or 'him' to refer to a person of unknown gender:

PERSON A: Whoever gets the job, I'm going to ask him to take responsibility for the duty rota.
PERSON B: How do you know it will be a man?
PERSON A: I don't.
PERSON B: So, why did you say 'him'?
PERSON A: Dunno, habit, I guess.

Voice of experience 8.2

I used to be an education welfare officer and I could see how the school worked as a microcosm of society. The labelling, the scape-goating, the in groups and out groups, they were all there, making life a misery for some students, and they were often the ones who would then absent themselves. I now work in a child care team and I can see the same things going on in the community. It's no wonder some people struggle to cope with life's pressures or react strongly against them.

Phillippa, a social worker in a family support team

These processes will sometimes act in isolation from one another, but more often it is likely to be the case that they can generally be seen to be operating in combination, with very profoundly significant effects on the people so affected. We should not underestimate the extent to which social and political processes have a bearing on the lives of the individuals, families and communities that we encounter in social work. We would be committing the fundamental error of 'psychologism' if we were to fail to recognize this. Such an atomistic approach, as we have already noted, is a dangerous one that should have no place in forms of social work that are based on sophisticated understandings of the world in which we work.

An understanding of processes is important for ensuring that people do not adopt a reductionist understanding of social divisions and discrimination. I have discussed elsewhere (Thompson, 2003a; 2003b; 2009e) how efforts to tackle discrimination and oppression have in many cases been characterized by a simplistic understanding of the processes involved and often by a degree of rigidity and dogmatism. The comments of Okitikpi and Aymer reflect some of these concerns:

there is an assertion by Sallah (2007), sometimes implicit, and some-times explicit, that white practitioners are incapable of working with black service users. Similarly, there are those who question the role of men in social work (Pringle, 2001), and others who advocate the need for a separatist provision for service users with disability (Barns, 2003). These essentialist and absolutist positions have caused a great deal of damage and eroded people's desire to incorporate anti-discriminatory practice into their approach.

(2008a, p. 36)

These are just some examples of many that could be put forward to support the argument that there is a danger that a simplistic, dogmatic approach to anti-discriminatory practice can do more harm than good and can, at best, confuse people and, at worst, alienate them. We shall revisit this argument in Chapter 12 when we explore the relationship between language and discrimination, as the development of the notion of 'political correctness' illustrates this point well.

Power revisited

It is very unfortunate that, in the social work literature, power is often either oversimplified or not discussed at all, as if it is somehow seen as not relevant. One thing that this book should make very clear is that power is an essential focus for social work. However, where power has been discussed in relation to social work in the past, a very common tendency has been the adoption of psychological models of power. For example, there has been a tradition of looking at the power dimension of discrimination purely or at least predominantly in terms of personal prejudice. This has failed to do justice to the complexities involved in the wider operations of power – for example, in terms of the cultural and structural dimensions of how power works and how it relates to processes of discrimination.

Practice focus 8.3

Tim was a social worker in children's services for many years before he moved into adult services to join a team working with older people. He felt the time was right for a change and a fresh impetus. At university he had learned about the personal, cultural and structural dimensions of power and the discrimination that arises as a result of the abuse or misuse of such power. However, working with older people suddenly brought all this to life for him. He could see how the poverty that so many older people lived in was so disempowering for them. He could also see how ageist attitudes and assumptions, so widely accepted as a 'normal' part of culture were so detrimental, and again disempowering. So, when it came to working with individuals at a personal level, he could see why what he so often encountered was what appeared to be a low-level depression, a very dispirited approach to life. He could see how power – and a sense of power-lessness – were so relevant to the lives of the people he was working with. Looking back at his career in child care he could see that the same issues had applied there too, but it had taken the change of scene by switching from children's services to adult services for the significance to strike him. He realized that he would have to think care-fully about how best to use this understanding to underpin his practice – in other words, how he would incorporate this knowledge into his theorizing.

The emphasis on psychological models of power was challenged by what I shall refer to as the structural critique. This refers to broadly marxist perspectives on power which were critical of the tendency to adopt an atomistic approach and which, in turn, have emphasized the significance of structural dimensions of power in terms especially of class, but also of race and gender. In turn, this structural approach has been criticized by what I shall refer to as the post-structuralist critique. This is something we shall discuss in more detail in Chapter 12 but, for now, I want to make the point that post-structuralists have argued that the emphasis on social structures in relation to power is misplaced. Under the influence of writers such as Foucault (see Faubion, 2000), the emphasis has been on the much more diffuse oper-ation of power – that is, the way in which power is much more common as part of everyday life on a micro level and is not simply a matter of broad macro-structural properties, such as class. Power, according to post-structuralism, is not a feature of social structures, but rather a dimension of social interactions channelled through language.

From an existentialist point of view, it can be seen that none of these approaches is adequate. What is needed in terms of our under-standing of power is a much more holistic perspective that takes account of personal/psychological dimensions of power, cultural levels in terms of, for example, the operation of discourses and culturally embedded norms of social interaction, as well as – but not instead of – structural considerations, such as the major social divisions discussed above. In later chapters, this aspect of existentialism will be discussed more fully, but for now it is important to note that, in theorizing our practice, we need to be attuned to different types of power, rather than get lost in essentialist and reductionist debates about which is the 'correct' or 'true' type of power.

Voice of experience 8.3

On one of my placements I felt a bit like piggy in the middle. My practice teacher was a strong trade unionist and very interested in marxist thinking. My tutor, though, was a post-structuralist and felt that marxist ideas were misconstrued. I could see benefits in both schools of thought, but it was a pity that they seemed more interested in doing down each other's approach, rather than seeing how they could learn from each other.

Janice, a social worker in an advocacy project

McNay's comments are instructive in this regard:

Using power relations as a unifying concept necessitates an exploration of the dimension of power whenever we consider explanations of social issues. It may not be necessary or appropriate to reject particular theories, but rather to understand how being set in a wider context of power would change their meaning.

(1992, p. 127)

This is a very significant passage for two reasons:

1. It makes the very important point that power is a fundamental dimension of social life and therefore needs to be a factor in any explanations of social life – whether formal, 'textbook' theories or the everyday theorizing of practitioners engaging in reflective practice.
2. It rightly argues that it is not simply a matter of accepting or rejecting a particular theory (looking for the Truth) but, rather, seeing whether it incorporates an understanding of power and, if it does not, considering what difference it makes to the theory's value in offering insights when the power dimension is introduced.

This does not mean that no theory should ever be rejected, but it does mean that all theories should be subjected to the 'power test' and that it is possible to gather different insights from different theoretical perspectives and seek to integrate them as part of our understanding of practice (our 'theorizing') – rather than simply decide which theoretical club we are going to be a member of (see Chapter 1).

Conclusion

It is to be hoped that this chapter has made it clear that, if we do not adopt a broad perspective informed by sociopolitical understandings, we run the risk of reinforcing discrimination and oppression – in effect, sealing people we are trying to help into their positions of social inequality, rather than playing a constructive part in processes of empowerment geared towards promoting emancipation. As we noted in Chapter 2, this notion of emancipation is one that has been criticized by postmodernist thinkers. This chapter has laid the foundations for the more in-depth discussions in Chapter 14 which will argue, *contra* postmodernism, that emancipation is a key concern for social work practice.

A major feature of our discussions in this chapter has been the further broadening of our focus, emphasizing that the individual, although a unique person in their own right, needs to be understood as part of a much wider social context. Our particular focus has been on the sociopolitical processes that are such an important part of the macro-structural context of social life in general and social work in particular. Social work is part of the wider social and political sphere. To understand social work, we therefore need to have at least a basic understanding of how our professional roles and activities are influenced and, to a certain extent, defined by that wider sphere. This chapter is not enough on its own to offer that level of understanding, but it should provide a basis for developing the fuller knowledge and understanding needed.

The wider sociopolitical sphere is not a fixed, static entity – it is dynamic and evolving. It can therefore be understood as a set of processes. We would do well to 'tune in' to those processes, so that we are able to make sense of how they are shaping our clients' lives, our professional context and how the two interrelate. Indeed, as social workers, we would do well to develop a sensitivity to processes in general: psychological, interpersonal, intragroup, intergroup, cultural, social and political. There are also organizational processes that we need to be able to understand if we are to be able to see how our practice is shaped by the workings of the organization we work for. Chapter 9 is therefore concerned with beginning to make sense of the organizational context of social work.

Points to ponder

1. Imagine a family seeking social work support. In what ways might wider social factors be playing a part in their situation?
2. What do you understand by the term 'alienation'? How is it relevant to social work?
3. List three ways in which power typically plays a part in shaping the situations we encounter in social work.

Further reading

Bauman and May (2001) is a useful general introduction to sociology. My own work on social divisions features mainly in Thompson (2006a) and (2003a), with Thompson (2007a) focusing in particular on power and empowerment. See also N. Thompson and S. Thompson (2008), Chapter 2.2. Callinicos (2007) and Mullaly (2002) are both interesting sources worth exploring, as are Ferguson, Lavalette and Mooney (2002) and Ferguson (2007).

The organizational context

Introduction

One of the things that we shall focus on in Chapter 10 will be the importance of the social work profession adopting a broad perspective that incorporates the moral-political dimensions of our work. In this chapter I argue that our perspective also needs to be broad enough to incorporate an understanding of organizational factors: how they affect us and how we can affect them (another example of the dialectic in action). The chapter is premised on the belief that an understanding of the workplace and the processes that go on within it is an essential part of the social worker's knowledge base. Here I am therefore concerned with exploring some of the key issues as they relate to the organizational context in order to provide a platform from which to develop a fuller understanding of the complexities involved.

We begin by looking at the important role of organizational culture and how it creates a set of expectations around how people should behave, think, feel and interact. We then move on to consider the structures, strategies and policies that shape the organizational environment in which we work. Finally, we explore what part social workers can play, individually and collectively, in influencing the organizations in which they work with a view to minimizing the problems that organizational life can generate and maximizing the potential for high-quality professional practice within a supportive and empowering environment.

It is worth re-emphasizing at this point the significance of managerialism (and its underlying political philosophy of neoliberalism), as this has proven to be a strong influence on organizational life in recent years. There is more to organizations than managerialism, but it none the less needs to be an important part of our considerations in trying to make sense of how the organizational context shapes social work practice.

Organizational culture

The notion of organizational culture is captured in the phrase: 'the way we do things round here'. That is, it refers to the unwritten rules and established habits that become part of the working way of life of a group of people, or indeed of a whole organization. The culture within an organization can either help or hinder in a variety of ways (in reality, it usually does a mixture of both). It can help by giving a great sense of solidarity and camaraderie, much as culture does in general within the wider society (see Chapter 7). But it can also cause problems in so far as aspects of the culture may be unhelpful in some ways. For example, some organizations, or some sections of organizations, can have a strong anti-learning culture – that is, anybody who is attempting to learn and improve their practice can be marginalized or even ridiculed. Such cultures can be captured in the phrase: 'Heads down, get on with it'. Even though, as Wenger (1998, p. 96) puts it: 'Learning is the engine of practice and practice is the history of that learning' (cited in Taylor, 2004, p. 79), many organizations develop cultures that are not supportive of learning and may actually discourage it in a spirit of defensiveness. I agree with Wenger's argument that the history of learning that becomes enshrined in practice can (and *should*) become embedded in the culture. Whether it is or not will depend to a large extent on the culture and the extent to which it values learning. Cultures that discourage learning therefore undermine good practice and act as an obstacle to progress.

Any sort of anti-learning culture can patently, then, be quite a disadvantage (with regard to both organizational effectiveness and career development for the individuals concerned) in terms of the opportunities afforded for learning and thereby improving their practice. Baldwin goes a step further in arguing that learning can help to manage the uncertainties of organizational life:

> One of the tenets of effective organizational learning is that it is there to manage the uncertainties of organizational life and, indeed, to use them as a positive force for change and development. To attempt to manage out uncertainty is to destroy the potential opportunities for dynamic creativity present in managing uncertainty.
>
> (2004, p. 48)

This is consistent with existentialism in so far as the need to address uncertainty (the 'contingency of being', as discussed earlier) is a key feature of the philosophy. It is also consistent with existentialism's emphasis on learning, recognizing human existence as a process of becoming, rather than a fixed entity. As we shall note below, learning (or its absence) is an important feature of the workplace.

Practice focus 9.1

Lisa was a social worker in an older people team. At first she liked working there, and the team members were very friendly. However, over time she felt less positive about the team. They were under a lot of pressure, with a strong, constant flow of referrals. Lisa was a highly competent practitioner and very committed to reflective practice. Her way of dealing with a heavy workload was to think carefully about priorities, to make sure she was being as effective as she could and trying hard to allow the pressures to push her into making mistakes. But this approach put her in a minority of one in the team. Everyone else just busied themselves in their work, trying to deal with the pressures by rushing and attempting to get the cases sorted out as quickly as possible. Lisa was not prepared to adopt that approach as she could see that it was dangerous in terms of both quality of practice and the health and safety of the staff, and so she stuck to her guns. As a result of this, the team started making sarcastic comments to the effect that: 'if you've got time to stop and think, then you haven't got enough work to do'. She was very disappointed about this attitude. The team had adopted a 'heads down, get on with it' mentality and were not open to new ideas or prepared to explore different ways of dealing with the high workload. She spent a year in the team trying to influence it in a more positive, learning-oriented direction, but, after achieving minimal success during that time, she decided to move on and to look for a post in a team more committed to learning.

A culture can be, and often is, a stronger influence than policy or management. What this means is that there may be policies in place that promote a particular form of practice, and there may be managers who are keen to develop that type of practice, but, if the culture does not support such practice, then it is unlikely to occur. This means that culture is something that has to be given careful consideration. It would be quite foolish to ignore the significance of organizational culture in shaping practice. Good practitioners can find that their work is sabotaged, in effect, by being filtered through an organizational culture that is problematic in one or more ways. Similarly, organizational cultures can discourage and demoralize where they are characterized by negativity, defeatism and cynicism. However, as mentioned above, there is also the positive side of culture, and so I do not want to paint too negative a picture of how culture operates and the effects it has. Teams can be extremely beneficial for their members where open, supportive learning cultures have been established. Indeed, this is one of the reasons why an understanding of culture is so important: if we have little idea of how cultures work, then we will easily be pushed here and there by them and be in a very weak position when it comes to trying to influence them in a more positive direction (or to maximize their positive potential where they are working well).

Given that cultures can be either largely positive or largely negative or a mixture of the two, it can be helpful to undertake what is known as a 'culture audit'. This can be carried out at an extended team meeting or an 'awayday' or other such team development event. It involves working together to draw up a list of those factors that can have a bearing on the culture. The following are some of the major ones to consider. The culture of the team (or organization) can be understood in terms of where it is located on a continuum between each of the two extremes in relation to each of the following criteria:

- *Negative vs. positive.* How would you characterize the team in terms of negativity and positivity? Are they mainly positive and upbeat, adopting a constructive approach or is there a lot of negativity, defeatism and cynicism? If being entirely negative and demoralized is 0 and being entirely positive and energized is 10, what score would you give your team?
- *Dependency vs. independence.* Are team members mainly self-starters who show initiative and take ownership of their work or do they rely too heavily on managers to give them guidance or even instructions? Where would you rate the team on a continuum between dependency (0) and independence (10)?
- *Tramlines vs. creativity.* Does the team 'push the envelope' or 'think outside the box' (to use two current clichés)? That is, are they creative in their work, looking for innovative solutions? Or do they stick to the tried and tested and never venture far from a narrow range of well-established responses to the situations they encounter? What rating, on a continuum from 0 to 10, would you

give your team between working in tramlines and working creatively?

- *Problem avoidance vs. problem solving.* Where difficulties are experienced is there a tendency for team members to attempt to brush the problems under the carpet – that is, to engage in avoidance behaviour? Or is it more characteristic of the team to pull together and work out possible strategies for addressing the difficulties being encountered? Where, again on a scale of 0 to 10, does your team fall between the two extremes of this continuum?

- *Resisting change vs. capitalizing on the opportunities presented by change.* While there is nothing inherently wrong in resisting ill-conceived or otherwise inappropriate change, teams can have problems if they resist even potentially helpful changes (for example, if the culture is a highly conservative one that places a high value on continuity and a low value on change). So, the key question is: does the team try to make the best of the changes that come its way or do they dig their heels in, even when they may benefit from the change? How would you rate your team on this dimension?

- *Unsupportive vs. supportive.* Can a member of the team who is experiencing difficulties count on the team for the support and assistance he or she needs? Or would other team members offer only the minimal level of support they can get away with without appearing rude, unfeeling or hostile? Where, on this continuum, would you place your team?

- *Closed vs. open.* Is the culture of your team one that is secretive and guarded, with hidden agendas and a lack of honesty and openness? Or is it more open and based on trust and integrity, with no tensions coming from unresolved conflicts or other undercurrents? Consider too how your team would be rated between these two extremes.

By rating the team according to these seven dimensions of culture, areas for development can be identified and strategies for addressing them developed. Similarly, areas of strength can be identified, so that they can be built on over time. Although this is not intended as a scientific tool (do not let the use of numbers lead you to assume otherwise), having an overall numerical score (out of 70) can give a rough and ready idea of how helpful or otherwise the team's culture is likely to be.

Voice of experience 9.1

We had been having problems in our team, so when we had an external consultant lead us through an awayday, we didn't know what to
expect. So, we were very pleasantly surprised when the 'culture audit'
she got us to do proved so helpful. It gave us some clear ideas about
what needed to change if we were going to get out of our bad patch
and go back to being a more supportive team.

Hannah, a social worker in a child care team

Once you have a clear picture of the culture in which you work
(whether this is done through a formal culture audit or just through
your own perceptions of the team or organizational culture), then this
raises the question of how the culture can be changed or improved.
One important point to note is that a culture is basically a set of
habits. It persists only if it is reinforced – that is, put into practice –
on a daily basis by members of the team or organization. Cultures can
and do change – they are fluid processes rather than fixed entities.
There are many questions that can be asked which will help to establish what direction the team or work group can move in. Let us
consider just two of them by way of illustration.

One particularly important question to ask is whether there is a
learning culture present. If not, then this raises questions about how
you can ensure that you continue to learn, so that, over time, you
become more knowledgeable, more skilled, more confident and more
committed – rather than the opposite scenario which involves no
learning (therefore over time becoming more routinized, more disillu-
sioned, more demoralized and therefore more likely to engage in poor
practice). Baldwin makes apt comment in discussing the significance
of 'double-loop learning' as an alternative to becoming bogged down in
working practices that fail to exploit the learning potential:

Routine learning in most organizations is described by Argyris and
Schön as single-loop learning, in which organizations and the individuals within them repeat procedures, learning in an uncritical fashion from
previous experience. Argyris provides considerable detail of the sort of
problems that such an approach leads to – 'defensive routines', 'games of
control and deception' and taboos on discussing key issues (1999: 6). It is
only by creating an environment in which these routines, games and
taboos which construct an organization's culture are critically evaluated
through double-loop learning, that they can be tackled and the organi-

zation can more effectively match its espoused theory with its theory-in-use.

(2004, p. 47)

Double-loop learning involves being able to adopt a critical overview of our work and drawing out the learning from it (Thompson, 2006c). As Baldwin's reference to 'espoused theory' and 'theory-in-use' signals, double-loop learning can help us to make sure that our theorizing (theory in use) is consistent with the professional knowledge base we claim to be using (espoused theory).

Another important question to address is the culture's approach to risk issues. Denney (2005) argues that an overemphasis on risk has developed in recent years (and, as we noted earlier, it is no coincidence that this has occurred in the context of managerialism). He comments that:

> Risk management and risk regulation can be seen as ways of diverting attention from system weaknesses and reducing the status of regulatory activities to little more than 'blaming mechanisms'. The over-emphasis on regulation and risk management can make regulatory systems unwieldy and ultimately self-defeating.

(Denney, 2005, p. 156)

What it is important to establish, then, when it comes to considering the future direction and development of the team or organization is the extent to which this overemphasis on risk has been incorporated into (or, conversely, resisted by) the culture of that team or organization. This is not to say that risk issues are not important and can be safely disregarded. It is, rather, a question of trying to ensure that such concerns are not dealt with in a heavy-handed and thus potentially counterproductive way (see the discussion of risk in Chapter 11 of *Practising Social Work*).

Some may argue that it is the job of managers, not practitioners, to worry about matters like culture and to seek to influence their direction and growth. There is an element of truth in this, in so far as managers do have such a responsibility. However, I would argue that practitioners – as professionals committed to maximizing the effectiveness of their practice rather than bureaucrats committed simply to doing the basics of what is required of them – share that responsibility to some degree. Indeed, as pointed out earlier, it is not only managers that can be leaders – practitioners can also make an important contribution to shaping positive and helpful working cultures.

Structures, strategies and policies

Organizations by their very nature have a structure, a network of interconnected elements. It can be very helpful for practitioners to understand that structure so that we are aware of who has power over what, what channels of influence exist, and so on. Without an overall understanding of organizational structure, we will be in a very weak position when it comes to influencing that organization positively. This means that we are less likely to be able to function as a professional and could be limited to acting bureaucratically, following instructions and administrative processes without having a wider picture of where they have come from and how they might change over time. Clarke and Newman note that professionalism is needed in welfare, that bureaucracy is not enough on its own:

> However, bureaucratic administration was not, by itself, sufficient for the public provision of social welfare. It needed to be tempered by forms of 'expertise' which were more than administrative competence and which drew on distinctive bodies of knowledge and skills about the causes and solutions of social problems. This marks the point at which bureaucratic administration and professionalism met in the development of the welfare state (Cousins, 1987: ch. 5).
>
> (1997, p. 6)

This is an important passage, in so far as it demonstrates nicely the coming together of bureaucracy and professionalism. As noted earlier, managerialism has served to emphasize the bureaucratic elements of welfare systems and, in not recognizing or valuing the professional elements, has undermined them considerably. Our understanding of the organizational contexts therefore needs to incorporate a recognition of the importance of professionalism and not just bureaucracy (Payne, 2000).

Given that social work is part of a much wider social policy field, the social worker needs to have a broad understanding of the organizational context and structure – for example, in terms of whether their employing organization fits into the broader field of local government, the health service, or the voluntary or private sectors. This will provide a platform for developing the basis of an understanding of the *formal* workings of power – how the hierarchy assigns power to certain postholders, for example. From this can be developed an understanding of the informal workings of power as well – for example, in terms of knowing who are the key players in getting things done or which policies have 'teeth' and must be followed to the letter and which are meaningless pieces of paper that are generally ignored. A social worker wishing to maximize their effectiveness will need to know about both formal and informal sets of power relations.

What is also important is the development of strategic thinking. This refers to the ability to understand what outcomes the organization is required to achieve and what strategies are in place for achieving them. Without this overview or macro-level perspective, much of what happens in an organization will make little sense to the worker concerned. They will then be in a very weak position when it comes to being able to use their knowledge and skills to make progress in their particular activities.

Practice focus 9.2

When appointed to his new post in the access team, Mark was pleased to be part of a group who had developed a reputation for very high quality practice. His previous team had been a disappointment to him, as morale was very low there and there seemed to be very little commitment to quality practice, let alone best practice. He was keen to find out what the differences were – what made one team so committed and the other far less so. He quickly realized that the leadership qualities of the respective team managers certainly made a big difference. Over time he also came to realize that another key difference was awareness of the wider context. In his previous team, staff basically got on with the job and there was no discussion of wider issues of policy or organization. They simply concerned themselves with their individual caseloads and that was it. However, in his new team, he could see that there was a much stronger emphasis on, and understanding of, organizational dynamics and how the team's work fitted into the wider picture not only of the organization itself, but also of the broader social policy field. He found this to be a much more professional approach and certainly gained much more job satisfaction from understanding his work role as part of this wider picture, rather than just a set of cases to work through without any real understanding of how his work was part of a bigger whole. He was so glad that he had made the switch, as he could see that the broader perspective that characterized the culture of his new team was a much better foundation for professional practice.

By having a fuller understanding of this broader context, we are not reliant on the often quite conservative perspectives of organizational theorists. Casey writes about how: 'Organization theorists and analysts became as in C. Wright Mills' (1959) view, "servants of power"' (2002, p. 11). In saying this, she is recognizing that much of the conventional understanding of organizational life lacks a critical edge. Because of this, there is a need for critically reflective practice – for social workers to look at the organizational context of their work with a critical eye in order to develop a fuller understanding of how power operates in organizations and how discrimination and oppression can be perpetuated through organizational processes that are allowed to continue because so many members of that organization remain unaware of them – this is the basis of institutional discrimination (see Chapter 6 of Thompson, 2003a).

Part of the underpinnings necessary for strategic thinking is also the need to understand and engage with processes of change. Organizations do not stand still; they are dynamic, evolving entities, and so a well-informed social worker needs to be able to understand what the factors underpinning change in an organization are and how they make a difference.

One of the reasons why strategic thinking is important is that strategy should guide practice. A strategy should not be seen as simply a glossy mission statement that has no connection with reality. It is important that we are clear about why the organization we work for exists, what its overall formal goals are and how, through our actions, we are helping the organization to fulfil those goals (while also recognizing that different factions within the organization may have different and competing goals). Without that understanding, it is possible for our efforts to be misdirected or for us to come into unnecessary conflict with our organization. Also, if we are not tuned in to that overall strategic direction, then we do not have a voice when it comes to challenging that direction if we think that it is not consistent with our professional values (see the discussion below of influencing organizations).

Strategic thinking, then, is about having an overall sense of direction, a sense of where we are heading and why. This is important in terms of motivation and morale. If we do not find our work meaningful, then it is highly likely that we will find it much more difficult to be motivated or to realize our full potential (Moss, 2007b). This links well with our discussions of spirituality which will form the basis of Chapter 12. Spirituality can be seen as a matter of, among other things, creating and sustaining a meaningful worldview that acts as a basis of our relationship with the world. This applies to the workplace as much as to any other aspect of our lives. Having clarity about the *purpose* of our work, the aims it is intended to fulfil, and the values on which it is based can therefore be an important part of making our work meaningful, bringing, in effect, a spiritual dimension to the workplace (Moss, 2009).

In addition to broad strategies, organizations will have policies on specific areas to support that overall strategic direction and to guide practice. It is clearly important, then, that social workers are aware of the policies that underpin their work. Without an understanding of these issues, we are again on fairly weak territory when the matter of having a voice arises. We disempower ourselves quite significantly if we fail to make the most of the opportunities available to us to influence aspects of the organization in a positive direction. Sitting back passively and hoping the organization takes the positive steps necessary is neither a strong nor desirable position to be in. Being so burned out and cynical about the organization and its work as to no longer care about what direction professional practice goes in is an even worse position to be in, but unfortunately that is precisely where some practitioners are to be found.

One very important factor in relation to strategy is the key role of leaders in keeping that strategy on course. As we have already noted, leadership is something that is an essential part of effective organizational operation. Leaders are expected to communicate the organization's goals and the strategies for achieving them, but, as the subtitle to Gilbert (2005) puts it, while also 'remaining human'. We would do well, then, to keep the idea of leadership in mind, particularly *professional* leadership, as this has a crucial part to play in shaping practice, the way that practice is organized and the direction it takes. We shall return to this point below.

Voice of experience 9.2

Our focus is on innovation so, when we are recruiting, we always look for people who show evidence of professional leadership, people who do more than just routinely go about their business ticking boxes. We find that these are the people who flourish in an organization like ours.

Solomon, manager of a voluntary organization

Influencing organizations

In an earlier work focusing on the processes involved in promoting equality (Thompson, 2003a), I wrote about the 'organizational operator'. I used this term to refer to staff and managers within organizations who have the knowledge, skills and commitment to making a positive difference within their organization by influencing the direction of the organization towards a greater emphasis on equality and diversity. However, that term can also be used more broadly, in the sense that an organizational operator can, in addition, be somebody who uses their knowledge and skills to influence the organization in a positive direction about other matters more generally, as well as about equality and diversity in particular. In this way, an organizational operator can be somebody who plays a part in shaping the culture, helping to move away from destructive aspects, such as blocks to learning, and focusing on developing a more value-driven form of professional practice within the organization. An organizational operator in this sense is a leader (as noted earlier, it is not necessary for leaders to be managers). Anyone who is able to play a positive role in communicating and supporting organizational (and professional) strategy can play a part in leadership.

A key part of this is the recognition that, central to professionalism is the acknowledgement that our primary accountability is to the profession (and therefore our clientele), rather than to our employer. This is what distinguishes professionals from bureaucrats. At times, professionals may come into conflict with their employing organizations where the culture or practices of the organization are contrary to professional values. Given that social workers in the UK are now registered and therefore committed to a code of conduct and related national occupational standards, this raises important considerations to address because, if a social worker chooses to simply go along with the organizational culture for a quiet life and does not promote best practice in terms of professionalism, he or she could potentially face de-registration if it were found that the practices were contrary to professional requirements. 'I was just doing what other people do' would be no excuse, just as a nurse who failed to meet professional standards could not use the failure of other nurses in this respect as an excuse.

Practice focus 9.3

At her developmental review, Vee was asked how she ensured that her practice met the national occupational standards. Vee was a very experienced senior practitioner who qualified in the days before occupational standards existed and she had not taken the trouble to find out about them. She was therefore very embarrassed to reply that she was not aware of what her obligations were under these standards. Chris, the service manager who was chairing the review was not surprised by her response – she knew Vee was not the only person who was in that boat – but she was disappointed. She pointed out to Vee that, while she was pleased with her overall standard of work, it was a pity that she had not kept up to date with professional developments. She explained to Vee that the standards were the minimum expected of social workers and that, while she often went far beyond the minimum expected, she needed to be aware of the professional standards she was required to meet. 'How', argued Chris, 'can you expect to influence the direction of our profession if you do not know the basics of what is expected of us as professionals?' 'How', she went on, 'could you possibly adopt a critical perspective on those standards when you have not engaged with them at all?' Vee took her point and decided that she would have to give some serious thought to what it means to be a professional.

Practice focus 9.3 illustrates the importance of professional accountability, being aware of how our actions have consequences, positive or negative, for which we can be held to account. Ironically, managerialism has had the effect of de-emphasizing professionalism by placing the emphasis on standardized bureaucratic processes. However, despite this playing down of professionalism in general, the accountability aspect has received greater attention, particularly in relation to the assessment and management of risk. As Duyvendak, Knijn and Kremer point out: 'Accountability itself is not the problem, but the fact that it has become a social neurosis' (2006a, p. 11). Webb's views illustrate this further when he writes about how a blame culture has come to be associated with managerialism:

Within blame culture, risk avoidance becomes a key priority for care managers and front-line practitioners. Ever tighter mechanisms of accountability and transparency are introduced. This in turn hardens the defensive tactics of front-line workers, resulting in secrecy and mistrust. People become scared. In local authority social services departments elaborate complaint systems are put in place, the purpose of which is to make definitions of responsibility specific, narrow and precise, rather than to nourish a sense of shared responsibility. In line with neo-liberal practice they put the question of responsibility into the context of a contest, not the context of common values. Cynics argue that rather than making professionals more accountable, these blame systems put a very high premium on avoiding responsibility and deflecting possible blame or legal liability onto someone else.

(2006, p. 70)

Of course, it is not only cynics who doubt the wisdom of this approach. It is possible to be sceptical about such matters without becoming a cynic.

As professionals seeking to influence the organization in which we work we would do well to bear in mind the significance of managerialism in creating a blame culture and try to undo its damaging effects, while not losing sight of the need for genuine professional accountability. Accountability provides the parameters for trust (in so far as it marks the limits of what professionals can and cannot do), but accountability – a positive ethical base for professionalism – becomes negative, demeaning, demoralizing and unduly restrictive where there is no trust. In short, accountability without trust is simply blame. It is therefore important that we challenge blame culture and the managerialism on which it rests whenever we can.

It is also important to note that the professional challenges of *influencing* an organization should not be equated with *fighting* that organization. If we are to engage in professional discussions about important matters of professional concern, then this should be done in a spirit of professionals working together (practitioners and managers), rather than employees biting the hand that feeds them by attacking their employers. These are important points to which we shall return in Part Three.

Ultimately, in terms of attempting to influence the organization, we can conclude that, if we cannot change the culture positively, we can at least bypass it. Each of us can focus on our professional values and pride and do what we think is right and just in the circumstances, rather than mindlessly following others because that is 'the done thing'. This is consistent with the existentialist concept – drawing on the work of Kierkegaard (Watts, 2003) and Nietzsche (Wicks, 2002) – of each person needing to find his or her own way forward, rather than simply adopting a 'herd' mentality.

Voice of experience 9.3

I used to work in an office that was very regimented and bureaucratic. I tried to change things by trying to get professional debates going, but it got me nowhere – they just didn't see the relevance. It was sad really; they had such a narrow view of what they were doing. I had to work very hard to make sure their attitudes didn't rub off on me. When I moved on to a much more positive team, I was so glad I had been able to hold on to my professional values despite the strongly bureaucratic culture I'd been working in.

Brenda, a social worker in a community care team

Conclusion

While all jobs in the social welfare field involve some degree of administration and managerial control, we are, of course, professionals, and not bureaucrats. All professionals have to wrestle with bureaucracy to some extent. For example, lawyers have to engage with the bureaucracy of the legal system, architects with town planning regulations, doctors with health service regulations, and so on and so forth. However, we must not allow organizational processes and interests to reduce us to bureaucrats. Lawyers, architects and doctors do not *become* bureaucrats just because they have to work within bureaucratic systems – they retain their professionalism despite such pressures. The same can and should apply to social workers: working in a bureaucratic system does not turn us into bureaucrats unless we abandon our professional values. There is therefore a need for organizational understanding to underpin our practice. Without this there is a danger that we will simply be carried along on the waves of an organization's functioning and lose sight of our professional ethics and commitments, and that is very dangerous terrain for us to occupy.

This chapter has sought to build on the process of broadening out developed in the preceding chapters. To be able to work effectively with people, we must not only recognize them as unique individuals, we must also take account of interpersonal relations, group dynamics, culture, sociopolitical structures and processes, and the organizational context. This helps us to appreciate the need for a holistic approach, one that helps us to appreciate the 'big picture', rather than get lost in the minutiae of the particular practice situations we engage with. Our theorizing needs to be broadly based and holistic if it is to do justice to the complexities of people's lives, the problems they encounter and the potential solutions that social work can help to develop.

Our theorizing also needs to take account of another set of broader phenomena, namely the role of values and ideology in shaping our experience. Such issues will form the subject matter of Chapter 10, the final chapter of Part Two.

Points to ponder

1. How might an organization's culture affect social work practice?
2. Why is it important to understand how your employing organization works?
3. In what ways can a social worker seek to influence the organization that employs him or her?

Further reading

Thompson (2003a), Chapter 6 and N. Thompson and S. Thompson (2008), Chapter 2.5 are both good starting points. Casey (2002) provides interesting food for thought about organizational life generally (rather than specifically social work organizations), as do Fulop, Linstead and Lilley (2006). Easterby-Smith and Lyles (2003) and Thompson (2006c) concentrate on the significance of learning in organizations. Gilbert (2005) is a good introduction to leadership, while Grint (2005) explores the issues in more detail. Payne (2000) provides a helpful analysis of bureaucracy. Thompson and Bates (2009) highlight the importance of staff well-being as part of organizational life.

10

Morality and ideology

Introduction

Practising social work is not simply a matter of providing technical fixes for people's problems. Rather, it is a complex array of moral and political factors which make a significant contribution to shaping the world of practice and, in turn, the practices carried out under the heading of social work can and do contribute to the moral and political domains of the social world. What I mean by this is that social work cannot be kept separate from the idea of ethics and values, for what we do involves the exercise of power and that, in turn, brings with it ethical considerations to ensure that such power is not (deliberately) abused or (unwittingly) misused.

Social work is a contested entity (Thompson, 2009a; b) in the sense that, as we noted in Chapter 3, how it is defined or conceptualized will significantly shape how it is practised. Such definitions will be influenced by, and will in turn influence, notions of morality and, more broadly, ideology. This chapter is therefore concerned with exploring some of the very subtle and intricate issues associated with ethical concerns and their relation to the role of ideology in shaping beliefs, attitudes and values, and thus both thinking and doing – that is, theory and practice. The chapter begins with a consideration of social work as a moral-political activity (Sibeon, 1991) which leads into an exploration of the social work value base which, in turn, is connected with an examination of the significance of discourse and ideology as fundamental factors that underpin social work.

Social work as a moral-political activity

Schön is generally regarded as one of the founders of modern reflective practice (Schön, 1983; 1987; 1992; Argyris and Schön, 1995). His work was based on a critique of what he referred to as 'technical rationality'. What he meant by this is that, despite common understandings to the contrary, professional practice in any discipline is not simply a matter of 'applying' the theory or knowledge base in a direct or simple way, as if the knowledge base provides straightforward technical solutions. The reality is far more complex than this, hence the growth of interest in recent times in the significance of reflective practice – particularly *critically* reflective practice with its emphasis on looking beneath the surface of the presenting issues and locating them in a wider sociopolitical context (what S. Thompson and N. Thompson, 2008, refer to as 'critical depth and breadth').

If social work is not simply a matter of technical rationality, then morality becomes a key factor because, if practitioners are not simply following instructions or some sort of putative 'guidebook' to practice, then matters of decision making come to be seen as the exercise of professional judgement, and therefore as a further example of the exercise of power. These therefore have ethical implications, thus introducing morality as a key factor. Consequently, we can see that social work is strongly influenced by values (as we shall see below) and is not a morally or politically neutral technical activity. Superficially, the work of social work practitioners could be seen as simply carrying out duties within the parameters of the legal and policy mandate to deliver services to disadvantaged groups and help them tackle the problems and difficulties they encounter. However, on closer inspection, such a view is seen to be woefully inadequate, grossly oversimplifying some highly complex issues and simply skating over the surface of some very profound matters relating to ethics, values and politics. Making sure that our theorizing of practice does not fall into this trap is precisely what this chapter is all about.

One key aspect of morality in social work is the recognition that our practice can do harm as well as good – for example, by unwittingly increasing tensions within a family. This fundamentally makes social work a moral activity, in so far as it means that there is a potential to be counterproductive, to make people's situations worse rather than better. This therefore places a moral duty on us to ensure that, as far as possible, our efforts produce positive outcomes rather than contribute to negative ones or exacerbate existing problems. Of course, this will always be the case, as it is inherent in the nature of social work, and so social work will always be a moral activity.

Practice focus 10.1

Carmel had gone into social work as it seemed a natural progression from the voluntary charitable work she had been doing for her church. She had a strong sense of compassion and wanted to make a positive contribution to the well-being of people who were less fortunate than herself. This provided a strong sense of commitment and a high level of motivation. However, what it did not do was prepare her for the fact that her efforts could be counterproductive at times. Her first recognition of this came when she worked with Kerry, a pregnant teenager. Once it became known that Kerry had a social worker, other young people at her school started making fun of her and calling her 'inadequate' and 'a loser'. Carmel had not realized that her involvement could bring stigma and thereby make the situation worse for Kerry. Carmel had to work very hard to reassure her that she could help her, as Kerry's initial reaction to the problems she encountered was to refuse any further help from her. This had been an important lesson for Carmel, and she realized that she would have to give more thought to how her work could do harm as well as good, albeit unintentionally.

At a broader level, social work can also be seen to either bolster or undermine the status quo, in so far as what we do will either reinforce existing social arrangements (for example, keeping oppressed groups 'in their place') or go some way towards weakening their hold (for example, by making a contribution to the empowerment of disadvantaged groups). This is a fundamental principle of emancipatory practice, and so we shall return to this point in Chapter 14 but, for present purposes, let us note that this makes social work a political activity in so far as the activities of social workers contribute to, at however small a level, the continuance or not of existing social relations. If we put these two sets of factors together – the ethical and the political – we begin to recognize that social work is a *moral-political* activity. Social workers who have little understanding of this can therefore be acting not only naively, but also dangerously in so far as their practice could unwittingly be leading to consequences that are both unethical and politically undesirable.

Voice of experience 10.1

At college we had a tutor who was always banging on about social work being a 'moral-political' activity. At first, I didn't really understand what it meant and just put it down to it being his hobby horse. But, when I went out on placement, my practice teacher was very hot on the ethical side of things and used the terms 'moral' and 'morality' quite a lot. So, one day in supervision I asked her about what she saw as the difference between 'moral' and 'moral-political'. We had a really interesting discussion about how values are not just professional or personal matters, they are also part of the wider political world. It made a lot more sense after that!

Pam, deputy team manager of a learning disabilities team

If social work is indeed a moral-political activity, then does this mean that social workers should subscribe to the views of a particular political party, moral philosophy or school of thought? The short answer to this is 'no', as that would reflect too simplistic a view of the complexities involved. An alternative question that is more appropriate would be: do social workers have to be alive to the moral and political implications of their activities? The answer to that is a very resounding 'yes' and, indeed, this is the basis of critically reflective practice, with its emphasis on being tuned in to how our actions have both moral and political consequences.

The social work value base

It is not my intention here to go through the specific values that are generally associated with social work as I have done that elsewhere (Thompson, 2009b – see also N. Thompson and S. Thompson, 2008), and so it is pointless repeating that exercise here. However, what I do want to do is to emphasize the significance of morality as more than simply following a set of rules. To adopt an approach to values that is little more than seeking to make sure that our actions do not breach any code of ethics is to return to a technical rationality form of thinking. Critically reflective practice helps us to understand that values and ethics are highly complex matters.

Part of this complexity is the fact that values are relatively fluid, albeit with a high degree of consistency and stability over time. This is because they are socially constructed and therefore reflect both changes and continuity in society. Values, though, are not written in tablets of stone in any absolute sense and will change over time. However, we should not allow this absence of an absolute approach to values to take us to the opposite extreme and assume that 'anything goes'. That form of moral relativism is in itself highly problematic (Rorty, 1991). Values are complex and 'slippery' matters (Shardlow, 2002), so we need to be careful that we do not come up with simplistic, dogmatic responses to the challenges values face (see Chapter 14 for a discussion of how this applies in particular to anti-discriminatory values).

A further factor that makes a social work value base quite complex is that there will often be clashes of values. These can be clashes between a person's individual values and his or her professional values. For example, consider the case of a Catholic social worker who is asked to assist a woman to deal with an abortion. The worker's personal values, drawn from their religious faith may be saying that abortion is a sin and should not be supported, while their professional values may be saying that the client should be helped in a non-judgemental and self-determining way.

There can also be clashes of values between worker and client, and these can be difficult to work through. For example, a client may express racist sentiments that are not acceptable to the social worker. However, even these types of conflicts do not exhaust the possibilities. There are also clashes between the worker and his or her agency and indeed between one agency and another. As we saw in Chapter 9, bureaucratic factors in an organization can often conflict with professional values. In addition, professional values can differ from professional group to group. For example, in a mental health context, there can be differences of perspective and values in terms of clashes between biochemical, medicalized approaches to mental distress and those based on more sociological and/or psychological understandings of the issues involved.

Practice focus 10.2

Ian was a strong advocate of the rights of patients receiving psychiatric services. He was critical of approaches to mental well-being that reduce complex problems to a simple diagnosis of an illness. He had learned over time that the mental health field is one that is characterized by a great diversity of perspectives and values among professionals. He had learned how to put his point of view across without offending others and without his own voice being lost in the web of competing perspectives. However, he found it quite a challenge when a new social work colleague, Janet, joined the team. Despite being a qualified social worker, Janet's approach was quite a narrow, biomedical one, and she regularly used terminology like 'illness', 'symptoms' and 'treatment'. Ian had worked very hard to reinforce the importance of psychosocial perspectives in mental health and he felt that Janet's uncritical acceptance of a medical model could potentially undermine the good work he had done. He therefore came to the conclusion that he would need to develop a strategy for working with Janet in such a way that he would be respecting her right to think in the way she did, but without watering down the social work commitment to more empowering approaches to mental health problems.

While it would be fruitless to try and come up with simple solutions to such clashes, the key conclusion we can draw is that it is important to recognize the need to be tuned into values issues. If we are not, then we will be in a very weak position when it comes to wrestling with the dilemmas and challenges of the subtle and intricate world of social work values. And it is no exaggeration to say that values dilemmas and challenges are never very far away in social work.

As a moral-political entity premised on values, social work is a vocation that brings with it professional accountability. That is, if our actions can have significant moral and political consequences, then it is vitally important that we are accountable for those actions in order to justify the position of trust that professionals occupy. This is not to encourage the sort of blame culture we discussed in Chapter 9 but, rather, to recognize that it would be unethical and politically unhelpful to practise in ways that cannot be justified by reference to a professional knowledge base and, indeed, a professional value base. Although what constitutes that professional value base may well be contested, it remains the case that professional accountability is very much needed.

Values, 'habitus' and culture

In Chapter 2 we discussed the significance of Bourdieu's concept of 'habitus' (Bourdieu, 1984; 1992). Lovell helpfully explains the idea in the following terms:

> By *habitus* Bourdieu understands ways of doing and being which social subjects acquire during their socialization. Their *habitus* is not a matter

of conscious learning, or of ideological imposition, but is acquired through practice. Bourdieu's sociology rests on an account of lived 'practice', and what he terms 'the practical sense' – the ability to function effectively within a given social field, an ability which cannot necessarily be articulated as conscious knowledge: 'knowing how' rather than 'knowing that'. *Habitus* names the characteristic dispositions of the social subject. It is indicated in the bearing of the body ('hexis'), and in deeply ingrained habits of behaviour, feeling, thought.

(2000, p. 27)

The reason I am reintroducing this concept here is that it can be a useful way of understanding how values become 'enmeshed' in our lives and social practices. One very easy mistake to make is to assume that values are simply the abstract entities that are discussed in relation to personal and professional morality, losing sight of the fact that, in reality, values are part and parcel of everything we do. Values are what we regard as important or meaningful to us. As such, they motivate our actions, inform our thinking and shape our emotional responses. Values, then, will manifest themselves in very subtle but significant ways. In this way, habitus is a helpful notion, as it captures the way in which values can and do emerge as part of our 'practical sense', our 'ways of doing and being' that we develop through our upbringing (our 'socialization').

In theorizing practice, the concept of habitus can help us to tune in to the subtle operations of values and thereby avoid the artificial separation between values (conceived as abstractions – thus operating at an *abstract* level) and everyday experiences (at a *concrete* level). More accurately, values are part and parcel of our day-to-day reality (our 'lived experience', to use the existentialist term) – they are enmeshed in everything we say and do, in our thoughts and feelings, and in our interactions with others. For this reason it is important that we understand that theorizing practice is not purely a matter of drawing on professional *knowledge* – it must also incorporate an understanding of *values* and how they are influencing the people we are seeking to help, the situations they are in, our responses to those situations, the decisions we make, and so on.

Voice of experience 10.2

I had a student on placement with me last year who was really keen on learning about values. She asked me a thousand and one questions about values issues and I had to have my wits about me not to get lost in all the complexities. She learned a lot, but I think I learned even more. All her questions made me think about values in ways I hadn't considered before. I knew they were important, but I suppose I hadn't thought them through in the way that her eagerness to learn forced me to do. I think it has made me a better practitioner, as I am much more tuned in to values now.

Colin, a practice teacher in a youth offending team

The idea of habitus can also be linked to culture, our subject matter in Chapter 7. Habitus can be seen as a 'personal' culture, in the sense that it comprises each individual's own set of taken-for-granted assumptions, habits and 'unwritten rules'. As such, habitus does not develop in isolation from the wider spheres of social life. Habitus at a personal level will therefore reflect the cultural context of the individual concerned and, of course his or her location in the social structure (see Chapter 8). The values that become apparent in our habitus will therefore reflect to a considerable degree the values of the wider cultural and structural levels. Those values will be part of the meaning systems that are key components of our culture.

In order to understand values, we therefore need to have some basis of understanding in relation to culture and how it creates frameworks of meaning which, as we noted earlier, are significant influences on our actions and interactions. Clarke (2004) discusses the 'cultural turn', by which he means the shift in social theory from an emphasis on social structures (as in marxism, for example) towards cultural explanations of the social world (as in post-structuralism). He points out that:

> one critical part of the 'cultural turn' has been an emphasis on culture as actively constructed by social agents. Meanings have to be made – and remade. They require practising agency. Much work in cultural analysis has championed active, practising agents against determinist views of social (or economic) structure. From E. P. Thompson's exploration of the 'making' of the English working class to examinations of cultural innovation, subversion and resistance, cultural analysis has celebrated the active production and contestation of meanings (e.g. Thompson, 1963; Hall and Jefferson, 1976; Hebdige, 1988; Duncombe, 2002; Holland and Lave, 2001b). This draws attention to culture as the *product of practice*.
> (Clarke, 2004, p. 39)

Culture provides the context from which we learn much of our value base, but, as a 'product of practice' culture is also created and recreated through the actions inspired by those values. Here we see two further dialectical relationships: (i) between values and the actions they lead to; and (ii) between values and the broader cultural context. In both cases, each of the 'poles' of the relationship has an influencing effect on the other, although not necessarily an equally balanced one – for example, the culture's impact on a person's values is likely to be much stronger than the influence of his or her values on the culture. Despite this relative imbalance, it would be a mistake to see the relationship as a linear one – that is, in one direction only.

One problem with the 'cultural turn', as Clarke calls it, is that it has had the effect of de-emphasizing the significance of social structures. That is, instead of *adding* cultural factors to our understanding of the relationship between the individual and wider social structures (as in PCS analysis – Thompson, 2003a; 2006a), the cultural emphasis of post-structuralism has tended to *replace* a focus on structure with one on culture. Rather than using insights about the significance of culture to extend and enrich our understanding of human experience, post-structuralism has sought to displace previous understandings – a further example of the process (described in Chapter 1) of theoretical 'clubs' competing with each other in their attempts to recruit adherents, rather than exploring ways of ironing out contradictions and seeking to build on connections.

Values, then, are not only part of each individual's habitus, they are also a reflection of the wider cultural context. Seeing values in this wider macro-level context, then, introduces the political dimension. Values are not only personal and/or professional – they can also be political, in the sense that they reflect and embody a commitment to a particular political outlook. Even people who do not regard themselves as 'political' will none the less subscribe to particular political values (in the same way that failing to vote amounts to voting for the status quo). Political values become part of frameworks of meaning (discourses or ideologies), and so, in order to appreciate this wider aspect of values, we need to explore the role of such meaning frameworks in shaping our thinking and our practice.

Discourse and ideology

The term 'discourse' in its literal sense refers to a conversation. The origin of the term is to be found in the study of language. However, over time, its usage in the social sciences has grown to be descriptive of more than simply conversational factors. Under the influence of post-structuralist thinking, it has come to mean forms of language and associated practices that have power implications. Just as a discourse in its original, linguistic sense involves a framework of meaning, so too in its broader sense a discourse also amounts to a framework of meaning. Sunderland explains discourses as follows:

> the primary meaning of *discourses* is equivalent to *broad constitutive systems of meaning* (from post-structuralism) and to 'knowledge and practices generally associated with a particular institution or group of institutions' (Talbot, 1995a: 43) or 'different ways of structuring areas of knowledge and social practice' (Fairclough, 1992: 3) (from critical social theory). I refer to these as 'interpretive discourses'. *Discourse(s)* in this third sense is (are) at times used indistinguishably from *ideology* – Eckert and McConnell-Ginet gloss this 'shared' use as 'projections of the interests of people in a particular social location', a useful reminder that we are not simply talking about 'perspectives' (2003: 412).
>
> (2004, p. 6)

'Ideology' is a term we shall discuss below, but for now it is important to note that what the different uses of the term 'discourse' have in common is the idea of the type of framework of meaning I referred to above. This is an important point to note from an existentialist perspective, as meaning and interpretation are key elements of phenomenology, which in turn is part of the philosophical foundations of existentialist thought. In line with Nietzsche's perspectivism and Gadamer's (2004) notion of 'horizon', phenomenology teaches us that there is no absolute, unmediated sense of reality – everything has to be filtered through our perceptions. In this way the frameworks of meaning we develop to help us make sense of our reality then play a key part in defining and thus shaping that reality. See the discussion of the dialectic of subjectivity and objectivity in Chapter 2.

The classic example of a discourse is 'medical' discourse. This refers to the 'common sense' conception of medical power in which it is assumed that the notion of 'doctor's orders' has some basis in reality. In actual fact, in very few cases do doctors have the power to give orders to patients, but the discourse of medicine creates language forms and thus patterns of behaviour that make quite acceptable the idea that it is legitimate for doctors to give orders to patients. It is the fact that it is widely assumed that 'doctor's orders' is a legitimate basis of medical practice that gives doctors the power to issue orders that they have no actual right to give. Because the discourse translates 'doctor's advice' into 'doctor's orders' a power relation is created. The fact that this power relation remains hidden, buried within the discourse, makes it all the more effective as a means of control.

Discourse therefore relates to the power of language to construct sets of meanings that can have profound implications for social life. Discourse, then, is very much about both power and language (language is central to meaning and the significance we attach to particular forms of meaning, in turn, influences power relations). The way in which social work is carried out, the linguistic forms practitioners use and the implications of these for people's lives are therefore key factors that we need to take into account when we attempt to theorize practice – that is, to practise from a well-informed position.

As Sunderland notes, closely linked to the idea of discourse is the concept of 'ideology'. An ideology is a framework of ideas that is used to promote particular sectional interests. Berger and Luckmann (1967) define ideology as the power of ideas serving the interests of power. Similarly, Forte, citing Thompson (1990, p. 7), describes ideology as: 'meaning in the service of power' (2001, p. 275). These are both helpful definitions. What they enable us to do is to recognize the links between discourse and ideology. This is because discourses can be used *ideologically* – that is, discourses, as frameworks of language and related practices, often serve to reinforce existing relations of dominance and subordination. For example, a heterosexist discourse which propagates the view that gay men, lesbians, bisexuals and transsexuals are 'unnatural' serves to support existing power relations by reinforcing their status as an 'undesirable minority'. In such an example, the discourse is functioning in an ideological way – it is reinforcing powerful ideas which, in their turn, reinforce existing social arrangements (that is, the marginalization of people whose sexual orientation is not that of the majority). We shall return to the point of ideology reinforcing discrimination in Chapter 14 when we discuss emancipatory practice.

As the quotation from Sunderland (2004) above pointed out, discourse and ideology overlap to a certain extent. A discourse, as a framework of meaning, has the effect of creating and sustaining a set of power relations. An ideology similarly involves having sets of ideas and meanings that reinforce power relations. The two concepts 'discourse' and 'ideology' have grown up from different theoretical traditions and have subtle differences of emphasis. However, the precise differences between the two need not concern us here, but it is important to note that ideas, particularly dominant ideas – the ones that are so often taken for granted as 'common sense' (such as the assumption that caring for children is women's work) – are not neutral in terms of power. They have the (ideological) effect of creating and sustaining a view that favours one group over others. In the case of dominant ideologies, it will be the position of the dominant group(s) they support. However, there are also what are known as 'counter-vailing' ideologies – that is, sets of ideas that seek to challenge and undermine the dominant ideas. Feminist ideas challenging the notion that caring for children is women's work would be a good example of this (Barrett and McIntosh, 1991).

The clashes of values mentioned earlier in this chapter can there-fore often be seen to be clashes of discourse or ideology, or at least manifest themselves in such clashes. For example, it is commonly the case that a social worker operating from a discourse of promoting a client's rights may clash with a nurse who is interested primarily in working within a discourse of care. For the nurse, therefore, the prior-ity may be care, and the person's rights may therefore be seen as subservient to this. The social worker may then be called upon to argue the case for the person's rights – for example, in a situation where an elderly dependent person prefers to live at significant risk in the community, rather than to be 'cared for' in a residential home. This does not mean that social workers are not caring, but the values discourse adopted makes a significant difference to how the situation is dealt with.

Practice focus 10.3

In trying to persuade Janet to adopt a broader perspective on mental health problems, Ian talked to her about the way discourses operate and the way a medical discourse of mental well-being has the ideo-logical effect of maintaining people in a position of subordination. Janet's response was that she had read about social perspectives, but did not accept them because she had seen just how 'ill' some of the patients had become at times. Ian tried to counter this by suggest-ing that the word 'ill' made certain assumptions about the client (the term 'patient', he pointed out, makes similar assumptions). He fully accepted how distressing and debilitating a 'psychotic episode' could be, but he tried to convey to Janet that being distressing does not make it an illness. He tried to show how disempowering it could be to describe psychosocial issues in medical or biochemical terms. He drew a parallel with grieving. He pointed out that grief could be very distressing and debilitating and could have a major impact on a

> person's well-being and on their life in the longer terms, but grief is not
> an illness. Janet, to Ian's great dismay, responded that she thought
> that grief is in fact an illness and pointed out that it is often dealt with
> by psychiatrists. Ian realized that challenging a discourse was not a
> simple matter and that it could take a very long time to make an
> impact

In trying to understand the significance of discourse and ideology in shaping people's thoughts and actions, it is important not to oversimplify the situation. For example, in considering attitudes towards gender, it is not simply a matter of men adopting one view (and therefore discourse) and women another. As Sunderland argues: 'Women can also produce sexist (anti-women) discourses and men feminist discourses' (2004, p. 8). What this indicates is that discourse, ideology and power (and their interplay) are very complex, multi-level issues, and so we need to be careful not to adopt reductionist approaches in our efforts to make sense of them. The guide to further reading at the end of the chapter offers some helpful signposts for developing your understanding further. However, for present purposes, we should note that frameworks of meaning (discourses, ideologies) are very significant in subtly shaping power relations and thus the interactions of individuals and groups. In seeking to understand the context of our practice (as part of our theorizing of that practice), we should not therefore neglect the role of ideas, meaning and power. We shall revisit some of these themes in Chapters 12, 13 and 14.

A key part of social work is helping people to construct a new 'narrative' of their lives, to throw off disempowering forms of understanding that can be limiting and undermining of confidence (Crossley, 2000 – see also the discussion in Chapter 12). A key part of contributing to empowerment is making sure that the social worker does not simply impose his or her discourse, but, rather, works within a range of discourses to look at positive ways forward. A key part of this is Foucault's notion of how discourses can be used to restrict people. For example, his writings (Foucault, 2001) talk of how madness became conceptualized as (that is, came to be instituted as a discourse of) an illness, and therefore justified the development of a significant institution of psychiatry geared towards dealing with the 'illness'. One of the results of this has been that people with mental health problems have been significantly disempowered by having the label of 'sick' attached to them. This, then, grossly oversimplifies a highly complex set of issues (see Practice focus 10.2 and 10.3 above) and while placing the major emphasis on bio-medical interventions ('treatment'), thereby de-emphasizing psychosocial aspects of the situation (and thus potentially more empowering, less pathologizing forms of help). The same argument can be applied to other client groups within the social work world. For example, ageist discourse presents older people as passive individuals likely to need care and support. This in effect pathologizes older people and, in doing so, distorts the reality of their lives. For example, it ignores the fact that the majority of older people manage to live their lives without any form of welfare support. It also fails to recognize that even those people who may need some form of care are likely to have something to offer, a contribution to make to society and other people's well-being by drawing on the insights afforded by their wealth of experience and wisdom, as well as having needs (that is, they have a capacity for 'reciprocity' – giving as well as receiving; Sue Thompson, 2009).

Voice of experience 10.3

I started my career as a nurse working with geriatric patients. The longer I worked there, the angrier I got about how disgracefully and disrespectfully older people can be treated by the system and by society in general. So, in the end, I decided to retrain as a social worker so that I could play a more active part in challenging ageist stereotypes and supporting older people's rights. It's not been as easy to do that in social work as I thought it would be, but I still feel I have played a part in breaking down barriers.

Sue, a social worker in an older people team

Underpinning these considerations is, of course, the significance of language. Once again, we see that language has a key part to play in shaping our interactions and the outcomes of those interactions in terms of whether they (i) reinforce existing dominant–subordinate power relations; or (ii) they challenge these in a spirit of commitment to empowerment. These issues will be revisited in more detail in Chapter 12.

Conclusion

Social work is a professional undertaking and cannot therefore be apolitical – it necessarily involves the exercise of power. As such, it also has ethical connotations and consequences. This being the case, social workers need an understanding and awareness of the moral and political context in which they operate. This chapter has, I hope, gone some way towards establishing a foundation for developing a much more sophisticated understanding of the moral-political aspects of the work we engage in, the ethical and political landscape in which we carry out our duties.

Earlier chapters in Part Two have sketched out how 'the person' should not be seen in atomistic terms – that is, in isolation from the wider aspects of the social context (interpersonal, group, cultural, structural and organizational). This chapter has further argued that all of these considerations also need to be understood in the context of the values and political factors that have a major bearing on social work activity not only at a macro level in terms of the nature and purposes of social work (see Chapter 3), but also at the micro level of actual practice interventions. In particular, we have seen how values relate to the wider cultural and political spheres and how frameworks of meaning (discourses, ideologies) play a critical role in shaping our understanding and thus our actions (our theory and our practice).

Our exploration of all of these complex, high-level issues could lead some people to conclude that they have little bearing on the actual concrete world of practice. However, such a conclusion would be a significant mistake, as close and careful scrutiny of practice situations readily reveals the workings of values and ideologies – we do not have to dig too deeply to find them once we know what we are looking for. To neglect these issues, to disregard the moral-political dimension of our work, would put us in a very weak position when it comes to developing an adequate basis from which to theorize our practice – that is, to engage in critically reflective practice.

Finally, one further mistake to be aware of is that of adopting a defeatist or quietist approach to the workings of discourse and ideology to (re)produce relations of dominance – an attitude I have often encountered ('Power structures are so deeply ingrained in our society and in people's minds, what can we possibly do about them?'). Clarke writes helpfully and insightfully about such matters. He counsels wisely:

> we should not tell stories that reproduce or reinforce the illusions that dominant forces try to construct. They want us to believe in the inevitability of their rule – so we should not describe their rule as inevitable. They want us to accede to their vision of how the world should

be – so we should not close out the possibility of other imaginings of how the world might be. They want us to succumb to the 'natural' conditions of competitive capitalism – so we should not reinforce its authority by attributing to it more reach, potency and effect than it has.

(2004, pp. 5–6)

This passage captures perfectly the significance of social work values. If we, as a profession committed to promoting social justice, empowerment and well-being, allow a surrender to discourses of dominance to dissuade us from furthering our aims, we are doing our clientele a considerable disservice. Our approach should be one of realism (Thompson, 2009a) – neither naively optimistic, nor cynically pessimistic – demonstrating commitment to making a positive difference when we can, recognizing that there will be significant limitations to what we can achieve, but also acknowledging that any gain we make is a step towards a more humane society.

Points to ponder

1. In what sense is social work a 'moral-political' activity?
2. What values influenced your choice to enter social work?
3. How does ideology reinforce power relations? Give an example or two.

Further reading

Moss (2007a) is the ideal introductory text when it comes to values. My own work has discussed values in Thompson (2009b) and N. Thompson and S. Thompson (2008b), while Thompson (2007a) focuses in particular on the value of empowerment. Buber (2004) is a classic text that raises important issues about values. Hugman (2005) is also a helpful text, as is Dean (2004). Callinicos (2007) provides a great deal of food for thought in relation to ideology. Clarke (2004) too is an important source.

Part Three

Developing Theory

Introduction to Part Three: Taking theory forward

Part One established the importance of theory and theorizing, with existentialism being proposed as a helpful way forward, and Part Two developed an overview of some of the main complexities of what social workers need to understand – again informed in large part by existentialism. Part Three has as its focus the *development* of theory. The basic argument underpinning this part of the book is that theorizing from a static or stagnant knowledge base is inadequate and potentially dangerous. If theorizing practice is to fulfil its potential as a foundation for high-quality professional practice, then it is necessary to make sure that the knowledge base on which it draws is one that keeps developing, one that stays in touch with the changing social world. Indeed, a key element of existentialism is its understanding of human existence as 'flux' – that is, as constant change and development.

The aim of this is not to suggest that practitioners need to be engaged in research or high-level theoretical debate (although these are legitimate activities for those practitioners who are interested in doing so). Rather, it is a matter of (i) keeping up to date with the knowledge base as it grows and develops over time (for example, through continuous professional development); (ii) engaging with theoretical issues in the context of practice; this involves playing a part in making sure that theory and practice connect up, that theory is tested in practice; and (iii) recognizing that theory 'belongs' to practitioners as much as it does to academics (Thompson, 2000a). Practitioners can and, in my view, should have a say in developing theory – especially as theory is such an important dimension of practice and not something separate from it.

11

Developing coherence: drawing on existentialism

Introduction

Postmodernism challenged traditional theoretical understandings, as we noted in Chapter 2. However, we also noted that proponents of this approach brought with them their own problems. This chapter revisits some of these themes and explores the importance of *coherence* – the need for elements of our understanding to be interconnected or unified in some way, providing a reasonably systematic (as opposed to random) understanding of the social world in general and the social work world in particular. Building on the use of existentialist concepts at various points in Parts One and Two of the book, I present existentialism as a theoretical approach which offers a sound foundation for achieving this. In many ways what I am proposing runs totally counter to postmodernism which has denied the value of a coherent approach, preferring instead to emphasize fragmentation and playfulness.

The chapter begins by exploring the importance of coherence as a basis for both theory and practice. From this we move on to consider, first existentialist theory as it applies to social work, and then existentialist practice. That is, we look more closely at how existentialist ideas can both inform our understanding of, and actually shape, the practice realities we encounter in our work. As explained in Chapter 1, my aim is not to present existentialism as another theoretical club to join. Rather, I see it as a unifying philosophical framework or, to use Sibeon's (2004) term, a 'sensitizing theory' – not one that offers specific analyses and explanations of particular phenomena, but rather an overall framework of understanding that enables us to link together ideas and insights from different theoretical sources and traditions in ways that provide a positive foundation for theorizing practice. As such, it is an approach that opens doors to new forms of understanding, rather than closing them by adopting one outlook as the 'Truth' and thereby rejecting all others.

The importance of coherence

The development of postmodernist thought in relation to the social world contains with it the rejection of coherence. I would regard this as, in effect, throwing the baby out with the bathwater. While there is much value in the notion of 'post-foundationalism' championed by postmodernists (that is, the rejection of the idea of an absolute Truth), to go so far as to deny the value of coherence as a theoretical property is clearly a step too far (see the discussion of these issues in Chapter 2).

It would be a mistake to equate a commitment to coherence with a dedication to the notion of absolute Truth or, to use the postmodernist term, 'foundationalism'. Here we need to return to Nietzsche's notion of truth (with a small t rather than a capital T). That is, while there is no absolute, overall, global or absolute Truth, there are certainly smaller-scale local truths. For example, while Nietzsche's emphasis on each person having to adopt a perspective, with no one having a privileged, unmediated view of the world, it does not make much sense to talk about absolute truth or Truth in the abstract. However, this is not to say that there are no truths at all. For example, it is true that, in my cultural context at least, Tuesday follows Monday. It is also true that two plus two equals four, but what can it realistically mean to say that 'Love is Truth' or 'Compassion is the true foundation of humanity'? Nietzsche's challenging of the traditional use of the notion of truth in philosophy and social thought has proven to be a major influence.

In some respects, the postmodernist incredulity towards metanarratives reflects Nietzsche's view but, to go so far as to deny coherence as a legitimate aim of theoretical understanding is not only to show incredulity towards metanarratives, but also to show incredulity towards any narrative, for coherence needs to be recognized as something stemming from the structure and focus that form the basis for making a narrative meaningful. In Chapter 13, we shall look more closely at the concepts of narrative, meaning and spirituality, but here we should note that there is an important link between the need for theoretical coherence and these fundamental aspects of making sense of human experience.

In Chapter 2 the validity and value of adopting postmodernism as a theory base for social work was strongly challenged. Ife's views add to that critique:

> A complete and uncritical adoption of a postmodernist stance, however, raises problems for social workers. These problems stem from postmodernism's rejection of the 'meta-narrative', in favour of relativism. Social work, in its commitment to something called 'social justice' and its insistence on a core value component for the profession, is grounded in meta-narratives, whether they be traditional commitments such as 'the inherent worth of the individual' or more structural positions informed by an analysis of class, gender and race, and an understanding of counter-oppressive practice. The very idea of 'counter-oppressive' social work assumes a meta-narrative of oppression, and hence to deny the meta-narrative of oppression is to deny much of what social work has traditionally held to be central to its practice.
>
> The impact of thereby weakening the meta-narratives of social justice, in the current political climate, is substantial and alarming. While academic discourse may celebrate the death of the meta-narrative and the emergence of multiple realities, the world of social work practice is confronted with a meta-narrative of frightening power, and with the imposition of a single reality which denies the very basis of social work.
>
> (1999, p. 215)

While I would not want to return to the idea of 'grand theories' that seek to explain everything in their purview, I would see the rejection of anything that provides an overarching framework of meaning and explanation as excessive and would therefore share Ife's view of the dangers of adopting a postmodernist perspective – particularly the postmodernist rejection of the value of coherence.

One key factor in terms of such coherence is the significance of professional accountability. This theme has already occurred more than once in earlier chapters. In the interests of such accountability, professionals are called upon to provide a coherent rationale to account for their actions, especially the decisions they make and the steps they take as a result of those decisions (or the steps they do not take as the result of such decision-making processes). To assume that we can have any meaningful notion of professional accountability without a commitment to a coherent rationale is naive in the extreme. Here the postmodernist emphasis on play can be seen to be very far removed from the very serious matters that helping professionals encounter, especially those of us in the social work world. In this respect, once again, postmodernism can be seen to be significantly lacking as a theoretical underpinning for practice. Malik reinforces this view when he argues, in effect, that the cynicism of postmodernism is bought at quite an expensive price for some, especially for those in less affluent parts of the world:

> Nanda observes 'postmodernism in modernising societies like India serves to kill the promise of modernity even before it has struck roots.' The rise of postmodernism 'has totally discredited the necessity of, and even the possibility of, questioning the inherited metaphysical systems, which for centuries have shackled human imaginations and social freedoms in those parts of the world that have not yet had their modern-day enlightenments.'

(2008, p. 284)

While the simplistic faith in scientific rationality as a basis for inevitable social progress and a return to positivism is not a position I would want to embrace, nor would I want to dismiss altogether the potential for social progress. In other words, while I would see postmodernism as being correct in its critique of the excesses of Enlightenment thinking around progress at an abstract, generalized level, I would not want to rule out the potential for specific elements of progress linked to deliberate efforts to secure positive change. Without recognizing such potential, social work as an attempt to contribute to a more humane society would – as Ife rightly acknowledges – becomes a doomed enterprise. Forte (2001) makes use of Dewey's term 'meliorism' which refers to the fact that, whatever the circumstances we find ourselves in, they can always be improved in some way. Social work, then, can be premised on a commitment to social progress and 'meliorism' without falling foul of 'modernist' notions of inevitable social progress through the 'enlightenment' brought by science and rationality.

The approach I am adopting here is again one of *realism* (as explained in Thompson, 2009a) rejecting both the unwarranted overoptimism of the Enlightenment faith in scientific rationality as the basis of human betterment and the postmodernist pessimism that rejects the potential for emancipation from oppressive social structures and discourses. As we shall see later, the 'healthy' balance of realism between these two unhelpful extremes is precisely where existentialism is located.

Practice focus 11.1

Paromita was a community development worker in an inner city project geared towards addressing some deeply ingrained social problems and disadvantages. She had always found the work quite challenging, but none the less did it very well and enjoyed it. However, after a particularly difficult period of about three months in which she had major problems at home as well as at work, she began to experience a high level of stress. One way that this manifested itself was that she became quite 'down' about the project. She began to doubt that it was doing any real good, as the problems were so intense and so deeply rooted. She wondered whether there was any point continuing. Once her heart went out of the job in this way, she became even more highly stressed and was soon on sick leave as she felt she could no longer cope. Fortunately, she had a very supportive line manager, Anne, who visited her at home to offer her support. Once Paromita explained about her feelings of negativity and pessimism about the project, Anne did a very skilful job of counterbalancing this with examples of very real differences the project had made, real 'nuggets' of significant success. She managed to do this without crudely or superficially just trying to 'cheer her up', as Paromita would have found that irritating and patronizing. What Anne had succeeded in doing was to help Paromita move from a position of pessimism to one of realism without going to the opposite extreme of a naive optimism. Paromita found this extremely helpful and reaffirmed for her that, while major change cannot be expected in the short term, the small positives steps taken are all very worthwhile parts of making a significant difference to some people in the short term and making at least a small contribution to broader, macro-level changes in the longer term.

While rational coherence is clearly an important part of making sense of social work situations, we should also not neglect the significance of emotions, as these have a very central role to play in shaping what happens in day-to-day encounters between social workers and their clientele and, indeed, between social workers and other professionals in terms of multi-professional collaboration (Howe, 2008; Thompson, 2009a). Furthermore, we can also note that it is often the case that emotional factors are high on the list of elements of a situation that have necessitated the involvement of a social worker in the first place. However, it would be a mistake to see rationality and emotions as opposites. In some respects, they are two sides of the same coin. The social work world revolves around a balance of heart and head, of rationality on the one hand and an understanding of the crucial part that emotional reactions play on the other.

Establishing a coherent framework of meaning (what we shall refer to in Chapter 13 as a 'narrative') is often what is necessary to deal with situations that are highly charged emotionally. For example, the work of Neimeyer and colleagues in relation to 'meaning reconstruction theory' as a means of understanding what is happening when someone is experiencing a major grief reaction has been recognized to have excellent potential for providing a basis of understanding (Neimeyer, 2001; Neimeyer and Anderson, 2002). According to this theory, helping someone deal with grief involves supporting them in developing a new understanding of their life, a new framework of meaning to replace the one that has been shattered by the experience of loss. A sense of rational coherence, then, is not an alternative to the emotional dimension of social work – it is a means of making sense of it, so that we are in a better position to help people deal with the significant emotional challenges they may be facing. Again, it is a matter of incorporating both head and heart.

Voice of experience 11.1

I had a lot of losses in my childhood and that was a major part of my motivation for wanting to work in the bereavement field. My clients are people who are grieving because they face a major loss or have already had a major loss. Either way, their world is turned upside down and they don't know whether they are coming or going. My job is not to try and give them easy answers – because there aren't any. It is more a case of helping them make sense of a situation that seems to have no sense at all. It is a difficult job, but a very worthwhile one.

Andrea, a social worker in a hospice

In trying to make sense of the need for coherence as a basis for theorizing practice, an important concept is that introduced by Max Weber, namely the notion of 'Verstehen'. This refers to the importance of *understanding* – that is, developing a meaningful picture of the aspect (or aspects) of society we are studying (Allen, 2004). Social science, from Weber's point of view, is not about achieving a positivistic, definitive Truth, but, rather, it is a matter of developing a systematic understanding of what is happening. In some respects, this is what coherence refers to: the ability to develop an under-standing based on grasping the (meaningful) interconnections of various aspects of a complex situation. Simply to regard the various factors as 'fragmented' and leave it at that, as postmodernism would have us do, is totally inadequate when it comes to trying to construct theoretical understandings that are helpful to practitioners in a meaningful way.

In terms of coherence, it can also be argued that postmodernism's emphasis on the cultural level is problematic, in so far as it has little to say about the personal level (rejecting an essentialist view of the person often crosses the line in postmodernist writings to become a rejection of the notion of person altogether) and even less to say about the structural level (which is largely dismissed as a 'metanarrative'). Post-structuralist writings, in particular, emphasize the significance of language and discourse. While there is nothing wrong with this *per se* (indeed, I would share the view that these are highly important – see Chapters 10 and 12), Houston argues that this can go too far:

> But by fixing our attention to the discursive and linguistic constructions of cultural experience which these approaches engender, we are in danger of losing sight of the material domain (that is, the world of economic structures) and its effects on culture (Harris, 1978; Nightingale and Cromby, 1999). Moreover, there is a risk of lapsing into postmodernism's celebration of the pastiche, where an array of variegated signs and images cohere to replace reality as the focus of enquiry and a surreal depthlessness emasculates critical analysis.
>
> (2002, p. 150)

This final comment, that 'depthlessness emasculates critical analysis', is particularly significant. The de-emphasizing of the personal and structural levels in favour of the cultural level reflects a superficial and incoherent approach to social life and human experience.

If, as we noted in Chapter 2, positivism does not provide the flexibility to account for the complexity, diversity and depth of what it means to be a person in a cultural and structural context. Postmodernism offers more scope for flexibility and dealing with diversity, but its lack of depth and coherence makes it a far from adequate basis for making sense of the social work world. In terms of *developing* theory, we need something more than what positivism or postmodernism can offer. In many ways existentialism offers the productive balance between these two extremes, incorporating some of the focus and structure of positivism and some of the flexibility and fluidity of postmodernism, but without taking on board the limitations and flaws of either.

My aim is not to present existentialism as *the* answer (as that would be inconsistent with the existentialist conception of truth, as derived from the work of Nietzsche). More realistically, what I am trying to do is show how existentialism can offer a fruitful way forward in developing our theory base. In large part, the basis of its value in this respect is its status as a philosophy or metatheory – in effect, a metanarrative, a coherent overview that helps us link together disparate elements of knowledge and understanding as a basis for theorizing practice (in a critically reflective way). As mentioned in the Introduction to this part of the book, despite the postmodernist rejection of metanarratives, they have a part to play in providing a metatheoretical framework for providing a degree of coherence – the coherence that is needed for theory to inform practice (and thereby to provide a platform for *theorizing* practice).

Existentialist theory

The point was made earlier that existentialism can be seen as a balance between the destructive extreme of positivism at one end of the continuum (because of its hyper-rationalism) and at the other extreme, postmodernism (with its rejection of rationality – its irrationalism). What existentialism teaches us is that what we need is to find the 'healthy' balance between the two, but this is not a straightforward compromise between the two extremes, simply plotting a midpoint between the two ends of the spectrum. It is more complex and sophisticated than that, involving the use of dialectical reason. In terms of the relative importance of rational and irrational (or emotional) elements, existentialism shows that these are best understood as interacting in a dynamic way, shaping new situations as they encounter one another.

Practice focus 11.2

Jan came from a very formal family background, with a strong emphasis on being rational and reasonable. Her parents were both teachers (one of mathematics and the other of history) and the way the family operated had encouraged her to keep her emotions in check rather than express them openly and fully. When she trained as a social worker she found it difficult at first to engage with the emotional aspects of people's lives and problems, even though she was intelligent enough to realize that this was necessary for effective practice.

The situation came to a head when she worked with Michael, a young man with mental health problems. In some ways he seemed to be the mirror image of her. The previous social worker had described him as 'lacking emotional boundaries'. If he felt an emotion, he expressed that emotion, and this caused him some difficulties in relating to others who would often want to distance themselves from him because they found his emotionality too raw and intense. Jan realized that, in trying to help Michael deal with his feelings in ways that did not cause him problems, she might learn something herself about dealing with her own feelings. This case helped her realize that what is needed in social work is a balance of emotion and reason, heart and head.

Existentialism can be seen to offer a number of important concepts that are very significant in terms of social work theory. In an earlier work I have described and exemplified these factors in terms of eight principles for practice as follows:

1. Freedom and responsibility are basic building blocks of human experience. Our lives are characterised by the constant pressure to make decisions and to live by their consequences. ...
2. Freedom is both liberation and heavy burden ... in the sense that it brings responsibility for our actions and their consequences. ...
3. Authenticity is the key to liberation while its opposite, bad faith, is the common (unsuccessful) strategy for coping with the burden. ...
4. Despite freedom, existence is characteristically experienced as powerlessness and helplessness. ... The task, therefore, is to attempt to overcome feelings of powerlessness by supporting people in establishing control gradually and steadily as part of a process of empowerment. ...
5. Existentialism proposes a shared subjective journey – a partnership in helping. ...
6. The dynamic tension between authority/control/statutory duties on the one hand and creative, non-directive work on the other is one to be recognised. It is a conflict that has to be managed in our everyday work rather than resolved once and for all. ...
7. Existence is movement. There is no 'natural' stability as our life-plans are constantly being reconstructed and so development, disintegration or stability are perpetual possibilities – contingency is ever-present. ...

8. Existential freedom – the process of self-creation – is a prerequisite to political liberty. To deny the former is to foreclose the latter and thus render an authentic social work impossible.

(Thompson, 2000b, pp. 119–22)

Existentialism is a very complex philosophy in its own right and seeking to link it to practice adds further difficulties, and so this brief overview should be seen as a 'taster', rather than an adequate account in its own right – see the guide to further reading at the end of the chapter.

Voice of experience 11.2

Two years after qualifying as a social worker I trained as a counsellor, as I felt the extra knowledge and skills would be very helpful in my job. When I studied the existential school of counselling theory I was fascinated by it; I could see how it explained so many of the experiences with people I had had in my professional role. It made me realize what a great pity it is that existentialist ideas are not so widely used in the education and training of social workers.

Nicky, a social worker in a child and adolescent mental health team

Also significant in terms of existentialist theory is the fundamental role of spirituality in people's lives. Existentialism can be seen as a theoretical approach that provides an important platform for understanding the subtleties and complexities of spirituality. As a philosophical approach it raises important questions about meaning and purpose and other such factors traditionally associated with spirituality. We shall return to this point in Chapter 13, where we discuss the significance of spirituality, narrative and meaning for social work.

Finally, in terms of existentialist theory, perhaps the most important point we should note is that its greatest strength is that it provides an overview of the nature and characteristics of human existence. It therefore acts as a 'sensitizing theory' (Sibeon, 2004) or metatheory, as discussed in Chapter 1. In so doing, it enables us to incorporate insights and understandings from a wide range of substantive theories, thereby facilitating critically reflective practice. Consider, for example, the passage below from Craib and substitute the word 'existentialism' for 'Marxism':

Marxism is able to revive itself in a consistent rather than an arbitrary or piecemeal way. Thus the superiority of Marxism does not lie in its individual statements about the world, but in its ability to revise those statements as soon as they become inappropriate without creating destructive internal contradictions, without fragmenting its insights, uniting each through its totalizing movement which is not achieved once and for all but is rather a ceaseless movement of totalization and retotalization. One could say that a science that could not recognize its own inadequacies and revise itself would be lost.

(1998, p. 22)

The existentialism on which my work is based (see, for example, Thompson, 1992) draws mainly from Sartre's work (Sartre, 1969; 1973; 1982), which is best understood as a combination of traditional existentialist notions with the more sociological understandings provided by Marx's early work. What Craib is saying about marxism can therefore also be seen to apply to existentialism. It is not so much about the 'individual statements' of the theory (although they have a part to play) as the 'totalization and retotalization' – that is, the use of dialectical reason to develop systematic and coherent (there is that important word again) understandings at a metatheoretical level, but without falling foul of rigidity or dogmatism.

Existentialist practice

Forms of social work practice premised on existentialist thinking would be characterized by a number of elements. Such practice would be:

- *Reflective.* The point has already been made that good practice needs to be reflective practice – and especially *critically* reflective practice (S. Thompson and N. Thompson, 2008). Existentialism is highly compatible with such an approach in so far as its status as a philosophy or metatheory provides a foundation for incorporating into meaningful (and practically useful) whole insights from a variety of sources. Such sources include formal theories from across the social science disciplines and their respective research bases, as well as informal theory developed from 'practice wisdom' or professional expertise, and the knowledge to be gained from hearing the voices of the individuals and groups we serve (McPhail, 2007; Thompson, 2007b). Such knowledge needs to be used *critically*, partly because different elements being drawn on may contradict one another and partly because an uncritical approach would leave room for discriminatory and oppressive assumptions to creep into our practice.

- *Holistic.* The term holistic is used to refer to approaches which are not prone to the criticism of being partial and therefore incomplete. A holistic approach is one that looks at the overall picture and tries to incorporate all elements. Existentialism is strongly characterized by such a holistic perspective due to (i) its reliance on dialectical reason which, by its very nature, serves an integrative or 'totalizing' purpose by showing how conflicting forces interact to produce new circumstances; and (ii) its status as a philosophy that seeks to understand the nature of human existence overall rather than just particular aspects of it. Without a holistic perspective we run the risk that our actions will be based on a picture lacking some vitally important aspect of the situation. This could lead to our practice being ineffective, or even counterproductive.

- *Dialectical.* Appreciating the wider picture is only part of the story. What we also need to understand is how that wider picture is based on processes involving conflict. Individuals, groups and other factors interact with each other and, in so doing, influence each other, thereby creating new realities over time. For example, the love of parents for their disabled son could enter into conflict with the exhaustion, frustration and resentment they feel as a result of the intense and prolonged demands of looking after him, creating a situation that could potentially involve abuse towards the child. A social worker who sees either the love or the pressures, but not both will not be in a position to recognize the interactions between the two and will therefore be ill equipped when it comes to preventing abuse from occurring or responding to it if it does arise.

- *Clear and focused.* In my other writings I have emphasized the significance of systematic practice (Thompson, 2008a; 2009b; c; N. Thompson and S. Thompson, 2008) which ensures that practitioners are at all times clear about what they are trying to achieve, how they are going to achieve it, and how they will know when they have achieved it. This emphasis on clarity and focus is very strongly associated with existentialism. This is because existentialism recognizes, in line with Nietzsche, that there is no underlying absolute reality. The reality is socially and personally constructed through a dynamic set of interactions. It is therefore easy to lose sight of what we are doing in a highly complex multi-faceted situation. Systematic practice enables us to retain clarity and focus, and not become swept away by the complexities involved. Existentialism takes account of the complexity, variability and constant change involved in human encounters, and therefore recognizes the need for a focused, systematic approach in order to establish a baseline of understanding as a foundation for addressing the needs and problems identified and building on the strengths that become apparent.

- *Partnership oriented.* One of the key concepts underpinning existentialism is the idea of *being-with-others*. This involves the recognition that human beings do not exist in a vacuum. We are part of an interacting world where what one person does relates to, and is influenced by, what other people do (see Chapter 5). Partnership is therefore an important part of making sure that, when we are working together with others, we are doing so positively and constructively and not allowing conflicts to pull people apart, with often highly detrimental results for all concerned. Existentialism recognizes that conflict is part and parcel of human existence and not a 'breakdown of normality', as common-sense understandings generally present it. This is not to say that harmony and consensus cannot be achieved, but rather that they must be established. Harmony is a potential *outcome* of human interaction – it is not something we can take for granted as a starting point.
- *Empowering.* It is very easy for uncritical forms of social work practice to make people dependent, to lock them into their problems. There is therefore an increasingly strong emphasis on the need for empowerment (Adams, 2008; Thompson, 2007a). This is because, if we are not aware of the power that we have and how it can be used, either constructively or destructively, there is a danger that we will unwittingly disempower people, making the resolution of their difficulties less likely, rather than more so. The recognition, as a key part of existentialism, that people are not static, fixed entities (see Chapter 4) helps us to understand that each of us can be helped to grow and develop by gaining greater control over our circumstances or we can be blocked and frustrated in our efforts by the actions of others (one of the reasons why Sartre, 1989, wrote that 'hell is other people'). When we encounter others professionally (and, indeed, in our personal lives) our actions can either help them to extend the range of choices available to them or can limit these. Similarly, our actions and attitudes can encourage them to

make choices and take greater control over their lives (empowerment) or can discourage them from doing so (for example, through dependency creation – disempowerment).

- *Focused on meaning.* Existentialism helps us to appreciate the significance of meaning as a phenomenological aspect of human existence. That is, existentialism is premised in part on the notion that reality is not simply given, but is constructed through a set of (personal, cultural and structural) processes. We actively make sense of our experience, rather than simply have it given to us ready made, as it were. Understanding this to be the case offers us a set of insights that cast light on people's motivations, behaviour, thoughts and feelings. This is a sufficiently important issue to justify a whole chapter devoted to the topic (Chapter 13). Trying to deal with situations 'objectively' without an adequate understanding of the subjective dimension – the meanings people attribute to their experiences – is likely to produce dangerously one-sided approaches to practice (see the discussion of the dialectic of subjectivity and objectivity in Chapter 4).

- *Premised on uncertainty.* Fundamental to existentialism is the notion of the 'contingency of being' – the recognition that human existence is characterized by constant change (or 'flux', to use the technical term) and thus a degree of uncertainty. Denney shows how some aspects of current professional practice run counter to this: 'Contemporary notions of risk appear to contain an illusory searching to conquer uncertainty itself. The certainty of security in all aspects of experience appears now to be a desirable and marketable commodity' (2005, p. 12). Existentialist thought warns us of the folly of this by arguing that uncertainty and insecurity are basic features of human existence. The existential challenge we all face is being able to develop the confidence, skills and networks of support we need in order to be able to cope with this effectively. Social work based on existentialist principles involves helping people respond to the challenges of uncertainty, rather than working towards the unachievable goal of eradicating uncertainty and establishing more or less complete security.

I have already made it clear that I am by no means suggesting that existentialist thinking is some sort of panacea for social work's ills, but I would argue that there are very strong indications that the insights offered can be very usefully applied, not only in the interests of developing theory, but also in developing practice. Indeed, this is a further strength of existentialism: it is a philosophy of *lived experience*, not simply a set of abstract thoughts. It is primarily concerned with what was referred to in Chapter 1 as 'praxis', the fusion of theory and practice. This further emphasizes its suitability as a basis for critically reflective practice.

Practice focus 11.3

Carla was a student on her first practice placement. She had found the theory discussed at university quite interesting, but had not been entirely confident that she would be able to use it in practice. She was, in effect, stuck in the gap between theory and practice that plagues so many people. Her practice teacher, Alicia, was an avid exponent of reflective practice and also quite interested in existentialist thought. Alicia quickly became aware of Carla's anxiety about relating theory to practice and therefore sought to reassure her by explaining to her about how reflective practice works and, in particular, about praxis and lived experience. Carla was still not entirely convinced, but the discussion did reassure her quite a lot. Alicia was pleased that Carla had found the ideas helpful but realized that, because her level of confidence was so low, she would have to be careful not to flood her with too many ideas all at once. She was aware that, while theoretical and philosophical ideas could be very useful for explaining the situations we encounter, many people find them quite daunting and therefore have to approach the subject at their own pace.

Conclusion

As we have noted, existentialism does not offer an answer for everything (and it would be dangerous to do so), but it does provide a basis for a highly sophisticated understanding that begins to do justice to the complexities involved. One of its great strengths is that it is not a theoretical 'club' for people to join that therefore excludes elements of understanding that are offered by non-members.

Existentialism attempts to be a holistic, dialectical philosophy that is therefore capable of (critically and not unquestioningly) incorporating elements from other theoretical perspectives, as appropriate. It is therefore not a rigid grand theory (or metanarrative in the postmodernist sense), but rather, as Sibeon (2004) puts it, a *sensitizing* theory that helps us to develop an overall picture which, in turn, gives a degree of coherence and meaning to what we are trying to do. Without that sense of coherence, social work would be prone to major difficulties in terms of finding any positive way forward in what is already a difficult and challenging professional field – what Schön (1983) called 'the swampy lowlands of practice'.

Voice of experience 11.3

Social work can be so messy at times; so many different things going on, with people having different perspectives on the situations and different ideas about what we should do about it. But, for me, that's part of the appeal – it can be really satisfying to get hold of a really complex, messy situation and work with people to make some sort of sense of it that will enable us to move forward. I couldn't do the sort of job where you just tick boxes or follow procedures. What's the point of that?

Kay, a social worker in an access team

The work of the existentialist thinker, Søren Kierkegaard, offers a significant insight with which we can usefully conclude this chapter. Watts captures the idea well when he explains that:

Kierkegaard definitely does not want anyone to adopt his, or any other, philosophy or understanding of life – the fundamental aim of his writing is to motivate his readers to form their *own* conclusions about life and choose their *own* way of existence.

(2003, p. 61)

Kierkegaard's ideas were instrumental in establishing what later came to be known as existentialism. The point we can deduce from what Watts is saying here about Kierkegaard is that theoretical or philosophical perspectives should provide us with tools for thinking and should not do our thinking for us by becoming rigid and dogmatic doctrines. This fits nicely with the idea of *theorizing* practice – developing our own specific understandings based on a critical understanding of the wider and deeper knowledge base, rather than a dogmatic, uncritical adherence to it or an anti-intellectualist rejection of it. Theory, then, should serve to facilitate developing coherent understanding, rather than attempt to provide definitive, ready-made answers that do not require any critical engagement with them (positivist science) or offer only superficial understandings that not only lack coherence, but also see no value in it (postmodernism).

Points to ponder

1. Why do you feel it is important for social work practice to be based on a degree of coherence?
2. What is meant by the term 'meliorism'? How relevant is this to social work?
3. In what ways do you think existentialist ideas could be applied to practice?

Further reading

Butt (2004) offers helpful insights into existentialist thought. My own work has drawn heavily on existentialist thought – see in particular Thompson (1992) as well as Thompson (2000b) and (2009c). Van Deurzen and Arnold-Baker (2005c) is an interesting collection of readings as is Tomer, Eliason and Wong (2008). Krill (1978) is a fascinating early attempt to link social work and existentialism.

12

The linguistic turn

Introduction

There has been a considerable development in social theory of a focus on language and its role in not only reflecting or describing reality, but also in constructing that reality. That is, it is increasingly being recognized that language is an active part of the development of our sense of reality (see the discussion in earlier chapters of the process of social construction). Language, then, is not simply a form of communication; its role in society generally and social work in particular, is much fuller than that. Although the significance of language has been recognized in social work theory up to a point, my argument in this chapter is that there is room for a much greater development of this theme.

In this chapter I will therefore emphasize the importance of language and point out how problematic it can be if we neglect the central role of linguistic factors in social work practice. This will lead on to a discussion of how our actions and interactions take place through the medium of language – that is, we work *through* language.

Finally in this chapter, we shall explore the important topic of developing 'linguistic sensitivity' (Thompson, 2003b; 2009e). This is fundamentally a discussion of the power of language to create problems for people, particularly for members of disadvantaged groups who may be stigmatized or discriminated against. I shall be particularly critical of oversimplified approaches to this highly complex subject. Once again, competence in this area of social work requires the ability to handle complexity, rather than look for simple solutions.

The importance of language

In Chapter 5, the point was made that language is an important part of communication. What we have also noted at various points in earlier chapters is the link between language, on the one hand, and issues to do with power and equality and diversity on the other. However, there are still other aspects of language that are worthy of our attention.

Although I have been critical of postmodernist thinking, its close cousin, post-structuralism, has some important positive features (for a discussion of the differences between the two and the tendency to conflate them, see Tew, 2002). One of the particular strong points is the emphasis on language. Although, in some respects, I regard the post-structural emphasis to be too extreme (in so far as it has a tendency to exclude non-linguistic factors), I am pleased that their efforts have helped to put language 'on the map', as it were, to make it part of the professional agenda. The title of the chapter, 'The linguistic turn', has been chosen because it reflects the development of post-structuralism as an important theory in the social sciences. The notion of a 'linguistic turn' refers to the shift of emphasis in philosophy and the social sciences to the significance of language as a key feature of social life (Rorty, 1992).

Returning to our earlier theme of the social construction of reality (that is, the notion that reality is not 'given' and cannot therefore be taken for granted), we can see that the relationship between language and reality is an important one, as language is a primary vehicle through which social construction takes place – that is, our sense of reality is in large part shaped by language. Grint also refers to the work of Rorty in discussing this: 'language does not so much describe reality as construct it. Or as Rorty (1999: xxvi) puts it, "languages are not attempts to copy what is out there but rather tools for dealing with what is out there"' (2005, p. 11).

We engage with the world through language, and the net result of this is that language plays a key role in shaping our sense of the objective world – the world 'out there'. Returning to the concept of the dialectic of subjectivity and objectivity, as discussed earlier, we can see that these dialectical interchanges that create our view of the world and our place in it are mediated through language. That is, my subjective perceptions will be shaped in part by language (how I use it towards other people and how they use it towards me), but the objective world I engage with will also be a linguistic world: I will understand it through concepts, and, in turn, I will understand those concepts through language (concepts are, after all, words).

An example of how language constructs reality would be a situation in which, by using friendly forms of language, I am giving a signal that

I want our interactions to be conducted on a friendly basis. If the person I am speaking to responds with friendly forms of language, then we will now have a consensus about the nature of our interaction and we will have created (constructed) an amicable situation. If, however, my friendly signals are met with forms of language that suggest distance or formality, then we will have a situation of conflict. The 'objectivity' I now encounter is a relatively unfriendly one; my subjective response to this now becomes important in shaping how it will develop. If I now abandon using friendly language and respond more formally, then the conflict will be resolved, but I may not be happy with this and may feel that I have lost face, that I have been 'snubbed'. Alternatively, I may choose to 'up the ante' in terms of the conflict, by continuing to speak in a friendly, informal way, thereby putting pressure on the other person to be less formal and more 'personal'. The ball will now be in their court in terms of how they respond. They may reinforce the conflict level by remaining formal and distant or they may choose to resolve the conflict by accepting my 'invitation' to be more informal. And so it may go on. The key point to note here, however, is that all this is done through language (including body language). Language, then, is not just a way of communicating about behaviour – it is, in itself, a set of behaviours. And, when we try to make sense of these interactions by thinking about them – our thinking will be done through language as well.

Language is, in effect, a key part of how we subjectively connect with the outside (objective) world. This will be an important consideration in Chapter 12 when we consider the fundamental role of meaning. Meaning is not 'out there' in the objective world; it arises from the interaction of subjectivity and objectivity, which, as we have already noted, is primarily linguistic. The comments of Harding should help us to understand this:

> In nature nothing is true or false. As physical objects, the tree, the stone and the fox exist as unnamed 'things' that we encounter, but when we name them we draw them into our own concerns and possibilities, and argue endlessly as to the truth or falsity of what we perceive them, and ourselves, to be.
>
> (2005, p. 93)

The idea of truth or falsehood is therefore a social construction, something that has developed historically from the interactions of human beings with their environment that has then become institutionalized into our cultural foundations, embedded in our shared understandings of the world. Truth, then, is not a feature of the objective world, a 'given', unmediated reality. Rather, it arises from our human (that is, personal, cultural and structural) interactions with the world. Compare this with Nietzsche's view of truth as discussed in earlier chapters. Our notion of truth, then, depends in large part on language and how we use it to engage with the world.

Practice focus 12.1

Gail was a social worker in a family support team. Although it was a pressurized job she enjoyed it and found it rewarding for the most part. She prided herself on the skills she had developed of engaging with families – that is, being able to connect with them at a level they understood but without being patronizing. However, when her elderly mother had a stroke and needed community care support services from their local office, Gail was both surprised by, and dismayed at, the interactions she had with Maureen, the social worker from the older people team. Gail found that she used lots of medical terminology she didn't understand and a lot of social work jargon she did understand, but which she would not have done if she had not been a social worker herself. But, it wasn't just the specific terminology; there was something about how Maureen's use of language in general came across as creating distance. Gail found it difficult to put her finger on it precisely, but one thing she was very sure about was that it made her feel uncomfortable. The incident spurred her to look at how she used language in her own work. She had always felt she had a good rapport with people, but she could see now that she was going to have to check that out. She came away thinking that the subtleties of language are much more important than she had realized.

I have presented at various points in the book my arguments as to why existentialism can be seen as a helpful, theoretical or, more specifically, metatheoretical basis for social work, but it must be acknowledged that existentialism has had relatively little to say about language. In fact, it has been pointed out that this is a significant weakness that merits close attention in terms of the potential for developing a much stronger version of existentialism – that is, one that is more attuned to the significance of language (Wicks, 2003).

Part of this development can come from learning lessons from how post-structuralism has picked up on what were originally existentialist themes and developed them with a greater appreciation of the role of language. This latter theoretical perspective hinges on the notion of discourse and is closely associated with the work of the leading theorist, Michel Foucault. As noted in Chapter 10, a discourse is literally a conversation, but the term is used in a specialist sense to refer to the way forms of language come to be associated with patterns of behaviour that, in turn, construct and maintain sets of power relations. That is, by using language in particular ways, sets of power relations are established and reinforced. We have already considered this in relation to the critique of the medical model, particularly in relation to mental health issues and mental well-being. However, there are many more examples that could also be developed.

One in particular that is worthy of mention is the way forms of language construct notions of gender and therefore gender role expectations. In this way, powerful 'rules' are established which can lead to significant social sanctions if men and women diverge from their expected gender roles. For example, a child who behaves, dresses or speaks in ways more associated with the opposite gender, can be exposed to intense pressure, including ridicule and even, on occasion, violence. This is an example of the power of language, but specifically language as operating through particular frameworks of meaning – that is, discourses.

Voice of experience 12.1

My work involves working with young offenders. For the boys, who are the majority, one of the things I focus on is how their ideas of masculinity can be getting them into trouble. For example, joyriding is a major problem in this town and a lot of that is around boys trying to 'prove themselves' as men. So, I do a lot of work around helping them to develop less problematic notions of what it means to be a boy or man. It has to be done very subtly and carefully, as part of their sense of masculinity would be to dismiss me as 'just a woman' if they found what I was saying too threatening or undermining for them.

Debbie, a senior practitioner in a youth offending team

Within a post-structuralist framework, the use of the notion of discourse has been criticized for being too deterministic (Sibeon, 2004; Tew, 2002) – that is, for overemphasizing the power of language and not taking enough account of the capacity of human agency to work against that. This fits well with an existentialist conception of power in terms of the dialectic of subjectivity and objectivity. That is, while a discourse creates an objective reality that we cannot completely escape, we are not complete prisoners of that discourse. It is possible to develop alternative discourses – what are sometimes called counter-narratives – that challenge the dominant discourse. We should therefore be wary of adopting a deterministic conception of discourse.

Provided that we are able to avoid such deterministic extremes, then the concept of discourse is one that offers us a great deal of scope for developing our understanding. This is particularly the case when we recognize that language is the basis of meaning, and therefore of the narratives that are an important part of our identity and our relations with other people. Indeed, as Parekh makes clear, our personal sense of identity is part of a wider context of social identities:

> The world looks different when seen from the standpoint of different social identities. Human beings and social relations appear in different shapes, assume different degrees of significance, and are classified and understood differently.

> (2008, p. 23)

Those social identities (in terms of gender, ethnicity, class, language group, and so on) form part of the social structure (the S level). The discourse which maintains them forms part of the cultural context or backdrop (the C level), and then both these sets of factors influence the individual person (the P level). However, the key word here is 'influence' – that is, these factors press heavily in a particular direction, but they do not *determine* the direction the person takes. The influences of culture and structure, however powerful, do not take away human agency – this is a key feature of existentialist thought. It can be captured in Sartre's well-known idea that we are 'condemned to be free' (Sartre, 1969). That is, while structural and cultural factors have a powerful bearing on the choices that are (or are not) available to us, they do not take away our capacity to choose. As Sartre puts it, even a prisoner in a cell can and must make choices.

This relates back to aspects of our discussions in Chapter 4 and also anticipates some of the themes that we shall be discussing in Chapter 13. But, for present purposes, it is to be noted that discourse is a useful concept for explaining aspects of social work practice, provided that we do not fall into the trap of using the term in a deterministic way, assuming that discourses remove human agency – our capacity to choose how we react to the situations we encounter.

One example of discourse is the way in which an uncritical use of jargon can produce social exclusion. I have come across many examples of this over the years, but will restrict myself to mentioning just two briefly (see also Practice focus 12.1).

In the first example, one social worker told me of a situation in which a form being completed in a particular way had led to a very upset client. The form related to a child who was receiving help from a social worker. One of the questions on the form was: Is the child looked after? This was a technical reference to the child care legislation and was basically asking whether or not the child was – to use the old terminology – 'in care'. However, when the social worker completed the form indicating 'no', signalling that the child was not 'looked after' (that is, not 'in care'), the parents interpreted this as an accusation of neglect, that they had been poor parents. Consequently, they had to be calmed down and helped to understand that this was an example of misleading jargon and they were not being accused of being poor parents who were failing to 'look after' their child. What is particularly interesting in this example is that the form had clearly been designed with bureaucratic intentions in mind and had lost sight of the professional imperative of making sure that communications with clients and carers are phrased appropriately.

Another example is the (also bureaucratic) tendency, when writing to parents about their child, to put the child's date of birth under their name as the heading for the letter. I have come across many parents who find this bureaucratic practice quite alienating (and annoying). It can cause a great deal of resentment that an official agency is telling parents the date of birth of their own child. Of course, from within the agency, it is probably simply an administrative device to make sure that if there are two children with the same name, they are distinguished by reference to their date of birth. But if that is how information is used internally, it gives a very different message when that practice leaves the organization via a letter to parents. These are both good examples of how problematic the careless, uncritical use of language can be. They are also both good examples of how the communication ends up being to serve the convenience of the more powerful partner in the communication (the organization) at the expense of the interests and needs of the client (who is, after all, the whole *raison d'être* of the organization).

However, these are examples of language as a form of communication but, as noted earlier, we also need to consider the way in which language creates a much bigger picture of our social reality, and so is not simply a technical tool for people to pass messages between themselves. Communication in general and language in particular have the effect of creating social reality, or at least strong aspects of it. This is particularly the case in social work, and so it is to this that we now turn.

Practice focus 12.2

Jenny was a newly qualified social worker in an older people team. One of the first cases she was allocated in her new job related to helping Mrs Leeson, who was struggling to cope in the community since her very supportive neighbour moved away. Mrs Leeson was quite an anxious person, and, although Jenny was very skilled at putting her at her ease, she remained quite tense about what was going to happen. Jenny explained that there were various possible sources of help for Mrs Leeson, but what help would be offered would depend on the outcome of the assessment. Jenny did a very good job of not letting Mrs Leeson develop unrealistic expectations of what could be done to help her in terms of provision of resources, while also reassuring her by making it clear that she was committed to helping her in whatever ways she reasonable could. However, all this work was undone to a certain extent by the use of one term. When Jenny talked about it 'all depending on the outcome of the assessment', Mrs Leeson's response was: 'But, what if I fail it?'. Jenny was puzzled by this comment as first, but then realized that Mrs Leeson was interpreting the term 'assessment' in the educational sense of a test or exam. The net result was that this unfortunate use of a technical term without explaining in what sense it was being used returned Mrs Leeson to her previous state of high anxiety. Jenny was back to square one because she had unwittingly used professional terminology without realizing what (detrimental) impact that could have on how Mrs Leeson perceived the situation – her sense of reality. The situation illustrated well how a social work discourse (as manifested in the use of professional jargon) had alienated Mrs Leeson who did not feel comfortable with what she perceived as a process of being 'tested' (an educational discourse).

Working *through* language

It is important to recognize that to a large extent language is central to whatever we do in life. We form relationships and fall in love through language. We also fall out through language. We learn through language. We bring up our children, we are entertained and plan through language, albeit not exclusively so. We become disappointed through language, celebrate and rejoice through language, and also worship through language – but, most importantly, we should recognize that:

1. We work through language (that is, the major part of what we do as social workers is verbal). In the days of behavioural social work beginning to gain ascendancy, social workers who favoured behavioural methods were often heard to dismiss other social work methods as 'talkotherapy' as if to dismiss the value of talking to one another. When we look more closely at not only social work, but also the other helping professions, we can see just how important a tool language is.

2. We make sense of our lives through language. This applies in a number of ways. Consider, for example, the following:

   - The language we use with clients can help us to engage with them or alienate them. There are some significant issues to consider here in terms of what forms of language are appropriate. Practice focus 12.1 and 12.2 both exemplify this, and, of course, other examples are not hard to find.
   - Similarly, the language we use when working with professionals from other disciplines can either bring us closer together or push us further apart. Where the latter occurs, of course, it makes effective multiprofessional collaboration much harder to achieve. The skills needed for matching the forms of language we use to the particular situation in hand is part of the communicative competence we need for social work – it is an aspect of linguistic sensitivity, which involves having the awareness needed to appreciate the likely impact of the language we use in each situation.
   - Language is, of course, the medium through which we produce written records and reports as part of our professional duties. Committing ideas to writing is an exercise of power. The language we use in exercising that power can be highly significant. For example, describing somebody in judgemental terms in a report may lead to that person being discriminated against at some future date. It may also highly distort the way that person is seen, and dealt with, now. Consider, for example, the difference between:

- 'Peter gets anxious very easily and, when he feels insecure, he will often tell lies to protect himself. His comments should therefore be handled with caution'; and
- 'Peter is a pathological liar and is not to be trusted.'

- To a large extent, language defines what we do and how we do it. For example, I referred earlier to the people we serve as 'clients'. Many people have adopted the more modern usage of 'service users', but one of the reasons I prefer to keep the use of that term to a minimum is that the very terminology implies that the focus of our intervention is the provision of services. As I have argued at length elsewhere (Thompson, 2009a), there are serious dangers in conceiving of social work as primarily a process of providing (or worse still, just rationing) services. Of course, how people are treated does not just come down to particular words or even to language usage more broadly, but it would be very naive not to recognize that language is an important part of the process.

- There is also the question of: which language? It is important to acknowledge that, within any linguistic group there will be factors that relate to their particular language, but there will also be key issues to consider in terms of situations that involve more than one language. This involves, for example, the use of interpreters in certain circumstances. In this regard, we should also not neglect the significance of nonverbal forms of language, such as British Sign Language and its equivalents in other countries. There is a significant danger in assuming that, when we are talking about language, we are talking about English. Even where people are quite fluent in English, their preference may be for a different language, especially if they are talking about sensitive, emotional issue. In Wales, for example, being able to have the facility to use the Welsh language is a legal right, rather than just a preference for some people (Drakeford and Morris, 1998).

Each of these points should contribute to painting a picture of just how important language issues are in social work.

It is also instructive to look at how significant language is in relation to culture. This is because languages are generally not directly equivalent to each other or directly translatable from one to another; they are embedded in different cultural contexts and will tend to reflect aspects of that context. For example, speakers of some languages (especially western ones) are more direct in their expression, while others (mainly eastern) tend to be more indirect – reflecting differences in the respective cultures about rules of politeness (Guirdham, 2005). In this regard, Parker, Fook and Pease make an important point when, in discussing the significance of language, they argue that:

> The implication for social work practice is that social workers should strive for 'communicative competence', rather than gathering 'objective' data, which may have limited cultural relevance (Pardeck et al. 1994: 116).
>
> (1999, p. 153)

Language and culture are closely intertwined, in so far as language is rooted in a cultural context, while culture is largely expressed in, and transmitted through, language.

Voice of experience 12.2

I am fluent in both English and Tamil, the language of my home area in India, so I feel equally at home in either, perhaps with a slight preference for English, as my wife speaks only English, so that is the language of the home these days as well as the language I use at work. But, for my parents, they would much prefer to deal with important issues in Tamil, even though their English is really good after all these years in the country. Some things just don't translate from one language to another, and the cultures are so very different too. It's about what you feel comfortable with.

Ganesh, a social worker in an access team

From the above discussions it should therefore be clear that language needs to be recognized as s a key feature of social work. As I mentioned in the introduction to this chapter, this has been taken on up to a point in our thinking, but as far as theory development is concerned, there is still considerable scope for taking matters forward in terms of both broadening and deepening our understanding of linguistic factors and the part they play. It would be too ambitious to attempt to achieve such development here, but we can at least map out possible avenues to pursue.

Developing linguistic sensitivity

The term 'linguistic sensitivity' is one that I introduced in an earlier work of mine (Thompson, 2003b) that focused specifically on issues of communication and language. My main argument in that book is that language has the power to discriminate and oppress, but, unfortunately, the recognition of this fact has often led to a grossly oversimplified response to the problem. This is often referred to as 'political correctness'. It seems to be assumed by many people that, if we can simply avoid the use of certain words, then the problem of the power of language to discriminate and oppress will be solved. This is an incredibly naive and woefully inadequate understanding of the complexities involved. For one thing, language is not just about words, but rather about meanings (hence the emphasis on discourses as institutionalized frameworks of meaning that operate ideologically to preserve power relations – that is, relations of dominance and subordination). Language, of course, plays a central role in constructing meaning, but it is often the case that we can change the actual words, but the meaning remains – even when that meaning is a discriminatory or oppressive one. For example, staff working with older people in a residential home may perhaps be banned from using patronizing terms like 'old dear', but their tone of voice may none the less convey a patronizing message and thereby maintain a relationship based on dominance and dependency creation, rather than respect, equality, empowerment and interdependence. Similarly, organizations may start to use terms like 'chair' instead of 'chairman' (because of the now long-standing criticism that the latter term gives a message that positions of power belong to, or are reserved for, men), and yet still remain male-dominated organizations that have made no substantive concessions to the need for gender equality. Language comprises a set of powerful symbols, and so changing those symbols can be a useful way of giving a message that inequality is something that will not be tolerated. However, if other changes do not back up the linguistic change, then the change of terminology quickly becomes seen as tokenistic and dismissed as yet another example of that well-worn cliché 'political correctness gone mad'.

There is also the danger that changes in terminology can be imposed from above without any real explanation given or understanding gained. For example, one organization I worked with banned its staff from using the term 'respite care' and insisted that they use 'short breaks' instead, but it offered no explanation whatsoever. This imposed change without briefing, let alone consultation, caused confusion and annoyance in equal measure. There are also many cases I have encountered where one person's idea of what is or is not appropriate terminology is not shared by other people and the result is again confusion and annoyance or alienation.

Practice focus 12.3

Ailsa was a social worker in a child care team. She was working with Robbie, a 13-year-old boy whose foster placement had broken down. It had been realized that, if he was placed with new foster carers straight away, there was a danger that placement would break down too, due to insufficient matching and preparation. Arrangements were made to admit Robbie to a privately run residential home for children and young people. Ailsa took him there to assist in the admission process and to help settle him in. At one point while Robbie was being shown around the grounds, Ailsa had a cup of coffee with two of the residential staff. In conversation she said that she had worked with kids for many years but never in a residential setting. One of the staff then said that she should not let any of the managers hear her using the term 'kids'. When she asked why not, she was told that the officer in charge had banned the use of the term on the grounds that it was demeaning to young people. Ailsa said that she saw it as a term of affection, and not the slightest bit demeaning. She also said she had never heard anyone else object to the term. 'No, nor have we', said the other staff member, 'but, if the boss says "Don't say it", then we don't say it.' That's political correctness for you. Ailsa, who had been a staunch supporter of the need to challenge discriminatory language over the years, was quite dismayed to find that it had come to this.

What is needed, then, is not a simplistic political correctness approach that bans the use of certain words. Rather, we need the more sophisticated notion of 'linguistic sensitivity'. That is, it is important that social workers are attuned to the significance of language and its power, in relation to certain groups, to:

- *marginalize* – 'All staff will receive cultural diversity training to help them understand black people's perspectives.' How might a black member of staff feel about seeing minutes of a meeting that say this?

- *stigmatize* – 'What do you expect from someone with an accent like that?' is an example of one of the less subtle ways in which certain groups can be stigmatized through language use.
- *exclude* – 'Following a manpower review, new job descriptions will be issued. Anyone who has any concerns about this should speak to his foreman.' What message does this form of language give women staff?
- *dehumanize* – 'John is an epileptic and an asthmatic' tells us little about John as a person and a lot about the speaker's way of defining John.
- *demean* – 'You work at the psychiatric hospital, don't you? Doesn't it worry you, working with all those nutters?' All disadvantaged groups can be demeaned through language but, for people with mental health problems, it is surprising how often such demeaning language is deemed acceptable in polite company.
- *stereotype* – 'That was an Irish way of doing it' is now heard less frequently than it was, but is still widely used, despite it being a highly inaccurate and offensive stereotype.

Linguistic sensitivity therefore involves being in a position to work towards forms of language that are more empowering and less problematic. There are no easy answers or set formulas to use in this regard. Linguistic sensitivity needs to be part of critically reflective practice.

However, another dimension to linguistic sensitivity is the ability to develop the knowledge and skills to use language constructively and appropriately. For example, the strengths perspective and the related practice modality of solution-focused work have emphasized the importance of using language in a positive, empowering way, rather than simply avoiding the use of negatives. Munford and Sanders comment as follows:

> As Norman (2000, pp. 1–2) argues, the historical preoccupation with dysfunction, deficit and disease has prevented social workers from harnessing the 'inherent push for growth' and problem-focused orientation can be ultimately counterproductive. We have argued elsewhere (Munford and Sanders 1999) that strengths approaches link individual troubles to public issues. They also challenge definitions of clients as mere consumers of services and critique the wider discourses that see those who seek support as 'failed families'.
>
> (2005, p. 163)

Voice of experience 12.3

When I trained as a social worker nobody ever mentioned the strengths perspective, but then I went on a course about solution-focused approaches and realized how useful an idea it was. It fitted in with my ideas about empowerment and not writing people off. That course proved to be a turning point for my practice. Now I always make sure that, in whatever I do, I am taking account of people's strengths as well as their problems and needs.

Gill, a social worker in a learning disability team

Jack helps us to develop our understanding of this important theme:

> Strengths-based practice is principled and empowering work, guided by the worker's attitudes and beliefs, which is characterized by collaboration and ensures the client is understood to have strengths, resources, capacities and abilities that when mobilized by the client's aspirations and the worker's relationship, can generate change (Saleebey 1997).
>
> Strengths perspectives do not seek to minimize or sanitize problems but rather seek to respond to problems in the context of the strengths, resources and wisdom of the people involved with that problem.
>
> (2005, p. 177)

This is a point to which we shall return in Chapter 13, where the emphasis is on the importance of spirituality which, in turn, rests on key issues around meaning and narrative which are, of course, linguistic matters. Conversely, the use of language is highly significant in relation to the strengths perspective, in so far as so much of the work we can do to build on people's strengths we do through language – we therefore have to make sure that we have enough linguistic sensitivity to make sure that our language use is positive and empowering and a foundation for genuine partnership.

Conclusion

It is sadly the case that language issues are often neglected or over-simplified in the social sciences generally, but especially within social work. It is to be hoped that this chapter has established a need for a more sophisticated understanding to be developed. If we are to take the 'linguistic turn' seriously and the insights it offers, then clearly our theory base needs to have a much stronger focus on the significance of language. Equally, we clearly need to build on the progress that has been made to date.

This chapter has emphasized both the importance of language as a primary feature of social interaction and the complexities involved in understanding it. In terms of its importance, the key message I have tried to convey here is that we need to develop a fuller and more sophisticated understanding of language use, so that we are better able to theorize its use as a fundamental feature of not only our work directly, but also of our social interactions more broadly. We therefore have much to gain by developing our understanding in this area. In terms of the complexities involved, then the message of this chapter is much the same: the need to develop fuller and better understandings of how language (and, indeed, communication more broadly) operates, so that we can steer clear of the reductionist and dogmatic approaches to language that have plagued us in the past.

Points to ponder

1. How would you feel if a professional used jargon you did not under-stand?
2. What links can you see between language and power?
3. List three ways in which inappropriate language use could cause problems in social work.

Further reading

Thompson (2003b) is a wide-ranging discussion of communication and language. Rorty (1992) is less easy to read, but none the less a very inter-esting and thought-provoking text. Tew (2002) is a helpful source on post-structuralism. Petersen and colleagues (1999) is also worth consulting.

Saleebey (2008) and Nash, Munford and O'Donoghue (2005) offer insight-ful analyses of the role of language, and Parton and O'Byrne (2000) is simi-larly helpful. There is a very large literature on language. Of particular interest and use, in my view, are Aitchison (2007) and Crystal (2003).

13

Spirituality and meaning

Introduction

In recent years we have seen the growing awareness of the importance of spirituality, partly as a dimension of an enhanced level of awareness of religion and partly as an important issue in its own right, separate from debates about religion. There is an important literature base now developing (see, for example, Coyte, Gilbert and Nicholls, 2007; Moss, 2005; Thompson, 2007b), but there is still considerable scope for extending our understanding of spirituality and how it relates to other aspects of the theory base of social work and associated practice issues.

Spirituality can be seen as a key issue for social work for various reasons, but I am particularly interested in it here in the context of this book for three reasons:

1. It links well with existentialism and the rejection of (i) the rigidity of positivism that loses sight of the human being at the heart of our enterprise; and (ii) the cynicism of postmodernism, with its failure to establish clarity and coherence as a basis of meaning making.
2. Holloway (2006) refers to the work of Nash (2002) who argues that '"spiritual practice" unites concern for the personal with concern for social and political justice and therefore deepens social work's therapeutic potential' (pp. 274–5). This highlights nicely social work's concern with the person, but as part of a broader picture of social justice, rather than in atomistic terms that neglect the wider context.
3. Spirituality is fundamentally about meaning making (Morgan, 1993), and so too are:

- *existentialism* with its roots in phenomenology and its concerns with perception, interpretation and thus meaning;
- *social work* which, as I have indicated at various points in this book, involves a strong element of helping people develop more empowering meanings, understandings or 'narratives'; and
- *theorizing* which is, in effect, a process of developing informed critical and reasonably rigorous understandings of (or meanings for) the activities we engage in as practitioners.

There should be no doubt, then, that spirituality is very much a relevant concern for social work theory and practice, and, given the relative neglect of such matters in the professional knowledge base of social work, it is also a very relevant concern when it comes to highlighting much-needed *development* of theory, which is, of course, what Part Three is primarily concerned with.

I shall begin by exploring similarities and differences between spirituality and religion, before moving on to look at the specifically spiritual issues of meaning, purpose and direction. This will lead on to the discussion of another important facet of spirituality, namely connectedness and, finally, I shall comment on the key spiritual issues of awe, wonder and hope.

Spirituality and religion

Although the two terms are often used as if they were interchangeable, they are actually quite different. Spirituality is the attempt to develop a worldview and that can be a religious worldview, but does not have to be. The focus is on having a meaningful understanding of the world and how we are a part of it. Religion, then, is a structured institutionalized form of spirituality, a framework that acts as a basis for making sense of human existence. However, our focus is on spirituality *per se*, rather than religion specifically. This is not to say that religion is not important, but rather to ensure that people who have no religious commitments are not excluded from the equation.

These days spirituality is often associated with the growing interest in well-being (Jordan, 2007; McGillivray, 2007; Searle, 2008), happiness (Haidt, 2006; Layard, 2006; McMahon, 2006) and positive psychology (Seligman, 2003; 2006). While there are important links to be made with these issues, we do not have space to explore them more fully here. We can, however, note that (i) spirituality is indeed closely related directly to well-being and happiness and indirectly to positive psychology (in terms of a critique of it – see for example, Thompson, 2009c); and (ii) as such matters have been prone to a certain degree of popularization and 'dumbing down' in recent years, we should be careful not to adopt a simplistic understanding of spirituality. As with the other key issues in social work, it is a highly complex topic, and we do ourselves no favours (and our clientele a considerable disservice) if we settle for an oversimplified understanding of it.

What, then, is spirituality? Moss defines a person's spirituality as what we do to give expression to our chosen worldview:

> This world-view may be specifically religious – we may belong to a Christian, Jewish, Muslim, Hindu or one of many other faith-based communities, which give us a sense of community and purpose, and an outlook upon the world which shapes our thinking and our social action. It also encourages us to undertake certain activities such as shared worship and prayer.
>
> This world-view may most definitely not be religious – we may feel more comfortable with being agnostic or atheist or humanist – we may define our position as being existentialist – this too will shape our outlook upon the world and our social action, and what we choose to do and not do to express our convictions.
>
> (2005, p. 13)

This is partly linked to identity, in so far as spirituality involves a sense of who we are and how we fit into the wider world. Consider, for example, the passage below from Parekh and, as you read it, think about Moss's conception of spirituality as a chosen worldview:

> Personal identity is not a possession which, once achieved can be cherished passively. It is expressed in and retains its vitality only in so far as it is exercised and affirmed in appropriate choices and actions. It is never a finished product either. New experiences, new insights into oneself, social changes, exposure to other ways of looking at the world, and deeper self-reflection might reveal its ambiguities and limitations, and lead to its revision.
>
> (2008, pp. 10–11)

Identity, as we noted in Chapter 4, is not a matter of having a fixed personality. It is more a case of who we are being the journey, the flow of our life as our existence unfolds over time. As such, identity is very much a spiritual matter.

As a chosen worldview, spirituality can, then:

1. be totally separate from religion – atheists can be very spiritual people, very interested in, and committed to, spiritual issues and values, despite having no religious faith;
2. run parallel with religion – for example, a non-devout charity worker who acts on behalf of the religion in his or her capacity as a charity worker, but does not practise the rituals of the religion or derive his or her primary sense of location in the world from the religion;
3. coincide almost entirely with religion, in the sense that someone's religious beliefs and spirituality are more or less completely synonymous.

Each of these possibilities is important, and to understand the people we deal with in a social work context we have to have a good understanding of the significance of spirituality in people's lives, even where people do not openly acknowledge the spiritual dimension of their existence. As Holloway helpfully points out:

> Patel *et al.*'s description of spirituality as 'the human search for personal meaning and mutually fulfilling relationships between people, between people and the natural environment and between religious people and God' (1998, p. 11) is, without the last clause, indistinguishable from social work literature which, in emphasizing the therapeutic power of the social work relationship and person-centred helping, characteristically addresses the search for meaning and purpose, re-valuing and achieving personal growth and maturity (e.g. Thompson, 1996).
>
> (2006, p. 274)

This re-emphasizes the point I made earlier: that spiritual concerns are very compatible with social work concerns; they overlap to a large extent and therefore merit our close attention.

Practice focus 13.1

Mandy had been a social worker in a child care team for about four years before moving to the mental health team. She had decided she needed a change of scene, a fresh impetus to keep her going. She found it quite a culture shock to begin with, because so many things were so different from what she was used to in a child care setting. One thing that struck her very strongly was what she first perceived to be the loneliness of so many of the clients she was now working with. The families she had worked with in her previous job had significant, often multiple problems, but loneliness as such featured very little if at all. However, in her new post, it struck her that most of the people she was supporting seemed quite lonely. However, over time, she started to realize that is wasn't just loneliness; there was more to it than that. It was a sort of emptiness, what she came to think of as a 'spiritual impoverishment'. It made her want to read up on the subject and try to find out just how significant this feature of people's lives was. It also made her wonder how much of an issue it had been with the families she had worked with previously, but had perhaps been less visible.

Spirituality is also about something bigger than ourselves or, to use the technical term, the 'transcendent'. This could be God, nature, humanity or a whole range of other things. What is important is recognizing that, as individuals, we fit into a wider picture; we are part of something bigger than ourselves.

Meaning, purpose and direction

All three of these terms – meaning, purpose and direction – can be difficult to pin down. It is worth exploring each in turn.

Meaning

Meaning refers to how we make sense of our experience, how we relate disparate parts together, so that they make sense for us in some way. It is only through having meaning that we are able to deal with such issues. In a sense, we are connected to the world through meaning, in so far as when we look out upon the world, we do not directly perceive the raw, unmediated objects of our senses. We invariably filter those objects through our own frameworks of meaning. For example, when we see a red light on the roadside, we are not simply seeing a source of illumination with a red hue, we are seeing a 'Stop' sign. However, someone brought up in an area of the world that does not have motorized traffic is not likely to register a 'Stop' sign. The sensory input is not accessed directly; it is interpreted by reference to our own meaning system, which is partly individual (drawing on my own personal life experiences to date) and partly social (for example, cultural understandings and discourses). Gadamer (2004) wrote of 'horizons', by which he meant that each of us sees the world from our own perspective (note the debt here to Nietzsche's idea of 'perspectives'). When people interact we have what Gadamer calls a 'fusion of horizons' and that produces dynamic interactions (sometimes in harmony, sometimes in conflict) which, in turn, shape people's experiences and how they make sense of those experiences – each person's attribution of meaning can influence everyone else's attribution of meaning. This is how spending time with certain people can result in their views and understandings (their meanings) rubbing off on you and vice versa. This also helps to explain how interacting with people who have different perspectives from our own can be quite challenging (in finding common ground, for example), but also very rewarding and enriching because of the insights gained that are outside out own sphere of reference, our own habitual ways of seeing the world.

It is important to recognize, then, that meaning is not something fixed or immutable. Different symbols mean different things in different settings (consider the red light example above, and how a red light can have a very different meaning at times – for example, in the term 'red light district'). Meanings also change over time. Consider, for example, how words can change their meaning over time. Gay, once used to mean cheerful, now means homosexual, and is increasingly being used by some groups to mean unsophisticated. But, there is not only the literal meaning to consider (its 'denotation', what it actually refers to), there are also the more subtle 'connotations' (what is implied or suggested by the term without actually spelling it out). For example, 'gay', as a term to refer to people whose sexual orientation is towards same-sex relationships, was once very derogatory and still to this day can be used as an insult or term of abuse or at least disapproval, but the negative connotations have diminished significantly in recent years and it is now a much more neutral term. The following passage from Clarke emphasizes this aspect of meaning:

> Rather than words (or signs) having one fixed meaning, this conception of articulation emphasizes their polysemic character: they have a potential to be given different meanings. In practice, a specific meaning is (temporarily) fixed by the connection of the word/sign into a chain of meaning. It is inflected – given a specific meaning – by where it is located and the associations which are generated by that location.
>
> (2004, pp. 37–8)

This fluid, 'polysemic' notion of meaning is at the heart of spirituality. If there is no fixed, unchanging meaning to life, human existence and our place in the world, then where do we get our meaning from? Where do we get answers to questions like: Who am I? What does it mean to be me? Where do I fit into the world? What does the world expect of me? What can I expect of the world? Our answers to these questions in effect construct our worldview, as Moss (2005) so helpfully writes about.

This emphasis on meaning helps to explain why religions are so often interlinked. This is because, in a sense, religions give a largely predefined framework of meaning. So, for many, their spiritual quest is in large part, if not entirely, resolved by their adherence to a particular faith. For others, their faith provides a foundation for their spirituality, but it does not provide them with the full range of answers directly. Their faith is therefore the basis of their worldview, but not the whole story for them (Kierkegaard, one of the key founders of existentialist thought, argued, for example, that Christians should try to find their own way, their own path, within the parameters of Christian faith, but not expect an uncritical acceptance of established ideas to be sufficient to meet their spiritual needs – Watts, 2003). For yet others, religion plays no part in their spiritual journey. They reject the idea that faith is a satisfactory (and satisfying) foundation for providing spiritual answers. This last group can be subdivided into two further groups. First, there are those who, although they reject religion as a basis for spirituality, none the less have faith in a particular movement or set of values (socialism, materialism, feminism, environmentalism, fascism or whatever) to make a major contribution to their spirituality. Second, there are those who regard spirituality as a personal quest, believing that everybody must find his or her own way forward and not look for ready-made prepackaged answers. Different existentialist thinkers adopt different perspectives on this, but all contain an element of emphasis on this final approach (what is sometimes called the 'solitary' approach) and all see the fundamental 'aloneness' of each person as a key factor (see the discussion of 'connectedness' below).

Purpose

Purpose is a term that is related to meaning. It refers to establishing clarity about something that we are trying to achieve – for example, goals in our life, whether these are major long-term goals (in terms of particular career aspirations, for example) or short-term ones (such as finishing a particular task or assignment on schedule). It should not be confused with the teleological use of the term 'purpose', as discussed in Chapter 1. By 'purpose' I do not mean that there is a grand design, a predefined role for us in life and our spiritual task is therefore to discover what that is. This is particularly important from an existentialist approach, because a fundamental part of the philosophy is a rejection of predestiny and an emphasis on the key role of human agency (the decisions we make, the actions we take) in shaping events.

The spiritual notion of 'purpose', then, is not a matter of *finding* our spiritual place in the world so much as *creating* it: defining it, negotiating it and constructing it, in accordance with our values (Moss, 2007a). It is for this reason that, within existentialist understandings, spirituality is not about finding *the* answer, *the* Truth. Rather, it is about finding answers and truths on an ongoing basis as part of our life process. Or, to put it in technical terms, spirituality is about becoming, rather than being. A sense of purpose is a key part of that becoming.

Direction

Direction refers to having a sense of where we are moving towards. This is linked to the idea of purpose and goals, but is a fuller concept, in the sense that it incorporates wider elements of the meaning of what we are doing with our lives and whether we feel that it is worthwhile. Some people may have a sense of *purpose* (for example, that they want to find expression for their commitment to compassion), but not have a sense of *direction*. Should they plan to work in the helping professions and to express their compassion in that way? If so, which of the helping professions – medicine, nursing, social work, counselling or what? Would it be better to seek less-demanding work outside of the helping professions and supplement this with voluntary, charitable work? If charitable work is the chosen direction, should it be 'hands-on' work (Do I have the skills? The patience?) or would their talents be better directed towards fund-raising efforts? These are all questions of direction.

Direction is again an existential issue. Some people look for ready-made directions (they may want their horoscope or a psychometric test to tell them what direction they should go in). Counsellors and advisers commonly encounter this issue – with clients often wanting to be given *the* answer, rather than helped to find *their* answer. The question of finding a direction can be a major existential challenge, and one that people can wrestle with for much of their lives.

From a social work point of view, all three of these sets of issues can be relevant to practice. We will often encounter people who are struggling to make sense of their lives (people who are grieving or who have been traumatized, for example) or who are dissatisfied with the meaning their life has for them at present: I am an addict; I am a failing parent; I am out of control. People we encounter in social work will often have little or no sense of purpose. Their life can seem empty and pointless. Others may have purpose (establishing a life free of depression or debt, for example), but be struggling to find a direction (not knowing how to earn sufficient money or how to fend off depressive feelings). The social work task, then, is very often in many ways a spiritual task.

Voice of experience 13.1

I came into social work because of my religious beliefs, wanting to make a positive difference to people's lives, especially members of disadvantaged groups. After both my parents died in close succession I don't mind telling you that I came close to a nervous breakdown. I lost my faith at that point, angry that two such loving people should be taken before their time. It affected my life a great deal, as you can imagine, and yet it made little difference to my work. While I had lost my religious faith, my spiritual values were still there; it was my faith that had gone, not my compassion or commitment. I have since regained my faith and am now fully back into membership of my church, but the fact that my spirituality was not lost with my faith really made me think. It was a painful experience, but one that I learned a great deal from.

Marie, a social worker in a large voluntary organization

Each of these three aspects of spirituality can be impoverished by social circumstances. For example, the experience of social exclusion, deprivation and discrimination can undermine a person's meaning, purpose and direction. These can also be impoverished by personal circumstances – for example, experiences of loss and trauma, conflict, debt, illness or abuse. We should therefore not see spirituality as something 'unworldly', something unconnected with the social context and concrete personal realities of our lives.

Experiencing problems, whether from social or personal roots, or a combination of both, can lead to confusion. The lack of clarity that such confusion brings can then lead to what I shall refer to as 'spiritual drift', a feeling of being lost or at sea. The people we encounter in social work will often be experiencing such a spiritual drift. This has important implications in terms of social work practice in relation to spirituality, as to fail to recognize the significance of spiritual drift can leave us ill-equipped to help people rise to the spiritual or existential challenges they face. Without such a recognition, we run the risk of 'pathologizing' people, of seeing problems as a reflection of some inadequacy within them, rather than understanding the situation in terms of (i) broader social factors; and (ii) deeper spiritual ones. The comments of Folgheraiter are helpful in this regard:

> Elsewhere (Folgheraiter, 1998), I have defined (in)capacity for action to be the subject matter of social work. By this I mean that a problem of interest to social workers is not a *pathology*, or a static state of affairs, but a dynamic difficulty: an impediment against the achievement of goals.
>
> (2004, p. 44)

Incapacity for action is something that can be closely associated with spiritual drift and, of course, the 'impediment against the achievement of goals' is very much a spiritual issue to do with purpose and perhaps also direction.

Connectedness

Social work is about people working with people. What I mean by this is that, as social workers, there are (at least) two main things we should never forget: (i) the people we serve, the clients and carers, are *people* first and last – not just cases, statistics, problems or the like; and (ii) we are people too – we must therefore not neglect our own needs and must make sure that we do not allow the work we do to harm us in some way (for example, through stress). The importance of human contact and concern cannot therefore be underestimated.

Connectedness is a term used in the spirituality literature to refer to the important ways in which having other people in our lives is a central part of shaping our identity and our feelings of security or otherwise in the challenges of human existence. It can be linked with the existentialist idea of 'being-with-others', a term intended to denote that, although each of us is a unique individual, we are also inevitably part of society, connected with other people, cultures and social institutions and processes. 'Connectedness' as a concept underlines the need to reject atomism, as I have mentioned at various points in earlier chapters, to avoid falling into the trap of seeing the person without also seeing the social context of that person and how it shapes to a certain degree who they are, how they behave and how they make sense of the world.

One feature of existentialist thought is the recognition that, however sociable we may be, we remain to a certain extent cut off from other people. For example, however much one person loves another, we cannot get beyond a basic separation between the two of them. Even in a crowd each of us is alone, in the sense that our own subjectivity is precisely that; it is our own. No matter how close somebody may be to us, emotionally and/or spiritually, we will always have our own subjectivity, our own perspective on the situation. This is often referred to as 'existential aloneness', but it should not be confused with 'loneliness'. Even someone who has a wide range of friends and contacts (see the discussion of social capital below) and is therefore not the slightest bit lonely, will none the less be subject to existential aloneness.

The idea of 'connectedness', then, derives in part from the notion of aloneness. It involves recognizing that, while no one else can 'share my skin' (I will always be the objective to their subjective and vice versa), I can form links with other people that can help me carry this burden of aloneness. These can be links of respect, trust, affection, friendship, intimacy or love – all of which prevent the aloneness from becoming loneliness or, indeed, any sort of problem.

The concept of connectedness can be closely linked with a sociological notion that has started to receive increasing attention in recent years, namely 'social capital' (Castiglione, Deth and Wellob, 2008; Lin, 2001). As explained in Chapter 5, this is a term that denotes the social resources a person can draw upon to help them cope with life's challenges and to make their lives meaningful and fulfilling. This includes personal relationships with friends, neighbours, relatives, (ex)-colleagues and other associates; membership of organizations, clubs, associations and other such groups. It can be a great source of stimulation, motivation, pleasure, reassurance and support as well as what was earlier referred to as 'ontological security' – that is, our capacity to deal with life's uncertainties. The basic idea is captured in a wide range of clichés: a problem shared is a problem halved; all for one and one for all; you scratch my back and I will scratch yours; and so on. Connectedness is also part of the wellspring of compassion.

The notion of social capital as part of the broader concept of connectedness is therefore an issue that social workers should take very seriously. It can make a significant difference – positively or negatively – to someone's life experience. This raises significant implications for social work practice. If we see people in isolation and fail to take account of the significance of (a lack of) social capital, we can be missing a significant aspect of their life and their problems. This could be very significant practically (for example, in terms of not seeing how the boosting of social capital in some way could be a very positive step for many people) and spiritually (in so far as we could be failing to meet someone's spiritual needs by not seeing connectedness as a key issue).

Practice focus 13.2

Jane was a social worker in an older people team. After she undertook an assessment with Mrs Kingston, it became apparent that, although she was depressed, she did not need residential care (contrary to what was claimed in the referral from the GP). However, it was clear that part of Mrs Kingston's problems was social isolation. She was a very nervous person and found it difficult to form relationships. Consequently, Jane arranged for her to attend a day centre two days a week. After three months a review meeting was held. It was chaired by the service manager with responsibility for older people's services. At the meeting the senior day care office commented that she felt it was not working for Mrs Kingston, because she spent most of her time at the day centre sitting on her own and not joining in the activities. She was steadily getting more depressed and had started to neglect herself. The service manager commented that, in her view, Mrs Kingston needed a fuller plan for addressing her needs and that, if anything, simply attending the centre was making her problems worse. More careful attention needed to be given to how her social isolation and her depression could be addressed. The service manager proposed that Jane and the senior day care officer work closely with Mrs Kingston to develop a more detailed plan. Mrs Kingston indicated that she would welcome this. Jane realized after the review that she had skimped on her original assessment and had looked for an easy answer. The service manager had been very tactful and supportive about the whole thing, but Jane none the less felt bad that she had not looked closely enough at Mrs Kingston's social connections or the effect of their absence on her mental health.

Related to this is the notion of reciprocity (Sue Thompson, 2009). This involves giving as well as receiving. If somebody is connected to other people, but the giving aspect of the relationship is in one direction only – that is, they feel dependent because the people in their life are simply 'looking after them' or doing things for them – then the result can be a lowering of self-esteem and feelings of being unworthy or of being 'a burden'. It is therefore important that social workers working with people with high levels of dependency try to help create opportunities for reciprocity, so that the person concerned can give as well as receive and can therefore have a more positive sense of connectedness.

Another important aspect of connectedness is the sense of being valued as a human being among other human beings. This involves affirmation or validation. This is to be contrasted with the damaging effects of stigma and stereotyping as discussed in earlier chapters (and to which we shall return in Chapter 14). Houston discusses this in the context of culturally sensitive social work:

> Culturally sensitive social work must also be attentive to the fundamental, existential ground of being. In contrast to Giddens, who stresses ontological security as the key existential problematic, Bourdieu points out that people are basically motivated by a need for recognition. Having a designated place in the social world, an acknowledged position, a recognized achievement or a particular skill, serves to lessen the effects of existential *angst*, he suggests. In this sense, our finitude is assuaged by the mark we make in life. However, for the culturally excluded, misrecognition is the defining experience. In existential terms, it is tantamount to an abnegation of self.
>
> (2002, p. 161)

This is an important passage, as it illustrates the significance of spirituality (recognition can be linked with connectedness and affirmation, as can the idea of having a 'designated place in the social world') and how, when those spiritual needs are not met (through cultural or social exclusion), the result can be detrimental to a person's identity (abnegation of self) and thus their well-being.

Voice of experience 13.2

I work with youngsters from very deprived backgrounds. They see all the bright lights and shiny new things that consumerism offers, but the only real chance they have to get anything like that is through crime.

So, our project is about teaching the kids how to get self-esteem and personal rewards linked to achievement without falling back on activities that will get them into trouble sooner or later. They have to get their recognition somewhere, so if they can't get it through legitimate means, they will get it through illegitimate means.

Sandy, a social worker in a community development project for young offenders

----

The question of being valued and affirmed is also important in relation to the workplace. The question of whether or not social workers are valued and affirmed by their employing organizations is an important one. Social work is a difficult and demanding job. It is therefore important that organizations support their staff rather than make the job more difficult. Unfortunately, managerialism can be seen to have had the effect (as noted earlier) of making the workplace a more bureaucratic and less trusting one. In this context, Clarke, Gewirtz and McLaughlin write about managerialist 'organizations being viewed as chains of low-trust relationships' (2000a, p. 6). The lack of trust seriously undermines the potential for employees (and the managers, who are also disempowered and demoralized by managerialism) to find meaning in their work. The workplace, then, should also be seen as a site of spiritual significance (Moss, 2007b; 2009).

Casey (2002) also discusses the significance of the workplace. She sees the emerging emphasis on spirituality as a reaction against changes in the workplace in recent years, changes that have made the workplace a less human and less satisfying place (see Ehrenreich, 2005; Stein, 2007; 2009). She argues that:

The manifest efforts in seeking expressions of self-identity, of spirituality, emotionality and meaningfulness occurring in organizational workplaces are signs of a wider cultural reaction against the totalizing ideology of modern, and postindustrial, productivism. The reduction of humans and their potentialities to instrumental resources as organizational producers and consumers is, in these new ways, being challenged from within, and beyond, the organizational sphere. Re-enchantment of one's own life at work is a new, and in the first instance non-political (that is, in the usual modern understanding of political expression), counter-practice.

(Casey, 2000, p. 173)

This can be seen as part of the emerging emphasis on workplace well-being (Bates and Thompson, 2007). An important lesson it can teach us is that we need to be aware of, and responsive to, our own spiritual needs.

Awe, wonder and hope

As was noted above, meaning, purpose, direction and connectedness are recognized as major features of spirituality, but it would be a mistake not to include discussion of other significant facets – namely, awe, wonder and hope. I shall comment on each of these in turn:

- *Awe.* This refers to a sense of specialness and privilege where we feel that we are in a situation that is out of the ordinary, where it is in some respect 'magic'. Children tend to have a much stronger sense of awe than adults; it is as if we lose part of our sense of awe as we grow up. We have to make sure that people's lives are not deprived of awe, for example, dependent older people whose lives can become a routine drudge if we are not careful.

- *Wonder.* This is about being captivated by the marvels of the world in which we live. It is about learning, growth and development. Again, these are factors that can be subdued or even removed altogether by people's social or personal circumstances.

- *Hope.* This is linked to trust which, of course, can be very fragile. Trust is unstable while mistrust is stable. What I mean by this is that, once trust is lost, it is very difficult to regain. Having relationships built on trust helps to provide hope for people. Social work can therefore be seen as a matter of (i) building on hope wherever we find it, making the most of whatever hope already exists; and (ii) trying to instil it where we do not find it – that is, helping to create hope where there is currently none or very little.

Practice focus 13.3

Sean had been taunted and bullied by boys at school and in the neighbourhood he lived in. He had entered a vicious circle. The more he was bullied, the more withdrawn he became, and the more withdrawn he became, the more he came to be seen as an easy target for the bullies. This went on for a long time, with Sean becoming increasingly depressed and withdrawn until he became suicidal and took an overdose of paracetamol tablets. Phil, a social worker who specialized in working with adolescents, was asked to work with Sean to try and ensure that he did not make any further attempts to take his own life. Once he had got to know Sean and had formed a picture of the situation, he felt that he needed something that would help to restore some hope to his life. He had used a facility with other teenagers in the past which offered a week-long camp in the mountains in which the participants were involved in a range of activities geared towards trying to give them some sense of awe and wonder. This was achieved by being close to nature and by having well-trained, experienced staff who were good at engaging with young people and getting them involved in activities, and they had a high success rate. Phil knew that this would not be a miracle cure, and that it would need to be supplemented by lots of other steps that would need to be taken, but he saw it as an important means of providing some of the spiritual nourishment Sean's (physically and emotionally) battered persona badly needed.

Clearly, all three of these are very important aspects of what it means to be human and that, of course, is precisely what spirituality is about. This in turn is precisely why spirituality is important in social work. If we are not tuned in to matters of spirituality, then we are failing to treat the people we seek to support in ways that do justice to their humanity. The relative neglect of spirituality in social work (in both theory and practice) is therefore a matter of considerable concern. Holloway links this with managerialism in arguing that:

In a service delivery culture driven by a focus on measurable outcomes and concerned to establish the evidence base for its practice, as is the case in the UK certainly, this is an obstacle to creating the culture in which social workers feel free to engage with spirituality.

(2006, p. 272)

She goes on to add that:

Perhaps one argument for introducing 'spirituality' into social work practice might be to act as the guardian of those core values and practice which are threatened by the market-driven service delivery culture in which social workers in most of Europe and North America currently operate.

(Holloway, 2006, p. 274)

There is certainly much to be said for linking spirituality to the value base of social work, as there are some very significant connections to be made (Moss, 2007a). In addition, I would argue that there is much to be gained from examining spirituality (and its role in helping) from an existentialist perspective (Thompson, 2007b), as there are many connecting threads and common themes.

Voice of experience 13.3

I attended a workshop on spirituality in social work at our local university. There were people from all over the country there and quite a strong wave of positive feeling towards the subject. I found the day really stimulating, inspirational in fact. We need far more days like that for putting spirituality on the social work map.

Gwenda, a social worker in a hospice

Conclusion

Over the decades, spirituality has been an area that has suffered from neglect in terms of receiving very little attention. However, there are now some very clear and positive signs that this situation is changing and the subject is beginning to be researched, explored and acted upon much more than was previously the case. While this is very much a step in the right direction, it has to be acknowledged that we still have a long way to go. Thus we can see that there clearly are excellent opportunities for theory development in relation to the role of spirituality in social work.

Indeed, a stronger emphasis on spirituality can be seen as more broadly helpful in developing not only the theory base of social work, but also the actual art of theorizing (or critically reflective practice, to put it another way). This is because spirituality is a dynamic concept, not just a fixed set of beliefs. It is about how we engage with the world, make sense of it, settle into our place within it (or challenge that place), relate to each other and to the demands of being a human being, with all the challenges that entails (what are often referred to as 'existential challenges'). Spirituality is an ongoing, evolving feature of our lives. Similarly, our understanding of what we do in social work, our *theorizing*, needs to be dynamic and evolving and not simply rooted in a static knowledge base or dogmatic set of assumptions. We could even go so far as to say that the challenge of theorizing social work, in the sense that I have been using it in this book, is in itself a spiritual challenge.

Points to ponder

1. What does the term 'spirituality' mean to you? How important is it in your life?
2. What dangers arise if, in our practice, we do not consider the role of spirituality in people's lives?
3. Why is hope such an important issue in social work?

Further reading

Moss (2005) is an excellent starting point. Coyte, Gilbert and Nicholls (2007) is an interesting set of readings. Brandon (2000) is also very important. Thompson (2007b) offers my perspective on the subject, with a particular focus on the spiritual aspects of loss and grief.

14

Developing emancipatory practice

Introduction

Social work has witnessed a historical development from a strong individualistic focus, based predominantly on psychodynamic thinking, to a much broader, more sociological perspective based on systems theory and, beyond this, to a more critical sociopolitical perspective based on a commitment to anti-discriminatory practice.

A strong element of theory in social work for some time now has been a focus on tackling discrimination and oppression in terms of promoting equality, valuing diversity and contributing to the development of social justice. It is this aspect of theory development that I shall be discussing here under the heading of 'Emancipatory practice'.

I shall look at two aspects of the legacy left to us by the radical social work movement. First I shall look at the positives that have emerged from this development from the late 1960s onwards, and then I shall consider the problems that have been associated with it. The discussion here builds on my analysis of these issues in *Practising Social Work* (2009a). It revisits similar themes and seeks to develop them further. This will lead on to a concluding discussion about the importance of developing emancipatory theory to such an extent that it does justice to the complexities involved.

The historical development we have witnessed has been very positive for the most part, bringing significant improvement and much higher levels of awareness, but there have also been problems associated with this. This chapter covers both the positive and negative aspects of developments in this area, so that we can be better informed when it comes to building on the former and avoiding the latter.

The radical social work legacy 1: The sociopolitical focus

Radical social work was very successful in getting sociopolitical factors onto the social work agenda. It came as quite a shock to the largely psychodynamically oriented establishment within social work in the late 1960s when quite a strong sociological and political emphasis was brought to bear, arguing in particular that issues of class, poverty and deprivation should be uppermost on the social work agenda. It helped to move away from judgemental notions, such as 'the problem family' or 'the dysfunctional family'. It helped also to move away from pathologizing individuals by no longer referring to them as 'maladjusted' or other such stigmatizing terminology. It achieved this movement by setting social work in the broader context of social problems, recognizing that these have structural, sociopolitical roots and are not simply the sum total of individual problems. (See Thompson, 2009a, Chapter 2.)

Practice focus 14.1

Gareth had been brought up in a middle-class family in a very pleasant village close to a large town. He had read about poverty and seen documentaries on television, but he had never really encountered it directly. One of the main reasons he had decided to go into social work was that his aunt was a counsellor and he felt that he could use the insights he had gained from her in helping a wide range of people. However, on the first placement of his social work degree he was working with a team that covered some very deprived areas of a nearby town. The more time he spent 'on the patch', the more he could see how prevalent poverty and deprivation were, how insidiously undermining they were, and how they were such an obstacle for people who wanted to find their way in the world. He found the whole thing quite disheartening. He began to feel quite guilty that he had had such a privileged upbringing and had never experienced any of the privations he saw as characteristic of the areas he was now working in on the placement. He discussed this with his practice teacher who was very helpful and supportive. She told him that guilt was a negative emotion that gets in the way of progress and she encouraged him to put those negative feelings behind him and develop a positive commitment to doing something about the problems – in effect, to translate the guilt into a passion for making a difference. Gareth found this very helpful and it freed him up from the feelings that were paralysing him, so that he could look now at how he could make sure that his career in social work was part of wider efforts to address the social problems that have their roots in poverty and deprivation.

Radical social work emphasized the significance of social divisions and, from this, the processes of unfair discrimination that give rise to oppression. By criticizing the individualistic focus of traditional social work, radical perspectives set the scene for the development of a much broader perspective on social work. In particular, radical social work laid the foundations for:

- *Working in partnership.* Radical social work helped us to leave behind the major focus on a medicalized approach to social work, with its use of medical terminology, such as diagnosis and treatment (rather than the now widely used assessment and intervention). Instead of adopting an elitist approach to professionalism that was based on the idea of 'We are the professionals; we know best', radical social work established the baseline for working alongside clients, engaging with them as far as possible on equal terms in a spirit of partnership (Thompson, 2009a, Ch 14).
- *Empowerment.* Instead of pathologizing individuals and seeing their difficulties as being within them, as if they were some sort of personal inadequacy, radical social work helped to strengthen the move towards a focus on helping people appreciate the often social roots of the difficulties they encountered. The idea behind this was that they would be in a better position to take greater control over their circumstances, both individually through greater levels of awareness of what was happening to them, and collectively through potential political action. Smith and Drower link this to the notion of resilience:

> Links may also be made between resilience and an *empowerment approach.* In the narrowest sense, empowerment connotes only a psychological and personal sense of well-being; it is depoliticized and not useful for institutional change. However, when including the concept of liberation in describing those processes and objectives that challenge oppression, empowerment is restored to its intended meaning.
>
> (2008, p. 146)

If we replace 'liberation' with 'emancipation', then this comment fits perfectly with what this chapter is all about. What it amounts to, in effect, is a critique of (i) medicalized approaches that do not engage with empowerment at all; and (ii) atomistic approaches to empowerment that recognize only the personal levels and not the cultural or structural (Thompson, 2007a). This is an important theme to which we shall return below.

- *Anti-discriminatory practice.* This became a core element of social work, largely but not exclusively as a result of the influence of the radical social work movement. The need to take account of discrimination as a factor in people's lives in general and the problems and unmet needs they are experiencing in particular, as well as the potential for our own actions (or inactions) to be discriminatory has been a mainstay of the social work value base for some time now. However, it was not always so. For very many years issues of discrimination did not feature in the mainstream of theory or practice in social work. In a sense, radical social work laid the foundations for developing anti-discriminatory practice by (i) critiquing atomism (although they did not use that specific term at the time); and (ii) raising awareness of the major impact of wider sociopolitical factors on people's lives, including the structural inequalities that lie at the heart of much of the discrimination oppressed groups encounter. The original emphasis of radical social work was on class and poverty, but later developments extended the analysis to incorporate a wider range of structural inequalities (gender, age, disability and so on).

All these points add up to paint a picture of an important movement in British social work which has parallels in other countries as well, although often to a lesser extent. The positives that we have gained from this are a weakening of some highly problematic aspects of traditional social work and a much clearer focus on recognizing the psychosocial nature of social work problems. Radical social work helped to make it clear that it is no coincidence that the term 'social work' begins with the word *social.*

Voice of experience 14.1

I did my Master's dissertation on the history of social work and I could not get over how individualistic and psychodynamic social work used to be. I came into the profession when anti-discriminatory practice and the need for a critical, sociological approach were firmly on the agenda and I suppose I took it for granted that it had always been like that. Just shows how wrong you can be. It is well worth dipping into some

of the older social work texts if you can get hold of them, just to see
how things have moved on.

**April, a social worker in a child and adolescent
mental health team**

It is clear, then, that radical social work was an important driving
force for today's more sociologically informed understandings of the
nature and purpose of social work – its moral-political basis as we
called it in Chapter 10. However, these developments were not
entirely positive or productive. The following passage from Parekh
casts some light on this:

> the politics of collective identity is a mixed blessing. It establishes soli-
> darity among marginalized groups, empowers them, gives focus and
> moral energy to their cause, and challenges and opens up the possibility
> of pluralizing the dominant culture. It also, however, has a tendency to
> become narrow, exclusive, authoritarian, positivist and to replace one
> form of domination by another that is no better and sometimes even
> worse. Since struggles are crucial for social change and often require
> organized groups with clear objectives, collective identities are a neces-
> sary part of political life. This raises the question of how to retain what
> is valuable in the politics of collective identity while avoiding its dangers.
>
> (2008, p. 37)

Parekh captures well what I too see as the challenge facing us: to build
on the positives but to avoid the negatives. In order to help us move in
that direction, I shall now give an overview of some of the problems
that have arisen from the influence of radical social work – or, to be
more precise, from the distortions of the radical social work project
that have marred its original promise. As I see it, there is nothing
inherently wrong with radical social work *per se*; the problems have
arisen from how it has been interpreted by many people in oversimplified and dogmatic ways.

The radical social work legacy 2: Dogmatic reductionism

Although there were clearly benefits that emerged from the fresh
insights radical social work brought, these came at a price and that
price was, in effect, what I shall refer to here as dogmatic reduction-

ism. In principle, what I mean by this is a tendency to adopt a very rigid and oversimplified perspective on some very complex issues. I shall discuss each of these aspects, the dogmatism and the reductionism, in turn.

Dogma

Within the radical social work movement in its heyday, there was often little scope for debate or analysis of the complexities involved. Variation from what quickly became the established orthodoxy was labelled as 'reactionary' and therefore seen as unwelcome. For example, there was considerable dogma around the issues of language use. Many people were required to attend training courses, on which they were given handouts on what came to be known as 'politically correct' terminology. These handouts simply listed taboo words to be avoided and preferable alternatives, generally with little or no debate or analysis about the nature of language or how certain forms of language could reinforce discrimination. The net result of this was to a large extent people becoming 'tongue tied' about what they said, fearing the consequences of saying the wrong word or using the wrong terminology unwittingly. In a sense, this misguided, unsubtle approach to language use had the effect of encouraging avoidance behaviour, a mentality of 'Let's only go there if we have to'. It was more of a block to learning than a means of facilitating it. Premised on the mistaken assumption that 'no pain, no gain' is a helpful approach to learning, what was actually produced was a situation of 'too much pain, no learning due to the defensiveness it instils' (see the discussion of the Yerkes-Dodson law of adult learning in Thompson, 2006c).

The training and, indeed, the handling of the issues more generally, tended to be quite confrontational much of the time. Such a confrontational approach created considerable tensions that have proved quite costly, not only in terms of blocking learning, but also as a result of the effect of distracting attention from the underlying, very significant issues of how language can play a key role in perpetuating discrimination and oppression (Thompson, 2003b).

This was strongly contrary to what today we would call critically reflective practice. It was certainly critical up to a point, but it was far from reflective, and the critical element was a dogmatic one, and therefore, ironically, could be criticized for being uncritical – that is, many people involved in the movement adopted a politically critical perspective, but did so without giving sufficient consideration to the implications of this, and therefore fell into the trap of adopting the dogma uncritically. Healy argues: 'Poststructural theorists call into question the authoritarianism that lies, often unrecognized, in emancipatory practice theories' (2000, p. 38). This is an important point, although it is not necessary to embrace post-structuralist thinking to recognize the problems and dangers associated with an overzealous, illiberal approach to the challenges of tackling discrimination and oppression.

Practice focus 14.2

Gemma was a newly qualified social worker who had recently joined a very experienced team in a large child care voluntary organization. She got on very well with her colleagues and was delighted that they had a wealth of experience that she could tap into. One day, she was talking to three of her colleagues while they were having their sandwiches together at lunchtime. The subject of language and discrimination came up in conversation. One of her colleagues gave an example of her experiences of attending a training course in the early stages of her career that ended in chaos because the way the issues were handled created so much tension in the group, and the trainer's quite rigid approach only served to make it worse. Gemma was amazed to hear about this, but she was even more amazed to hear her other two colleagues give similar examples of a very heavy-handed, confrontational approach to issues relating to discrimination in general, but in relation to language use in particular. The upside of the situation, though, was that her colleagues were keen to learn from Gemma about the much more sophisticated approach that had been taken to language and discrimination issues on her degree course. This made Gemma feel good that she was, in part, returning the favour for the great deal of learning she had gained from them.

Reductionism

As we noted in Chapter 1, reductionism is a form of oversimplification. It involves taking complex multi-level issues and presenting them as if they were relatively straightforward single-level issues. One example of this to begin with was the emphasis on class in the earlier forms of radical social work, where it was argued that socioeconomic class is the primary factor in creating inequality in society, and is therefore the basis of discrimination and oppression (Corrigan and Leonard, 1978). Critiques from both feminists and anti-racist activists helped to move us beyond this form of class-based reductionism (Ahmad, 1990; Ungerson, 1985). However, in many ways, that was replaced by feminist and anti-racist forms of reductionism. There was therefore a parallel with the first wave of attention given to issues of discrimination and oppression: a lot of important insights were gleaned and we were able to develop a much more sophisticated understanding of the role and significance of gender, not only in people's lives in general, but also more specifically in relation to the problems they were experiencing that brought them to our professional attention.

Verkeuyten comments in particular on the tendency to allow essentialism (the idea of people being fixed entities rather than evolving processes, as discussed in Chapter 1) to creep into the way the issues were conceived and dealt with: 'anti-racism and critical social analyses have been criticized for subverting their own anti-essentialist project by defining majority group members as essentially oppressive and racist (Bonnett, 2000)' (2003, p. 388). The worst manifestations of this essentialism were outrageously simplistic comments that almost gained the status of slogans for a while: 'If you are white, you must be racist'; 'All men are rapists' and 'The problem is white men'. Now, some 20 to 30 years later, the idea that such views were being voiced in social work strains credibility, but that is in fact what happened.

The great irony here is that these problems were arising from social work (quite rightly) adopting a more sociological approach to its subject matter, and yet the direction many people were taking, the supposedly sociologically informed thinking, ran counter to what sociology has taught us about the workings of society, of power and related matters. No credible sociologist would have embraced such an oversimplified view of social issues. It was no surprise that many sociologists criticized this aspect of social work. For example, Roger Sibeon has been a consistent critic of the reductionist tendencies in social work thinking over a long period of time (Sibeon, 1991). He is also critical of attempts to combine forms of reductionism – for example, where efforts have been made to link different forms of discrimination together in ways that fail to do justice to the complexities involved in either – let alone in how they interrelate (Sibeon, 2004).

There were also unfortunate elements of essentialism appearing in the literature, with phrases like 'white racist social workers ...'

grossly oversimplifying some very subtle and intricate issues. This tendency added to the major concerns being felt at that time about whether it was safe to address such issues. The major consequence of this use of essentialist terminology was people avoiding what they saw as territory that was far too threatening. A key part of this was the unfortunate tendency to make do with paying lip service to issues of discrimination and oppression, because to engage with them at a deeper, more meaningful level was seen as too threatening. This again contributed to a fairly widespread reliance on avoidance behaviour.

Voice of experience 14.2

I used to work in a team where you just didn't dare open your mouth for fear of saying the wrong thing. I am so much happier in my current team where we discuss issues openly and supportively. We are all aware of how easy it is to slip into making discriminatory assumptions, but we see that as a learning issue for us all and not something to get uptight about. Getting uptight doesn't help anyone.

Colin, a social worker in an access team

Thankfully, there are now clear signs that we are moving away from the impact of the dogmatic reductionism that was an unfortunate and unintended by-product of the radical social work movement and what flowed from it. We still have problems associated with elements of both dogma and reductionism that become apparent at times, but it is a positive development that we are now able to note that such problems appear to be getting less frequent and significant as time goes on, with more and more people entering the profession who were not subject to the frightening levels of anxiety that were once associated with dogmatic reductionism. The problem, then, has not completely gone away, and we still have to be on our guard, but there is room for cautious optimism in terms of establishing more flexible and more sophisticated understandings of discrimination and oppression that can provide a solid foundation for a realistic approach to tackling the problems involved – without watering down our commitment to emancipatory forms of practice. We will also need to ensure that, in moving away from dogmatic reductionism, we do not go too far in the opposite direction and reintroduce the naive complacency that radical social work so vehemently attacked (Thompson, 2009e).

Developing emancipatory theory

The task of developing emancipatory theory is a major one, and so I cannot realistically expect to do full justice to the issues in one relatively short chapter. However, what I can more realistically do is to summarize what I see as some key issues as a potential platform from which to develop fuller understandings over time of the issues raised.

Developing PCS analysis

My own work has contributed to this area in a number of ways, primarily the development of PCS analysis as a contribution to developing a theory of anti-discriminatory practice. This topic has been well covered elsewhere, and so I shall not repeat the issues here. However, at its simplest, it is a matter of noting that discrimination and oppression are highly complex matters and therefore need to be considered in terms of the three levels of analysis: personal, cultural and structural, and of equal importance, how those three levels interact. For example, I have discussed elsewhere the importance of the notion of the 'double dialectic' (Thompson, 2003a). This refers to the way in which there is one set of dialectical interactions between personal and cultural factors and a further dialectic operating between the cultural and structural factors, resulting in a highly complex set of interactions that create a much more complex situation than radical social work thinking gave credence to.

PCS analysis has informed much of the discussion in this book, as in many of my other writings. It is also widely used by many others, whether as a teaching tool to assist learners or as a theoretical model to develop understanding. However, there remains considerable scope for developing this analytical tool a great deal further, as it offers a useful way of appreciating the complexities involved in discrimination and oppression.

Beyond postmodernism

I have also written elsewhere about the steps that need to be taken towards developing a theory of emancipatory practice (see, for example, Thompson, 1997). However, it is important to note that progress towards such goals has been seriously hampered by the growth of interest in postmodernist thinking, due to the fact that this approach to theory regards emancipation as not a feasible goal. As I have mentioned earlier, some writers argue for a watered-down version of postmodernism that allows scope for emancipation, but I argued in Chapter 2 that this represents an unrealistic undertaking as a consequence of the fact that this is a contradictory perspective to adopt.

Houston is also critical of the adoption of postmodernist thinking, particularly its emphasis on the cultural level at the expense of the attention that needs to be paid to the structural level:

> If the social work profession fails to grasp this point – that culture is inextricably tied to capitalism's evolution – then its sensitivity and competence will be undermined. Put in another way, if we view culture through a postmodern lens there is a danger of reducing our analysis to linguistic narratives, signs and disembodied discourses. The cost is palpable because what is at stake is the effects of material reality, of class conflict, work-induced alienation, polluted environments and, lastly, loss of contact with the corporeal domain. Culture, Bourdieu reminds us, may provide the ground for symbolic interaction, but it is also a source of domination and power relations which serve to reproduce institutionalized hierarchies.
>
> (2002, p. 153)

What Houston's important comments reflect is that the progress made by radical social work's focus on the inequalities deriving from social structures has been largely eclipsed by the postmodernist rejection of structural factors in favour of a concern with how discourses operate at the cultural level. This reflects my concerns voiced in Chapter 1 that progress in developing our understanding is hampered by the competitive operation of theoretical 'clubs'. The postmodernist club wins the battle for popularity against the marxist-influenced radical club, instead of the cultural and structural insights of both perspectives influencing each other to broaden and deepen our understanding.

Practice focus 14.3

Paula was a social worker in a children's centre. A major part of her job was forming links with the local community with the aim of being able to support parents in bringing up children in difficult circumstances. Her work had shown her that much of the difficulty families encountered was linked to structural factors to do with poverty, social exclusion and racism – and, for some of the mothers she worked with, sexism was also an issue, especially in relation to domestic violence. However, when the centre had an inspection she was surprised to note that one of the inspectors was dismissive of the team's emphasis on structural factors and was more interested in cultural issues – how, for example, a culture of poverty could be seen to be operating in the local community. In discussion with the inspector, Paula made a comment to the effect that she did not want their focus on structural aspects to be lost. The inspector described her approach as 'outmoded' and said that the discourses that feed into the local culture were what they should be focusing on. Paula was dismayed by this. Why can't we take account of cultural *and* structural factors? Why do we have to choose between the two?

Although some would see existentialism as just another club vying for dominance, this would be a misrepresentation of the existentialist position I am advocating here. Existentialism is not a closed theoretical system. It has the potential to incorporate competing perspectives dialectically (and through the use of the existentialist concept of paradox, the technical complexities of which need not concern us here).

Existentialist realism

Postmodernism's pessimism about the potential for emancipation in particular has served to hamper progress when it comes to theoretical development. While the postmodernist rejection of coherence, as discussed in Chapter 11, undermines the very notion of theory development in general, its view that emancipation is not a legitimate goal to aim for stands in the way specifically of the development of *emancipatory* theory.

An existentialist understanding of discrimination and oppression is that they have developed historically through human actions (de Beauvoir, 1972; Fanon, 2008; Sartre, 1969; 1982) and can therefore change through human actions. This is not to say that they will simply disappear if we want them to – the reality is far more complex than that. However, it does mean that an attitude of pessimism is not called for. As Clarke points out:

To the extent that strategies don't work as intended and people fail to come when they're called, domination is always fragile, always needs to be reproduced, always needs to search for better, more efficient and effective ways of securing its rule.

(2004, p. 159)

This short but informative passage tells us that there is scope for positive change. Marx recognized that the seeds of the destruction of oppressive systems are to be found within those systems, although he was not able to envisage the developments at a structural level that have occurred since his day that protect those seeds of destruction from being nurtured. The potential for change is none the less there.

Once again it is a matter of *realism*, in the sense of a healthy balance between the unhelpful extremes of cynical pessimism and defeatism on the one hand and a naive, rose-tinted optimism on the other. Healy's view is instructive. She argues that: 'Postmodernists reject visions of massive social transition as a chimera [an unrealistic ideal] and demand, instead, greater caution and constraint in the formation of critical practice objectives and processes' (2000, p. 2). I commented, in response to her earlier comment that post-structuralists are wary of the potential for authoritarianism within emancipatory theory, by saying that it is not only post-structuralists who are wary of claims to massive social change. I would want to make a similar point here. I agree with the thrust of what Healy is saying, but would not see this as being specifically a postmodernist insight. For example, Sartre (1982) argued, long before postmodernism was on the scene, that understanding of the shape, scope and scale of social change has to be developed through a dialectically informed understanding of the situation as it unfolds. It cannot realistically be left to a simple, generalized or non-specific approach to major social change.

This can be linked to his notion of 'counterfinality' (Sartre, 1969) – that is, the potentially disastrous unintended consequences of acting in a particular way without thinking through in detail the potentially very detrimental outcomes arising from the steps taken. In other words, a counterfinality is a situation that backfires on us. The bigger the step we take, the bigger the risk of a counterfinality, and so major social transformation brings enormous risks that have to be thought through very carefully and handled with caution.

Voice of experience 14.3

There is a need for clarity about the politics of what we are doing. We are not just putting sticking plasters on gaping wounds, but nor is it a case of just sitting back and spouting about 'come the revolution'. It's not that simple. We need to be clear about where we are trying to get to and then make sure that we take people with us, not replace one authoritarianism with another.

Martina, a service user participation development worker

An existentially realist view would therefore reject both extremes of, on the one hand, a simplistic and idealistic call to revolution (the optimistic end of the spectrum) and, on the other, a postmodernist rejection of emancipation as a realistic goal (the pessimistic end of the spectrum). Realism helps us to recognize that we can make progress in challenging discriminatory and oppressive practices, assumptions and structures, but that such change need to be worked towards over time. It is a matter of 'revolutionary' practice in the sense of working towards the full range of changes needed to end the institutionalized discrimination and inequality embedded within our cultures and structures, rather than simply settling for superficial changes that do not get to the heart of the matter.

Individuality without individualism

One of the major themes of postmodernist and post-structuralism is the rejection of the 'sovereign subject', the traditional essentialist notion of the individual self. However, as Craib comments:

> One does not have to be a postmodernist to recognize that most of us inhabit multiple roles involving different sorts of behaviour and a constant process of negotiation. The self fulfils these roles and negotiates between them and is not a simple entity.
>
> (1998, p. 112)

One (further) criticism of postmodernism is that it does not have an adequately developed model of the self. In his earlier works, Foucault seemed to reject the idea of self altogether. However, in his later works, he acknowledges the importance of such matters when he starts to discuss 'technologies of the self' (Martin, 1998).

One of the points emphasized in Chapter 4 was that identity or selfhood is a very important concept (in social life generally, but especially in social work), but that it needs to be understood as (i) fluid rather than fixed, a self 'process' rather than a set personality; and (ii) shaped in large part by interactions with others, culture and structure (in other words, the self is necessarily a *social* self – our identity is not what separates us off from society but, rather, what makes us part of society). What is needed, then, is a much fuller understanding of the individual in terms of his or her self or identity which recognizes their uniqueness (individuality), without neglecting the wider social aspects of that unique identity (that is, not falling into the trap of *individualism*, or what I have preferred to call 'atomism'). Casey's comments cover similar terrain:

> Touraine's subject and its process of *subjectivation* is clearly differentiated from *subjectification*, which is at the heart of Foucault's criticism of the subject; and from naive individualism that does not recognize social determinants or that dissolves the subject into the rationality of economic choices.
>
> (2002, p. 190)

'Subjectivation' refers to the process of developing a self, becoming a unique individual (what Bauman, 2001, refers to as 'individuation'), while 'subjectification' refers to the process through which individuals are made 'subjects' – that is, rendered insubordinate and thus subject to relations of dominance that lock them into less powerful positions. This captures nicely how wider social issues can, through the subtle workings of discourse, create 'willing slaves', people who accept without protest a position of subordination which is ultimately against their own interests.

Forte adds a further dimension of complexity when he comments, in relation to the work of Wolf (1990), that: 'Reflexive legitimation is her term for internalizing an identity as inferior and internalizing a set of meanings designating the oppressive social arrangements as appropriate' (2001, p. 274). I have elsewhere referred to this as 'internalized oppression' (Thompson, 2006a). The area relating to selfhood and identity, its links with discrimination and oppression, and its significance for social work is one that merits much fuller attention than it has been given to date, and so we can identify this as another significant area for theory development – and one on which existentialism has the potential to cast a great deal of light.

Reclaiming existentialism

In terms of taking forward our understanding of the steps that can be taken towards making social work practice a form of emancipatory practice I would argue that we need to 'reclaim' existentialism. By this I mean two forms of development: one is to reclaim existentialism from marxism. By seeking to merge existentialism with marxist thinking, Sartre succeeded in showing that existentialism is capable of being a holistic perspective that takes account of sociopolitical factors and is not simply an individualistic perspective. However, Sartre in my view, took this project too far, in so far as he sought to submerge existentialism within marxism, rather than to incorporate some of the key insights from marxism into existentialism. Sartre's adoption of the structural and dialectical elements of marxism have enriched earlier versions of existentialism and is therefore, in my view, something to be welcomed. However, a marxist approach without existentialism as a counterbalance has a tendency (i) to dehumanize and become deterministic; and (ii) to become reductionist (see Thompson, 1992, for a fuller discussion of these issues).

There is therefore a need to revisit existentialism as a sociopolitical philosophy without returning to the traditional notion of existentialism as an individualistic concern. Second, we need to reclaim existentialism from postmodernism. For example, even though, as I have indicated earlier, so many of the (valuable) key themes of postmodernist thinking have their roots in existentialism, one postmodernist, Hollinger (1994), simply dismisses existentialism as 'modernist', without any further explanation or justification.

Conclusion

What should be clear from this chapter is that significant progress has been made since the early radical social work days, but we still have a long way to go in terms of developing both emancipatory theory and emancipatory practice. Whatever steps we take, though, we need to take together in a spirit of partnership and mutual support, not one of competitiveness and division. I share Parekh's view of how we can helpfully move forward:

> One of my main concerns is to argue that we need to approach our problems in the spirit of human solidarity, and that this requires us to ener-

gize and consolidate our shared humanity, or what I call our human identity. Identity politics has so far been defined and conducted in terms of particular collective identities, such as those based on gender, ethnicity and nationality. While this is important, it is just as crucial to affirm our universal human identity, locate particular identities within its framework, and engage in what I call a new politics of identity.

(2008, p. 2)

There are, of course, no easy answers, no formula solutions to rely on, just a whole host of highly complex factors that we need to wrestle with if we are to be equipped to make sense of what we have to deal with. Social work values have at their heart a commitment to promoting equality and social justice – an especially important consideration, given that social work's clientele is to be found mainly in social groups who are particularly prone to discrimination and the oppressive degradation that goes with it. We have suffered from simplistic approaches to these complex issues. We now need a more sophisticated approach, theoretically, politically and pragmatically.

Points to ponder

1. Why is it important for social work to have a sociopolitical focus?
2. What are the dangers of oversimplifying issues relating to discrimination and oppression?
3. How can PCS analysis be used to inform practice?

Further reading

My own work has had a major focus on these issues – see, for example, Thompson (2003a; 2006a; 2007a). Mullaly (2002) is also helpful, as is Moss (2007a). Other useful texts include: Baker, Lynch, Cantillon and Walsh (2004); Crowley (2006); Ferguson (2007); Ferguson and Woodward (2009); Kallen (2004); Price and Simpson (2007); Tew (2002); and Wilkinson and Pickett (2009).

15

The challenges we face

Introduction

This final chapter serves two purposes. It acts as a conclusion to Part
Three, with its emphasis on theory *development* and also as a conclusion to the whole book, with its emphasis on *theorizing practice*. The
chapter is in four parts. First, we revisit the theme of the nature of
theory and theorizing. Next, we examine how theory relates to the
current demands of practice and look in particular at the National
Occupational Standards for social work. Third, I summarize the
particular issues arising in Part Three as they relate to the need for
theory development. Finally, I summarize how I see existentialism as
a (meta)theoretical foundation for not only meeting the requirements
of a well-informed, critically reflective practice, but also for developing
the underlying theory base over time.

Theory, theorizing, knowledge and truth

The need to 'apply theory to practice' has haunted generations of
students and practitioners who have been misled into thinking that
there can be a direct link between the two – what Schön (1983)
referred to as the 'technical rationality' approach. The development of
reflective practice has shown us that what is required is a much more
sophisticated understanding of the relationship between theory and
practice – it is not simply a matter of taking one and 'applying' it to
the other. It is more a case of integrating the two, of theory informing
practice, while practice is also informing and testing theory
(Thompson, 2000a; S. Thompson and N. Thompson, 2008).

Theories are basically attempts to explain. They need to be systematic (that is, not random, disconnected or incoherent), but not 'systematized' (that is, rigid and overly formalistic). They help us to establish 'truths', but not *the* Truth in any absolute or overall sense. They can be flawed and misguided (see the discussion in Chapter 1) and therefore have to be evaluated quite rigorously, rather than uncritically accepted ('It must be true, it said so in the textbook'). They can also offer extremely important and valuable insights that can be exceptionally helpful in dealing with the highly complex, multi-level situations that are characteristic of much of social work practice.

Theory, then, provides a foundation of professional knowledge, a set of understandings that illuminate particular aspects of human psychology, social life, personal and social problems, and so on. The knowledge base is growing and changing all the time due to the publication of policy papers, theoretical analyses and research studies (especially those research studies that draw out the lessons to be learned from actual practice). This formal knowledge base is supplemented by the informal knowledge base that practitioners build up over time from their own experience and insights (what is often called 'practice wisdom'). It has the disadvantage of being less rigorous and therefore potentially flawed or biased, but its strong point is its authenticity – it has arisen from, and is directly applicable to, actual practice situations. It is not at one step removed, as the formal knowledge base inevitably is. It is therefore potentially very valuable, but again needs to be used *critically* and reflectively and not just used unthinkingly or dogmatically.

This professional knowledge base – the theory base – is therefore an important foundation for making sure that our practice is *informed* practice and is not just based on guesswork, habit, copying others or just random chance. But simply having a knowledge base available to us is not enough. We have to be able to use it. As mentioned above, the traditional idea has been an expectation that professionals 'apply' theory to practice – that is, start with theory and head towards practice. The approach taken in this book has been very different from that, in so far as it is premised on the idea of starting with practice and then draw on the knowledge base to suit the circumstances of the situation (what situation am I in here? What knowledge do I need to help me make sense of it and deal with it effectively?). In a sense, this is a process of *operationalizing* theory, rather than 'applying' it.

What knowledge is needed and accessed will, of course, vary from situation to situation, and this then becomes the basis of critically reflective practice. The practitioner is called upon to work out how best to respond to the challenges and demands of the situation in hand, to be, as Krill (1978) aptly termed it many years ago, a 'spontaneous strategist'. This is where the idea of 'theorizing' comes in. Instead of simply having the noun of 'theory' (the actual knowledge base itself), we also need the verb of 'theorizing' – the actual process of drawing on that knowledge base to make sense of the situations we encounter, putting the theory to work, as it were. This involves:

1. *Being familiar with the knowledge base.* Trying to manage complex situations without an adequate level of understanding of what is involved is potentially disastrous. Imagine, for example, a social worker trying to deal with a child protection case without an adequate understanding of child abuse.
2. *Keeping our knowledge up to date.* The knowledge base is changing all the time and so, to make sure that we are basing our work on the best available understanding, we need to make sure that we do not allow our knowledge to become static and stagnant. A good example of this is grief theory. The idea that people grieve in stages was once the recognized wisdom, but in recent years that approach has been discredited (see the discussion in Thompson, 2002a), and yet I regularly encounter people who are still basing their work on what has now been shown to be an unhelpful way of understanding what happens to a person when they are grieving
3. *Using analytical skills.* Being able to 'operationalize' theory – that is, being able to work out what knowledge is needed and when – involves being able to use analytical skills. Some social workers will have developed these through their general life skills development – for example, through their experiences of education – while others will need to work at developing them (for example, by attending relevant training courses where available, seeking the support of a supervisor or other mentor and/or reading up on the subject – see, for example, Cottrell, 2005).
4. *Using practice skills.* This applies in two senses. First, we need the skills of being sufficiently 'tuned in' to the subtleties of the situations we are dealing with, to have the pragmatic skills of engaging with the people and their issues that we are concerned with. Second, we need the presence of mind to be able to think through situations as we are dealing with them, to 'think on our feet' as it were. This is what Schön called 'reflection in action'. It also links in

well with what I referred to earlier as being a 'spontaneous strategist' (Krill, 1978).

5. *Having confidence and self-belief.* None of the above will be much use if we do not have at least a basic level of confidence and self-belief. Social work is an important undertaking, and so those of us who are involved in it have to have a degree of faith, individually and collectively, in the value of what we do and our ability to do it. If we do not have faith in ourselves, we cannot expect other people (clients, carers, other professionals, managers, policy makers and politicians and the general public) to have faith in us either.

Theorizing practice, then, is a skilled activity, and we would do well to devote the necessary time and attention to developing those skills as fully as we reasonably can.

To develop those skills, and especially to develop the confidence and self-belief, it is important that we work together, that we support each other in our personal and professional endeavours. Folgheraiter not only captures the significance of this in the following passage, where he discusses the importance of 'networking' (that is, working in partnership), but also goes a step further in suggesting that this is a necessary way of engaging with theory:

> networking – the authentic social relation with reciprocal learning among the parties involved in the helping processes, not the unilateral application of some theory or some technique – is the real key to 'success' in social work.
>
> (2004, p. 22)

Practice focus 15.1

Hannah was a social worker in a multidisciplinary mental health team. At first when she joined the team she felt very nervous and unconfident, as she was the youngest and least experienced member of the team. She was particularly concerned about getting things wrong and showing gaps in her knowledge. However, she was soon reassured about this, as the team members proved very helpful in supporting her, making suggestions and generally doing a great job of creating an atmosphere of collaboration and mutual support. What was particularly helpful was when Simon, a very experienced community psychiatric nurse in the team, told her about his anxieties when he first joined the team and how they had proven to be unfounded. 'We all know something', he said 'and nobody knows everything, so we will all do

---

better if we pool our knowledge and help each other learn, rather than compete with one another or pull rank based on experience.' Hannah knew of friends she had known from university who were not so lucky and were working in teams where people were precious about their knowledge and kept it to themselves.

The demands of practice

If theory is to develop over time, then it needs to remain attuned to the needs of actual practice, while also adopting a critical perspective on the practice world. A good example of this is the development of managerialism in recent years. It has presented new challenges to social work practice, given that maintaining professional approaches in an environment that is becoming increasingly bureaucratic is quite difficult (Ferguson, 2008; Thompson, 2009a; 2009b). However, there are also challenges to social work theory. How can our knowledge base be developed to respond to the challenges of managerialism without becoming a managerialist theory? In other words, how can the theory be relevant to today's challenges while also retaining a critical edge in addressing those challenges?

One aspect of managerialism has been the development of National Occupational Standards in social work in the UK. These involve the need for social workers to fulfil six key roles (see below). Having the basis of our work predefined by governmental bodies is a relatively new phenomenon, but is increasingly becoming the norm for professional groups.

One danger is that these standards, which are intended to be the *minimum* standards of professional practice, become the targets for people to aim for. For example, I have already come across many students whose concerns about their practice on placement revolve primarily if not exclusively around the national occupational standards. What we should be aiming for is professionally defined *optimal* standards and recognize the occupational standards as the bare minimum. I shall return to this point below when I consider how theory development can be related to these standards.

Managerialism is part of what Grint refers to as the 'audit society', with its bureaucratic emphasis on counting and measuring and makes the important point that:

The development of the 'audit society' (Power, 1999), itself rooted in 'the tyranny of numbers' (Boyle, 2001) has various manifestations of the debilitating effect of conformance, including universities who concentrate on satisfying government demands rather than those of their profession (research and teaching), hospitals that shift resources around in time to comply with specific medical audits rather than concentrate on medical improvements, and the removal of non-ISO 9000-registered companies from authorized suppliers' lists. In sum, achieving the *required* results may not be the equivalent of achieving the *desired* results and the same shift from trust to conformity often inhibits leadership.

> (2005, p. 67)

Theory development therefore needs to respond to the challenges presented by the significant shift in an audit-led, low-trust, deprofessionalizing direction. This is because having a professional knowledge base is an essential part of professionalism. If we are to safeguard our professionalism in the face of bureaucratizing tendencies, then we need to make sure that the knowledge base is as sound as it can be and as fully geared up to addressing the challenges of managerialism as it reasonably can be.

This also involves reaffirming professionalism, especially forms of professionalism premised on partnership and empowerment rather than elitism (Duyvendak, Knijn and Kremer, 2006b; Thompson, 2007a; 2009a). Part of this is revisiting the idea of expertise. In the days of radical social work, professionalism came to be seen as a dirty word and the idea of being an 'expert' was dismissed as elitist and disempowering. However, this was an oversimplification of some very complex issues. What was (and still is) needed was expertise in engaging with people at the levels of partnership, expertise in problem solving in general, and contributing to the facilitation of empowerment in particular. As Parton and O'Byrne put it:

> But, as Cade (1992) writes, 'the role of expert can be taken in a way that doesn't disempower' (p. 30). He takes the view that he is an expert mainly in what does *not work*, and that what *does work* is 'infinitely more varied and personal than anyone could possibly imagine'.
>
> (2000, p. 68)

The question of expertise and therefore 'expert' status is clearly a complex one and we do not have sufficient space here to address it fully. However, for present purposes, we need to note that the demands of practice require a degree of expertise and professional knowledge from us. Managerialism has sought to undermine our professionalism, and so what is needed now is a reaffirmation of professionalism in general and of the vitally important role of professional knowledge in particular.

Voice of experience 15.1

I have been in social work for 20 years now and there has always been the challenge of stopping the bureaucratic elements from taking over. But it is worse than ever these days, so I am hoping that, as a group of committed professionals, we will be able to resist the push in the direction of conformity and hold on to our professional values and our professional pride. It's a big ask, but the alternative doesn't bear thinking about.

Marcia, a social worker in a child protection team

If we now return to the subject of the National Occupational Standards, we can briefly outline some of the theoretical developments that can help to ensure that practice goes beyond the minimum standards towards the optimal standards wherever possible. Let us now look at each of the key roles in turn:

1. **Prepare for, and work with individuals, families, carers, groups and communities to assess their needs and circumstances**

   At a bare minimum level this can be done mechanistically without any real engagement with the client or carers as human beings. There is already a wealth of literature around the knowledge, skills and values that can be used to 'engage' with people in a meaningful way and to work in genuine partnership. Some busy practitioners may object that they do not have time to do more than the basics of an assessment, but I would argue in response that this is a short-sighted approach and that skimping on this important work will lead to lower standards of practice and therefore more complaints, more re-referrals, less job satisfaction and fewer successful outcomes. In terms of theory development, two issues strike me as important. One is that this type of work often involves managing conflict – for example, conflicting expectations (see *Practising Social Work,* 2009a, Chapter 12) – and yet social work education and the theory base on which it draws has little to say about conflict management. This is a significant omission and an important area for further development. Similarly, given the high level of pressure on social workers generally, there is an important issue in relation to the development of time and workload management skills. This is another area largely neglected in the professional knowledge base and therefore another suitable target for investment of time and effort in theory development.

2. **Plan, carry out, review and evaluate social work practice, with individuals, families, carers, groups, communities and other professionals**
   Again there is a large literature base relating to the potential range of methods that can be used to work effectively with the people we are seeking to help. The gap here is not so much knowledge of methods as the ability to 'theorize' practice by drawing on that knowledge base. While critically reflective practice has seen a significant growth of interest in the past decade or so, there remains much development work to be done to establish it as a mainstream approach to practice. In particular, the obstacles to critically reflective practice and how to deal with them is a matter requiring significant attention if the benefits of this approach are not to be wasted.

3. **Support individuals to represent their needs, views and circumstances**
   The role of advocate is one that was previously much higher up the social work agenda than it is now. A reason for the relative lack of focus is no doubt the increasing emphasis on managerialism and more bureaucratic and (therefore less sociopolitical) approaches to practice. There is therefore considerable scope for developing the theory base underpinning the role of advocate in social work.

4. **Manage risk to individuals, families, carers, groups, communities, self and colleagues**
   Managerialism has also had the effect of putting risk management high up the social work agenda, and, as I have argued elsewhere (Thompson, 2009a) led to a distinct tendency for risk issues to be dealt with in quite a defensive way. This is highly problematic all round, and so, if we are to aim for optimal standards rather than just minimum ones, then we need to develop a much more sophisticated understanding of risk, how it can be assessed and managed.

Given the emphasis on 'contingency' in existentialism, this is an approach that can be particularly well equipped to provide an understanding of the complexities of risk.

5. **Manage and be accountable, with supervision and support, for your own social work practice within your organization**
   This fits well with the idea of critically reflective practice (we have to take responsibility for our actions 'on the spot' and cannot simply expect to follow instructions) as well as that of professionalism. This therefore adds weight to my earlier comment about the need for a fuller understanding of how to make critically reflective practice a mainstream approach.

   The question of 'with supervision and support' is also significant. This is because some organizations do an excellent job of supporting and guiding their staff, while others, in my experience, can be very poor indeed. There is therefore considerable scope for developing our knowledge base in relation to what is now increasingly being referred to as 'workplace well-being' (Thompson and Bates, 2009).

6. **Demonstrate professional competence in social work practice**
   In a sense, this underlines the need for theory development. We cannot simply rest on our laurels in terms of the knowledge base available to us. If we want to aim for optimal rather than minimum standards, then our professional competence needs to be based on the best available knowledge – and that cannot be done if our knowledge development is lacking.

Practice focus 15.2

Jim was a practice teacher in a family placement team. He had supervised students for many years now and felt very confident in what he was doing. However, he struggled with Moira, a student who had no prior social work experience. He found her to be quite anxious to the point that her anxiety seemed to be paralysing her. In particular, Jim was concerned about how she seemed to be obsessed with the six key roles of the National Occupational Standards. Whatever they discussed in supervision, whatever work he allocated to her, or whatever developmental visits she went on as a part of the placement, she always wanted to relate them directly to the key roles. Jim soon worked out that this was because she had been told at university that she needed to demonstrate competence in relation to these roles if she was to pass the placement. Jim therefore had to find ways of weaning her off her dependency on these standards, but to do so in ways that would not increase her anxiety. The great irony was that her anxiety about failing was going to lead to failure if she could not learn to see further than the minimum requirements. Jim therefore decided he would have to impress upon her somehow that she must broaden her focus and concentrate on learning, and that way she should have no difficulty meeting the minimum standards.

National Occupational Standards, then, can be seen as providing a useful, if rather limiting and limited, overview of what is required of social workers. However, what they cannot do is help us engage with practice at *optimal* levels, as the complexities, variables and moving foundations are so great as to make such an approach far from adequate. To aim for optimal practice rather than 'just about good enough', we therefore need to adopt a more professional approach, in particular one that values the underpinning knowledge base and appreciates the need to keep developing it.

The need for theory development

Developing theory has been the main focus of Part Three of the book. To reassert the importance of such development I shall briefly summarize the key messages from each of the preceding four chapters within Part Three:

Chapter 11   Developing coherence: drawing on existentialism

This chapter was critical of the postmodernist embracing of incoherence. It argued that both the theorizing of practice and theory development need to rely on coherence. It was also argued that existentialism is a theoretical approach that captures some of the fluidity, diversity and variability on which postmodernism is based, but without the drawbacks of postmodernism, as highlighted in Chapter 2.

Chapter 12   The linguistic turn

In this chapter the focus was on how language has taken on consider-able extra significance in the social sciences in recent years, and it was argued that the social work theory base could benefit from a greater understanding of the complexities of language without falling foul of the simplistic distortions of 'political correctness'. It was proposed that existentialism has the potential to develop a fuller understanding of language, drawing in part on some insights from post-structuralism but without going to the extremes the latter has been criticized for.

Chapter 13   Spirituality and meaning

Meaning is at the heart of both social work and spirituality. It is, of course, also a key feature of social work. This chapter therefore argued for a greater emphasis on spirituality in social work and for the development of our knowledge of this vitally important, yet often neglected aspect of theory and practice. Spirituality needs to be seen as a key issue for everybody and not simply for those who are members of a particular faith community.

Chapter 14   Developing emancipatory practice

Social work has a long-standing commitment to promoting social justice by combating discrimination and oppression. This chapter outlined how good progress has been made over the years in this regard, but there have also been significant obstacles to progress, particularly a tendency to rely on dogmatic reductionism. The key argument here, then, was that there is a need to by-pass dogmatic reductionism in order to develop more sophisticated understandings better suited to the major challenges we face.

Voice of experience 15.2

When I first started working in the disability field it was all very medical-ized and, frankly, quite patronizing. Now things have really moved on, what with the social model of disability and a much more politicized understanding of the issues. The medical stuff hasn't gone away, but the ideas available to us now to make sense of people's lives and problems are much better. I fell much better equipped to do my job now without adding to the disablism that is already so rife in our society.

Christine, a senior practitioner in a disability team

Existentialism as a basis for theorizing

I have been critical at various stages in the book of the tendency of supporters of one theoretical perspective or other to form a theoretical camp or 'club', with the effect of devaluing ideas and insights that do not belong to members of the club, in effect creating a competitive, us-them mentality. At times this can become quite extreme, with people adopting quite closed minds to ideas arising from outside their particular theoretical terms of reference. By contrast, what I am proposing is that existentialism has the benefit of offering a theoretical foundation that is open to ideas and insights from other areas too. This is because it is mainly a sensitizing theory (or metatheory), rather than a substantive theory (although it does have some substantive aspects). What makes existentialism different from other perspectives is that it encourages independence of thought. It does not seek to close down theoretical debate by trying to offer the 'Truth'. Rather, it provides tools for making sense of human experience and challenges by providing a philosophical foundation to facilitate breadth and depth of thinking around human issues.

Much of this facility comes from the approach of one of the very earliest of existentialists, Søren Kierkegaard, whose way of addressing these concerns is summarized nicely by Watts:

> Like his beloved model Socrates, Kierkegaard wished to make people think for themselves, use independent judgement and act with deliberate choice. This approach was based upon his realisation that existential truth – truth that potentially can transform a person's outlook and manner of living – couldn't be communicated directly in an effective manner. For existential truth presents insights that all people must adapt to their own unique experiences and outlook ...
>
> (2003, p. 65)

Existentialism, then, while having certain concepts that do form a theoretical framework in their own right, is primarily a way of facilitating exploration and understanding, rather than a specific theory. Or, to put it another way, it is more of a mode of theorizing than a theory in its own right. And this notion of it being a *mode of theorizing* is what makes it, in my view, an excellent basis for theorizing social work practice and thereby developing critically reflective practice.

In order, therefore, to appreciate more fully what existentialism has to offer as a theoretical foundation for social work, let us explore – by way of conclusion – what its status is as a theory or philosophy. I shall do this in two parts. First, I shall relate existentialism to the different dimensions of theory as conventionally defined in the literature and, second, I shall summarize what I see as the strengths of existentialism as a basis for both theorizing practice and developing the theory base which forms the wellspring for such theorizing.

Dimensions of theory

Existentialism can be understood in relation to the dimensions of theory in the following ways:

- *Ontology*. This refers to the study of being or reality. To ask what the ontological basis of a theory is involves enquiring as to what model of reality it adopts. Existentialism adopts a complex ontology but it is characterized by two main features:

  (i) it is *phenomenological* – that is, it emphasizes perception, interpretation and meaning as the basis of our reality. The concept of the dialectic of subjectivity and objectivity captures well this aspect of existentialist ontology;

  (ii) it is *psychosocial* – that is, it recognizes that human reality is simultaneously individual and social. This is one of the main reasons why I believe it is well suited as a basis for social work.

- *Ethics*. This refers to the value base underpinning the theory. Positivists would perhaps argue that a theory should be value free, but there is a strong argument that values cannot be separated out from our understanding of the world. The position relating to existentialist ethics is complex (see Thompson, 2008b), but I can make two important points, namely:

(i) a key part of existentialist ethics is a commitment to *authenticity*, which involves avoiding 'bad faith' and self-deception, trying to pretend that we are not responsible for our actions or for ourselves;

(ii) existentialism sees ethics as necessarily linked to politics and, in particular, a commitment to challenging oppression.

- *Politics.* Sartrean existentialism in particular is openly committed to a politics of fighting oppression and supporting emancipation. This is another reason why existentialism is a very valuable foundation for social work thinking. Unlike positivism which tries (but fails) to claim political neutrality or postmodernism which, at best, is ambivalent about emancipation, existentialism is openly and explicitly committed to creating a more equal society.

- *Epistemology.* This is the aspect of theory that is concerned with the status of knowledge. For example, positivists claim a scientific epistemology; they argue that their work produces scientific fact and truths. Existentialist epistemology owes a great deal to Nietzsche, another of the earliest existentialist thinkers, and his notion of the importance of perspectives and the absence of an absolute Truth. The fact that existentialism operates as a metatheory that facilitates understanding, rather than a discoverer of the Truth, is an example of existentialist epistemology. As such it provides a foundation for critically reflective practice.

These brief comments should help to paint a picture of existentialism as a potentially very good ally in our efforts to theorize our practice, to make sense of the highly complex issues we encounter.

Practice focus 15.3

Julie had studied philosophy at university before undertaking postgraduate studies in social work. She had particularly enjoyed studying existentialism as she found its emphasis on 'lived experience' both interesting and useful in her own life. This promoted her to read widely about existentialism. When she trained as a social worker, she used her philosophical knowledge wherever she could. Sometimes she struggled to make a connection to her practice, but at other times, there were very helpful links to be made, especially when it was existentialism that she was drawing on. She didn't talk much about this to anyone, as she thought it didn't fit well with the ethos where she was working. It would have been seen as 'weird'. Her team manager, in

particular, saw himself as a 'pragmatist' and would not have appreciated how much benefit Julie was getting from using these ideas to
inform her practice. She felt that was a great pity, as she believed
other people would have benefited too if they had been open to using
philosophical ideas to wrestle with the very complex cases that sometimes kept them awake at night.

Existentialism as a metatheoretical foundation

The following features are what I see as the building blocks that can
be used to develop a theoretical foundation for social work informed by
existentialism:

- *Handling complexity.* The need for social workers to handle
  complexity is now well established. Existentialism acknowledges
  the complexities of human existence and the existentialist challenges we face. It provides a range of concepts that can be usefully
  applied to make sense of the complexities. It does not shy away
  from them by trying to offer simple solutions or dogmatic or reductionist understandings.
- *Handling conflict.* Existentialism draws on dialectical reason to
  make sense of the interaction of conflicting forces. It recognizes
  conflict as a basic part of human existence and teaches us that this
  is something we need to engage with constructively and skilfully,
  rather than be frightened of and therefore shy away from.
- *Handling change.* Dialectical reason also provides us with a basis
  for making sense of change. By seeing change as arising from the
  interaction of conflicting forces, we are able to develop a fuller
  understanding of the subtle processes that shape and are shaped
  by, change. This also gives us cause for hope, in so far as the dialectic helps us to understand that the current far from satisfactory
  situations we encounter – in relation to equality and social justice,
  for example – were created historically through human action and
  can therefore be changed by human action. They are not fixed and
  immutable.
- *Handling power.* Existentialism provides a sound foundation for
  making sense of the subtle and intricate workings of power.
  Through PCS analysis, for example, we can understand that power

operates at personal, cultural and structural levels (Thompson, 2007a). Existentialism, especially in its later incarnations, is politically committed to promoting social justice, and that involves addressing power relations and inequalities.

- *Handling uncertainty.* A basic concept within existentialism is that of the 'contingency of being'. This refers to the fact that human existence is characterized by uncertainty and insecurity – this is often expressed succinctly as 'no guarantees'. Our ability to cope with this is something that we generally learn as we grow up, but some people struggle with this aspect of their lives (consider people who are schizophrenic, for example), while everyone can feel overwhelmed by insecurity at certain times (a major loss or trauma, for example).

- *Handling competing perspectives.* As we have already seen, existentialism is able to incorporate insights from other perspectives to help cast light on people and their problems. It is not an exclusive club. It will, of course, reject certain ideas that are not consistent with its basic principles (deterministic concepts that deny human agency, for example), but it has an open approach to seeking understanding, rather than a closed, dogmatic one.

Voice of experience 15.3

What I try and do in using theory to inform my practice is to adopt a holistic view, making sure that I am not just looking at somebody's feelings *or* their behaviour *or* their family dynamics *or* their experiences of oppression. I am wanting to know about all of these things – and more. You have to have a full picture to work with.

Amy, a social worker in a project for sexually abused children

Conclusion

Social work can be incredibly demanding, but it can also be immensely rewarding. It is also constantly changing, as the social issues it addresses are constantly changing. To try to make sure that we are well equipped to rise to the challenges and to maximize the rewards, we need to have a solid foundation of knowledge to make our practice *informed* practice. We also need to have the skills and confidence to be able to use that knowledge in practice – to be able to *theorize* practice. This is the foundation for critically reflective practice, for being able to engage with the complexities of practice, equipped with not only a helpful knowledge base to cast light on the various aspects of practice, but also the ability to 'put the theory to work', to enlist its support in taking things forward in ever-changing circumstances.

Existentialism does not offer any magic answers, but I have made the case that it can provide a sophisticated basis for developing our understanding and for using that understanding in our work. Whether or not you share my view of the value of existentialism, there remains a need for us to theorize our practice, to make sense of it as it unfolds. Without that commitment to, and capacity for, theorizing practice, we are likely to find ourselves facing some very difficult and challenging situations without the wherewithal to make sense of them or deal with them confidently and effectively. The commitment required to build up the knowledge base and the confidence and skills to theorize it in practice should therefore be seen as a very worthwhile investment of time, effort and energy.

Points to ponder

1. What steps can you take to make sure that you keep developing your knowledge base over time?
2. How can you make sure that you do not lose sight of what is expected of you in terms of what is expected of you as a professional (whether through occupational standards or social work values more broadly)?
3. How might you draw on the insights of existentialism to develop your practice?

Further reading

Ferguson (2007) presents a helpful analysis of the challenges we face in social work. In terms of developing critically reflective practice as a means of rising to those challenges, see S. Thompson and N. Thompson (2008); Fook and Gardner (2007) and White, Fook and Gardner (2006). Thompson (2009a) is also concerned with rising to the professional challenge of social work. Finally, I would ask you to ask yourself what inspired you to pursue a career in social work. If it was a commitment to social justice, then I would urge you to read as much as you can on social justice. If it was, for example, a desire to support people experiencing major losses and trauma in their lives, then make sure you read as much as you can about loss and trauma. Whatever it is that formed (and, it is to be hoped, still informs) the basis of your inspiration and motivation, do not lose touch with that crucial source of renewal to keep you going in what is, as well as being a rewarding career, also a very demanding one.

References

Adams, R. (2008) *Empowerment, Participation and Social Work*, 4th edn, Basingstoke, Palgrave Macmillan.

Adams, R., Dominelli, L. and Payne, M. (eds) (2002) *Social Work: Themes, Issues and Critical Debates*, 2nd edn, Basingstoke, Palgrave Macmillan.

Ahmad, B. (1990) *Black Perspectives in Social Work*, Birmingham, Venture Press.

Aitchison, J. (2007) *The Articulate Mammal: An Introduction to Psycholinguistics*, 5th edn, London, Routledge.

Alexander, J. (1987) 'The Centrality of the Classics', in Giddens and Turner (1987).

Allen, K. (2004) *Max Weber: A Critical Introduction*, London, Pluto.

Archer, M. S. (2000) *Being Human: The Problem of Agency*, Cambridge, Cambridge University Press.

Argyris, C. (1999) *On Organisational Learning*, 2nd edn, Oxford, Blackwell.

Argyris, C. and Schön, D. F. (1976) *Theory in Practice: Increasing Professional Effectiveness*, San Francisco, CA, Jossey Bass.

Argyris, C. and Schön, D. A. (1995) *Organizational Learning: Theory, Method and Practice*, Englewood Cliffs, NJ, Prentice Hall.

Baker, J., Lynch, K., Cantillon, S. and Walsh, J. (2004) *Equality: From Theory to Action*, Basingstoke, Palgrave Macmillan.

Baldwin, M. (2004) 'Critical Reflection: Opportunities and Threats to Professional Learning and Service Development in Social Work Organizations', in Gould and Baldwin (2004).

Barrett, M. and McIntosh, M. (1991) *The Anti-Social Family*, 2nd edn, London, Verso.

Bates, J. and Thompson, N. (2007) 'Workplace Well-Being: An Occupational Social Work Approach' *Illness, Crisis & Loss*, 15(3).

Bauman, Z. (2001) *The Individualized Society*, Cambridge, Polity.

Bauman, Z. (2005) *Work, Consumerism and the New Poor*, 2nd edn, Maidenhead, Open University Press.

Bauman, Z. and May, T. (2001) *Thinking Sociologically*, 2nd edn, Oxford, Blackwell Publishers.

Beauvoir, S. de (1972) *The Second Sex*, Harmondsworth, Penguin.

Beck, U. (1992) *Risk Society: Towards a New Modernity*, London, Sage.

Beckett, C. (2006) *Essential Theory for Social Work Practice*, London, Sage.

Beresford, P. and Croft, S. (2001) 'Service Users' Knowledges and the Social Construction of Social Work', *Journal of Social Work*, 1(3).

Berger, P and Luckmann, T. (1967) *The Social Construction of Reality*, Harmondsworth, Penguin.

Blauner, R. (1967) *Alienation and Freedom,* Chicago, University of Chicago Press.

Blumer, H. (1969) *Symbolic Interactionism,* Englewood Cliffs, NJ, Prentice Hall.

Bonnett, A. (2000) *Anti-racism*, London, Routledge.

Bourdieu, P. (1984) *Distinction*, London, RKP.

Bourdieu, P. (1992) *The Logic of Practice,* Cambridge, Polity.

Boyle, D. (2001) *The Tyranny of Numbers: Why Counting Can't Make Us Happy*, London, Flamingo.

Boyne, R. and Rattansi, A. (eds) (1990) *Postmodernism and Society*, Basingstoke, Macmillan – now Palgrave Macmillan.

Brandon, D. (2000) *Tao of Survival: Spirituality in Social Care and Counselling*, Birmingham, Venture Press.

Brooks, V. and Sikes, P. (1997) *The Good Mentor Guide*, Buckingham, Open University Press.

Brown, R. H. and Lyman, S. M. (eds) (1978) *Structure, Consciousness and History*, Cambridge, Cambridge University Press.

Buber, M. (2004) *I and Thou*, 2nd edn, London, Continuum (originally published 1958).

Burnham, J. B. (1986) *Familiy Therapy*, London, Routledge.

Burr, V. (2003) *Social Constructionism*, 2nd edn, London, Routledge.

Butt, T. (2004) *Understanding People*, Basingstoke, Palgrave Macmillan.

Byng-Hall, J. (1995) *Rewriting Family Scripts: Improvisation and Systems Change*, New York, Guilford Press.

Cade, B, (1992) 'I am an Unashamed Expert', *Context*, 11, pp. 30–1.

Callinicos, A. (2000) *Equality*, Cambridge, Polity.

Callinicos, A. (2007) *Social Theory: A Historical Introduction*, 2nd edn, Cambridge, Polity.

Carr, A. (2000) *Family Therapy: Concepts, Process and Practice*, Chichester, Wiley.

Casey, C. (2002) *Critical Analysis of Organizations: Theory, Practice, Revitalization*, London, Sage.

Castiglione, D., Deth, J. W. and Wellob, G. (eds) (2008) *The Handbook of Social Capital*, Oxford, Oxford University Press.

Clarke, J. (2004) *Changing Welfare, Changing States: New Directions in Social Policy*, London, Sage.

Clarke, J. and Newman, J. (1997) *The Managerial State*, London, Sage.

Clarke, J., Gewirtz, S. and McLaughlin, E. (2000a) 'Reinventing the Welfare State', in Clarke, Gewirtz and McLaughlin (2000b).

Clarke, J., Gewirtz, S. and McLaughlin, E. (eds) (2000b) *New Managerialism, New Welfare?*, London, Sage/The Open University.

Collins, B. E. and Guetzkow, H. (1964) *A Social Psychology of Group Processes for Decision-Making,* New York, Wiley.

Constantine, M. G. and Sue, D. W. (eds) (2005) *Addressing Racism:*

Facilitating Cultural Competence in Mental Health and Educational Settings, Chichester, Wiley.

Cooley, C. H. (1902) *Human Nature and the Social Order*, New York, Scribner.

Corby, B. (2005) *Child Abuse: Towards a Knowledge Base*, 3rd edn, Maidenhead, Open University Press.

Corrigan, P. and Leonard, P. (1978) *Social Work Practice under Capitalism*, London, Macmillan.

Cottrell, S. (2005) *Critical Thinking Skills: Developing Effective Analysis and Argument*, Basingstoke, Palgrave Macmillan.

Cousins, (1987) *Controlling Social Welfare*, Brighton, Wheatsheaf Books.

Coyte, M. E., Gilbert, P. and Nicholls, V. (eds) (2007) *Spirituality, Values and Mental Health: Jewels for the Journey*, London, Jessica Kingsley.

Craib, I. (1998) *Experiencing Identity*, London, Sage.

Crawford, F. R., Dickinson, J. and Leitmann, S. (2002) 'Mirroring Meaning Making: Narrative Ways of Reflecting on Practice for Action', *Qualitative Social Work*, 1(170).

Crook, S. (1990) 'The End of Radical Social Theory? Notes on Radicalism, Modernism and Postmodernism', in Boyne and Rattansi (1990).

Crossley, M. L. (2000) *Introducing Narrative Psychology: Self, Trauma and the Construction of Meaning*, Buckingham, Open University Press.

Crossley, N. (1999) *Intersubjectivity*, London, Sage.

Crossley, N. (2005) *Key Concepts in Critical Social Theory*, London, Sage.

Crowley, N. (2006) *An Ambition for Equality*, Dublin, Irish Academic Press.

Crystal, D. (2003) *The Cambridge Encyclopedia of the English Language*, 2nd edn, Cambridge, Cambridge University Press.

Cunningham, S. and Tomlinson, J. (2006) 'Children, Social Policy and the State: The Dichotomy of Care and Control', in Lavalette and Pratt (2006).

Dean, H. (ed.) (2004) *The Ethics of Welfare: Human Rights, Dependency and Responsibility*, Bristol, The Policy Press.

Denney, D. (2005) *Risk and Society*, London, Sage.

Doel, M. (2005) *Using Groupwork*, London, Routledge.

Doel, M. and Sawdon, C. (1999) *The Essential Groupworker: Teaching and Learning Creative Groupwork*, London, Jessica Kingsley.

Doel, M. and Shardlow, S. (2005) *Modern Social Work Practice: Teaching and Learning in Practice Settings*, Aldershot, Ashgate.

Doka, K. (ed.) (1989) *Disenfranchised Grief,* New York, Jossey Bass.

Doka, K. and Morgan, J. D. (eds) (1993) *Death and Spirituality*, Amityville, NY, Baywood.

Dostal, R. J. (ed.) (2002) *The Cambridge Companion to Gadamer*, Cambridge, Cambridge University Press.

Drakeford, M. and Morris, S. (1998) 'Social Work with Linguistic Minorities', in Williams, Soydan and Johnson (1998).

During S. (ed.) (2006) *The Cultural Studies Reader*, 3rd edn, London, Routledge.

Duyvendak, J. W., Knijn, T. and Kremer, M. (2006a) 'Policy, People, and the New Professional: An Introduction', in Duyvendak, Knijn and Kremer (2006b).

Duyvendak, J. W., Knijn, T. and Kremer, M. (eds) (2006b), *Policy, People, and the New Professional: De-Professionalisation and Re-Professionalisation in Care and Welfare*, Amsterdam, Amsterdam University Press

Eagleton, T. (2000) *The Idea of Culture*, Oxford, Blackwell.

Easterby-Smith, M. and Lyles, M. A. (eds) (2003) *Handbook of Organizational Learning and Knowledge Management*, Oxford, Blackwell.

Eckert, P. and McConnell-Ginet, S. (2003) *Language and Gender*, Cambridge, Cambridge University Press.

Ehrenreich, B. (2005) *Bait and Switch: The (Futile) Pursuit of the American Dream*, New York, Metropolitan Books.

Elkjaer, B. (2003) 'Social Learning Theory: Learning as Participation in Social Processes', in Easterby-Smith and Lyles (2003).

Elliot, J. (1991) *Humana conditio: Beobachtung zur Entwicklung der Menschheit am 40 Jahrestag eines Kriegsendes*, Frankfurt am Main, Suhrkamp.

England, H. (1986) *Social Work as Art: Making Sense for Good Practice*, London, HarperCollins.

Esping Anderson, G. (1990) *The Three Worlds of Welfare Capitalism*, Princeton, NJ, Princeton University Press.

Fairclough, N. (1992) *Discourse and Social Change*, Cambridge, Polity Press.

Fanon, F. (2008) *Black Skin, White Masks*, London, Pluto Press.

Faubion, J. D. (ed.) (2000) *Power: Essential Works of Foucault 1954–1984*, Harmondsworth, Penguin.

Featherstone, M. (1988) 'In Pursuit of the Postmodern', *Theory, Culture and Society*, 5, pp. 195–215.

Ferguson, I. (2006) 'Living in a Material World: Postmodernism and Social Policy', in Lavalette and Pratt (2006).

Ferguson, I. (2007) *Reclaiming Social Work: Challenging Neo-Liberalism and Promoting Social Justice*, London, Sage.

Ferguson, I. and Woodward, R. (2009) *Radical Social Work in Practice: Making a Difference*, Bristol, The Policy Press.

Ferguson, I., Lavalette, M. and Mooney, G. (eds) (2002) *Rethinking Welfare: A Critical Perspective*, London, Sage.

Folgheraiter, F. (1998) *Teoria e metodologia del servizio sociale. La prospettiva di rete*, Milan, Angeli.

Folgheraiter, F. (2004) *Relational Social Work: Towards Networking and Societal Practices*, London, Jessica Kingsley Publishers.

Fook, J. and Gardner, F. (2007) *Practising Critical Reflection: A Handbook*, Maidenhead, Open University Press.

Forte, J. A. (2001) *Theories for Practice: Symbolic Interactionist Transactions*, Lanham, NY, University Press of America.

Foucault, M. (1991) *Discipline and Punish: The Birth of the Prison*, Harmondsworth, Penguin.

Foucault, M. (1998) *The History of Sexuality: The Will to Knowledge vol. 1*, Harmondsworth, Penguin.

Foucault, M. (2001) *Madness and Civilization*, London, Routledge.

Fowler, B. (ed.) (2000) *Reading Bourdieu on Society and Culture*, Oxford, Blackwell.

Frankl, Viktor E. (1984) *The Unheard Cry for Meaning: Psychotherapy and Humanism*, New York: Washington Square Press.

Freire, P. (1972a) *Pedagogy of the Oppressed*, Harmondsworth, Penguin.

Freire, P. (1972b) *Cultural Action for Freedom*, Harmondsworth, Penguin.

Freire, P. (2007) *Pedagogy of Hope*, London, Continuum.

Fulop, L., Linstead, S. and Lilley, S. (2006) *Management and Organization: A Critical Text*, Basingstoke, Palgrave Macmillan.

Gadamer, H.-G. (2004) *Truth and Method*, 2nd edn, London, Continuum (first published 1989).

Gane, M. (2006) *Auguste Comte,* London, Routledge.

Gergen, K. J. (1999) *An Invitation to Social Construction*, London, Sage.

Giddens, A. and Turner, R. (eds) (1987) *Social Theory Today*, Cambridge, Polity.

Gilbert, P. (2005) *Leadership: Being Effective and Remaining Human*, Lyme Regis, Russell House Publishing.

Goffman, E. (1990) *Stigma: Notes on the Management of Spoiled Identity*, Harmondsworth, Penguin.

Gould, N. and Baldwin, M. (eds) (2004) *Social Work, Critical Reflection and the Learning Organization*, Aldershot, Ashgate.

Grint, K. (2005) *Leadership: Limits and Possibilities*, Basingstoke, Palgrave Macmillan.

Guirdham, M. (2005) *Communicating Across Cultures at Work*, 2nd edn, Basingstoke, Palgrave Macmillan.

Habermas, J. (1986) *Theory and Practice*, Cambridge, Polity.

Haidt, J. (2006) *The Happiness Hypothesis: Putting Ancient Wisdom and Philosophy to the Test of Modern Science,* London, Arrow Books.

Hamer, M. (2006) *The Barefoot Helper: Mindfulness and Creativity in Social Work and the Helping Professions*, Lyme Regis, Russell House Publishing.

Harding, M. (2005) 'Language', in van Deurzen and Arnold-Baker (2005c).

Harre, R. (1978) 'Architectonic Man: On the Structuring of Lived Experience', in Brown and Lyman (1978).

Harris, M. (1978) *Cannibals and Kings: The Origins of Cultures*, London, Fontana.

Healy, K. (2000) *Social Work Practice: Contemporary Perspectives on Change*, London, Sage.

Healy, K. (2005) *Social Work Theories in Context: Creating Frameworks for Practice*, Basingstoke, Palgrave Macmillan.

Holliday, A., Hyde, M. and Kullman, J. (2004) *Intercultural Communication: An Advanced Resource Book,* London Routledge.

Hollinger, R. (1994) *Postmodernism and the Social Sciences: A Thematic Approach*, Cambridge, Polity.

Hollis, F. (1966) *Casework: A Psychosocial Therapy*, New York, Random House.

Holloway, M, (2006) 'Spiritual Need and the Core Business of Social Work', *British Journal of Social Work*, 37(2).

Houston, S. (2002) 'Reflecting on Habitus, Field and Capital: Towards a Culturally Sensitive Social Work', *Journal of Social Work*, 2(2), pp. 149–67.

Howe, D. (2008) *Emotional Intelligent Social Worker*, Basingstoke, Palgrave Macmillan.

Howe, D., Schofield, G., Brandon, M. and Hinings, D. (1999) *Attachment Theory, Child Maltreatment and Family Support: A Practice and Assessment Model*, Basingstoke, Macmillan – now Palgrave Macmillan.

Howells, C. (1992a) 'Conclusion: Sartre and the Deconstruction of the Subject', in Howells (1992b).

Howells, C. (1992b) *The Cambridge Companion to Sartre*, Cambridge, Cambridge University Press.

Huang, Y. (2007) *Pragmatics,* Oxford, Oxford University Press.

Hugman, R. (2005) *New Approaches in Ethics for the Caring Professions: Taking Account of Change for Caring Professions*, Basingstoke, Palgrave Macmillan.

Hunt, S. (2005) *The Life Course: A Sociological Introduction*, Basingstoke, Palgrave Macmillan.

Hyman, H. H. and Singer, E. (eds) (1968) *Readings in Reference Group Theory and Research*, New York, Free Press.

Ife, J. (1999) 'Postmodernism, Critical Theory and Social Work', in Pease and Fook (1999).

Jack, R. (2005) 'Strengths-Based Practice in Statutory Care and Protection Work', in Nash, Munford and O'Donoghue (2005).

Jandt, F. E. (2006) *An Introduction to Intercultural Communication: Identities in a Global Community*, 5th edn, London, Sage.

Janis, I. L. (1982) *Groupthink*, 2nd edn, Boston, MA, Houghton Mifflin.

Jones, C. (1996) 'Anti-Intellectualism and the Peculiarities of British Social Work Education', in N. Parton (ed.), *Social Theory, Social Change And Social Work*, London, Routledge.

Jordan, B. (2007) *Social Work and Well-Being*, Lyme Regis, Russell House Publishing.

Kallen, E. (2004) *Social Inequality and Social Injustice: A Human Rights Perspective*, Basingstoke, Palgrave Macmillan.

Karvinen-Niinikoski, S. (2004) 'Social Work Supervision: Contributing to Innovative Knowledge Production and Open Expertise', in Gould and Baldwin (2004).

Kinsella, P. and Garland, A. (2008) *Cognitive Behavioural Therapy for Mental Health Workers: A Beginner's Guide*, London, Routledge.

Krill, D. F. (1978) *Existential Social Work*, New York, Free Press.

Laing, R. D. (1972) *Knots*, Harmondsworth, Penguin.

Langan, M. and Day, L. (eds) (1992) W*omen, Oppression and Social Work*, London, Routledge.

Langan, M. and Lee, P. (eds) (1989) *Radical Social Work Today*, London, Unwin Hyman.

Lavalette, M. and Pratt, A. (eds) (2006) *Social Policy: Theories, Concepts and Issues*, 3rd edn, London, Sage.

Lawler, S. (2008) *Identity: Sociological Perspectives*, Cambridge, Polity.

Layard, R. (2006) *Happiness: Lessons from a New Science*, London, Penguin.

Lesnik, B. (ed.) (1997) *Change in Social Work*, Aldershot, Arena.

Liebenberg, L. and Ungar, M. (eds) (2008) *Resilience in Action*, Toronto, University of Toronto Press.

Lin, N. (2001) *Social Capital: A Theory of Social Structure and Action*, Cambridge, Cambridge University Press.

Linstead, S., Fulop, L. and Lilley, S. (2004) *Management and Organisation: A Critical Text*, Basingstoke, Palgrave Macmillan.

Lovell, T. (2000) 'Thinking Feminism with and Against Bourdieu', in Fowler (2000).

Lyotard, J.-F. (1968) *Political Writings*, trans. B. Reading and K. P. Geiman, Minneapolis, University of Minnesota Press.

Malik, K. (2008) *Strange Fruit: Why Both Sides are Wrong in the Race Debate*, Oxford, Oneworld Publications.

Martin, L. (1998) *Technologies of the Self: A Seminar with Michel Foucault*, Amherst, MA, University of Massachussets Press.

McDonald, C. (2006) *Challenging Social Work: The Institutional Context of Practice*, Basingstoke, Palgrave Macmillan.

McGillivray, M. (ed.) (2007) *Human Well-Being: Concept and Measurement*, Basingstoke, Palgrave Macmillan.

McMahon, D. (2006) *The Pursuit of Happiness: A History from the Greeks to the Present*, London, Penguin.

McNay, M. (1992) 'Social Work and Power Relations: Towards a Framework for an Integrated Practice', in Langan and Day (1992).

McPhail, M. (2007) *Service User and Carer Involvement: Beyond Good Intentions*, Edinburgh, Dunedin Academic Press.

Mead, G. H. (1967) *Mind, Self and Society*, Chicago, University of Chicago Press.

Merleau-Ponty, M. (1962) *The Phenomenology of Perception*, Chicago, University of Chicago Press.

Merleau-Ponty, M. (1965) *The Structure of Behaviour*, London, Methuen.

Merleau-Ponty, M. (2002) *Phenomenology of Perception*, London, Routledge.

Midgley, J. (1999) 'Postmodernism and Social Development: Implications for Progress, Intervention and Ideology', *Social Development Issues*, 21(3).

Mills, C. W. (1959) *The Sociological Imagination*, New York, Oxford University Press.

Morgan, J. D. (1993) 'The Existential Quest for Meaning', in Doka and Morgan (1993).

Moss, B. (2005) *Religion and Spirituality*, Lyme Regis, Russell House Publishing.

Moss, B. (2007a) *Values*, Lyme Regis, Russell House Publishing.

Moss, B. (2007b) 'Illness, Crisis and Loss: Towards a Spiritually Intelligent Workplace', *Illness, Crisis & Loss*, 15(3).

Moss, B. (2008) *Communication Skills for Health and Social Care*, London, Sage.

Moss, B. (2009) 'Spirituality in the Workplace', in Thompson and Bates (2009).

Mullaly, B. (2002) *Challenging Oppression: A Critical Social Work Approach*, Oxford, Oxford University Press.

Munford, R. and Sanders, J. (1999) *Supporting Families*, Palmerston North, Dunmore Press.

Nash, M. (2002) 'Spirituality and Social Work in a Culturally Appropriate Curriculum', in Nash and Stewart (2002).

Nash, M. and Stewart, B. (eds) (2002) *Spirituality and Social Care: Contributing to Personal and Community Well-Being*, London, Jessica Kingsley Publishers.

Nash, M., Munford, R. and O'Donoghue, K. (eds) (2005) *Social Work Theories in Action*, London, Jessica Kingsley Publishers.

Neimeyer, R. A. (2001) *Meaning Reconstruction and the Experience of Loss*, Washington DC, American Psychological Association.

Neimeyer, R. A. and Anderson, A. (2002) 'Meaning Reconstruction Theory', in Thompson (2002b).

Nightingale, D. and Cromby, J. (1999) *Social Constructionist Psychology*, Buckingham, Open University Press.

Noble, C. (2004) 'Postmodern Thinking: Where is it Taking Social Work?', *Journal of Social Work*, 4(3).

Norman, E. (2000) *Resiliency Enhancement: Putting the Strengths Perspective into Social Work Practice*, New York, Columbia University Press.

Okitikpi, T. and Aymer, C. (2008a) 'The New Challenges of Anti-Discriminatory Practice in Social Work', in Okitikpi and Aymer (2008b).

Okitikpi, T. and Aymer C. (eds), (2008b) *The Art of Social Work Practice*, Lyme Regis, Russell House Publishing.

O'Neill, J. (1995) *The Poverty of Postmodernism*, London, Routledge.

Pardeck, J. T., Murphy, J. W. and Min Choi, J. (1994) 'Some Implications of Postmodernism for Social Work', *Social Work*, 19(4).

Parekh, B. (2006) *Rethinking Multiculturalism: Cultural Diversity and Political Theory*, 2nd edn, Basingstoke, Palgrave Macmillan.

Parekh, B. (2008) *A New Politics of Identity: Political Principles for an Interdependent World*, Basingstoke, Palgrave Macmillan.

Parker, S., Fook, J. and Pease, B., (1999) 'Empowerment: The Modernist Social Work Concept *Par Excellence*', in Pease and Fook (1999b).

Parton, N. and O'Byrne, P. (2000) *Constructive Social Work: Towards a New Practice*, Basingstoke, Palgrave Macmillan.

Patel, N., Naik, D. and Humphries, B. (1988) *Visions of Reality: Religion and Ethnicity in Social Work*, London, CCETSW.

Payne, M. (2000) *Anti-Bureaucratic Social Work*, Birmingham, Venture Press.

Payne, M. (2005a) *Modern Social Work Theory*, 3rd edn, Basingstoke, Palgrave Macmillan.

Payne, M. (2005b) *The Origins of Social Work: Continuity and Change*, Basingstoke, Palgrave Macmillan.

Pease, B. and Fook, J. (1999a) 'Postmodern Critical Theory and Emancipatory Social Work Practice', in Pease and Fook (1999b).

Pease, B. and Fook, J. (eds) (1999b) *Transforming Social Work Practice: Postmodern Critical Perspectives*, London, Routledge.

Petersen, A., Barns, I., Dudley, J. and Harris, P. (1999) *Poststructuralism, Citizenship and Social Policy*, London, Routledge.

Pietroni, M. (1995) 'The Nature and Aims of Professional Education for Social Workers: A Postmodern Perspective', in Yelloly and Henkel (1995).

Powell, F. (2001) *The Politics of Social Work*, London, Sage.

Power, M. (1999) *The Audit Society: Rituals of Verification*, Oxford, Oxford University Press.

Preston-Shoot, M. (2007) *Effective Groupwork*, 2nd edn, Basingstoke, Palgrave Macmillan.

Price, V. and Simpson, G. (2007) *Transforming Society: Social Work and Sociology*, Bristol, The Policy Press.

Pullen, A., Beech, N. and Sims, D. (eds) (2007) *Exploring Identity: Concepts and Methods*, Basingstoke, Palgrave Macmillan.

Rock, P. (1979) *The Making of Symbolic Interactionism*, London, Macmillan Press.

Rorty, R. (1989) *Contingency, Irony and Solidarity*, Cambridge, Cambridge University Press.

Rorty, R. (1991) *Objectivity, Relativism and Truth*, Cambridge, Cambridge University Press.

Rorty, R. (ed.) (1992) *The Linguistic Turn: Essays in Philosophical Method*, 2nd edn, Chicago, University of Chicago Press.

Rorty, R. (1999) *Philosophy and Social Hope*, London, Penguin.

Rorty, R. (2007) *Philosophy as Cultural Politics: Philosophical Papers*, Cambridge, Cambridge University Press.

Ross, D. (2005) *Ireland: History of a Nation*, 2nd edn, New Lanark, Geddes & Grosset.

Rubinstein, D. (2001) *Culture, Structure and Agency: Towards a Truly Multidimensional Society*, London, Sage.

Ryan, W. (1988) *Blaming the Victim*, 2nd edn, New York, Random House.

Saleebey, D. (1997) *The Strengths Perspective in Social Work Practice*, New York, Longman.

Saleebey, D. (2008) *The Strengths Perspective in Social Work Practice*, 5th edn, London, Allyn & Bacon.

Sardar, Z. (1998) *Postmodernism and the Other: The New Imperialism of Western Culture*, London, Pluto Press.

Sartre, J.-P. (1969) *Being and Nothingness: An Essay on Phenomenological Ontology*, London, Methuen.

Sartre, J.-P. (1973) *Search for a Method*, New York, Random House.

Sartre, J.-P. (1982) *Critique of Dialectical Reason,* London, Verso.

Sartre, J.-P. (1989) *No Exit and Three Other Plays*, New York, Vintage.

Sartre, J.-P. (1995) *Anti-Semite and Jew*, New York, Schocken.

Schön, D. (1983) *The Reflective Practitioner: How Professionals Think in Action*, New York, Basic Books.

Schön, D. (1987) *Educating the Reflective Practitioner*, San Francisco, Jossey Bass.

Schön, D. (1992) 'The Crisis of Professional Knowledge and the Pursuit of an Epistemology of Practice', *Journal of Interprofessional Care,* 6(1).

Scott, J., Treas, J. and Richards, M. (eds) (2007) *The Blackwell Companion to the Sociology of Families*, Oxford, Blackwell.

Seale, C. (ed.) (2004) *Researching Society and Culture,* London, Sage.

Searle, B. A. (2008) *Well-Being*, Bristol, the Policy Press.

Seligman, M. E. P. (2003) *Authentic Happiness: Using the New Positive*

Psychology to Realize Your Potential for Lasting Fulfillment, London, Nicholas, Brealey.

Seligman, M. E. P. (2006) *Learned Optimism: How to Change Your Mind and Your Life*, New York, Vintage.

Shardlow, S. (2002) 'Values, Ethics and Social Work', in Adams, Dominelli and Payne (2002).

Shotter, J. (1993) *Cultural Politics of Everyday Life*, Buckingham, Open University Press.

Sibeon, R. (1991) *Towards a New Sociology of Social Work*, Aldershot, Avebury.

Sibeon, R. (2004) *Rethinking Social Theory*, London, Sage.

Smith, L. and Drower, S. J. (2008) 'Promoting Resilience and Coping in Social Workers: Learning from Perceptions about Resilience and Coping among South African Social Work Students', in Liebenberg and Ungar (2008).

Stein, H. (2007) *Insight and Imagination: A study in Knowing and Not-Knowing in Organizational Life*, Lanham, MD, University Press of America.

Stein, H. (2009) 'Understanding and Consulting with Inconsolable Organizations', *Illness, Crisis & Loss*, 17(3).

Stepney, P. and Ford, D. (eds) (2000) *Social Work Models, Methods and Theories*, Lyme Regis, Russell House Publishing.

Stepney, P. and Popple, K. (2008) *Social Work and the Community: A Critical Context for Practice*, Basingstoke, Palgrave Macmillan.

Sunderland, J. (2004) *Gendered Discourses*, Basingstoke, Palgrave Macmillan.

Tajfel, H. (1981) *Human Groups and Social Categories*, Cambridge, Cambridge University Press.

Talbot, M. (1995) *Fictions at Work*, London, Longman.

Taylor, C. (2002) 'Gadamer on the Human Sciences', in Dostal (2002).

Taylor, I. (2004) 'Multi-Professional Teams and the Learning Organization', in Gould and Baldwin (2004).

Tew, J. (2002) *Social Theory, Power and Practice*, Basingstoke, Palgrave Macmillan.

Thompson, J. B. (1990) *Ideology and Modern Culture*, Stanford, CA, Stanford University Press.

Thompson, N. (1991) *Crisis Intervention Revisited*, Birmingham, Pepar.

Thompson, N. (1992) *Existentialism and Social Work*, Aldershot, Avebury.

Thompson, N. (1996) *People Skills*, Basingstoke, Macmillan – now Palgrave Macmillan.

Thompson, N. (1997) 'Towards a Theory of Emacipatory Practice', in Lesnik (1997).

Thompson, N. (2000a) *Theory and Practice in Human Services*, 2nd edn, Buckingham, Open University Press.

Thompson, N. (2000b) 'Existentialist Practice', in Stepney and Ford (2000).

Thompson, N. (ed.) (2002a) *Loss and Grief: A Guide for Human Services Practitioners*, Basingstoke, Palgrave Macmillan.

Thompson, N. (2002b) *Building the Future: Social Work with Children, Young People and their Families*, Lyme Regis, Russell House Publishing.

Thompson, N. (2003a) *Promoting Equality: Challenging Discrimination and Oppression*, 2nd edn, Basingstoke, Palgrave Macmillan.

Thompson, N. (2003b) *Communication and Language*, Basingstoke, Palgrave Macmillan.

Thompson, N. (2006a) *Anti-Discriminatory Practice*, 4th edn, Basingstoke, Palgrave Macmillan.

Thompson, N. (2006b) *People Problems*, Basingstoke, Palgrave Macmillan.

Thompson, N. (2006c) *Promoting Workplace Learning*, Bristol, The Policy Press.

Thompson, N. (2007a) *Power and Empowerment*, Lyme Regis, Russell House Publishing.

Thompson, N. (2007b) 'Spirituality: An Existentialist Perspective', *Illness, Crisis & Loss* 15(2).

Thompson, N. (2008a) 'Focusing on Outcomes: Developing Systematic Practice', *Practice: Social Work in Action*, 20(1).

Thompson, N. (2008b) 'Existentialist Ethics: From Nietzsche to Sartre and Beyond', *Ethics and Social Welfare*, 2(1).

Thompson, N. (2009a) *Practising Social Work: Meeting the Professional Challenge*, Basingstoke, Palgrave Macmillan.

Thompson, N. (2009b) *Understanding Social Work: Preparing for Practice*, 3rd edn, Basingstoke, Palgrave Macmillan.

Thompson, N. (2009c) *People Skills*, 3rd edn, Basingstoke, Palgrave Macmillan.

Thompson, N. (2009d) *Loss, Grief and Trauma in the Workplace*, Amityville, NY, Baywood.

Thompson, N. (2009e) *Promoting Equality, Valuing Diversity*, Lyme Regis, Russell House Publishing.

Thompson, N. and Bates, J. (eds) (2009) *Promoting Workplace Well-Being*, Basingstoke, Palgrave Macmillan.

Thompson, N. and Thompson, S. (2005) *Community Care*, Lyme Regis, Russell House Publishing.

Thompson, N. and Thompson, S. (2008) *The Social Work Companion*, Basingstoke, Palgrave Macmillan.

Thompson, S. (2005) *Age Discrimination*, Lyme Regis, Russell House Publishing.

Thompson, S. (2009) 'Reciprocity in Crisis Situations', *Illness, Crisis & Loss* 17(1).

Thompson, S. and Thompson, N. (2008) *The Critically Reflective Practitioner*, Basingstoke, Palgrave Macmillan.

Tomer, A., Eliason, G. T. and Wong, P. T. P. (eds) (2008) *Existential and Spiritual Issues in Death Attitudes*, New York, Lawrence Erlbaum Associates.

Tuckman, B. (1965) 'Developmental Sequence in Small Groups', *Psychological Bulletin* 63(6).

Twelvetrees, A. (2008) *Community Work*, Basingstoke, Palgrave Macmillan.

Ungerson, C. (ed.) (1985) *Women and Social Policy*, London, Macmillan.

van Deurzen, E. and Arnold-Baker, C. (2005a) 'The Self', in van Deurzen and Arnold-Baker (2005c).

van Deurzen, E. and Arnold-Baker, C. (2005b) 'Introduction', in van Deurzen and Arnold-Baker (2005c).

van Deurzen, E. and Arnold-Baker, C. (eds) (2005c) *Existential Perspectives on Human Issues: A Handbook for Therapeutic Practice*, Basingstoke, Palgrave Macmillan.

Verkeuyten, M. (2003) 'Discourses about Ethnic Group (De)-Essentialism: Oppressive and Progressive Aspects', *British Journal of Social Psychology*, 42, pp. 371–91.

Vetere, A. and Dowling, E. (2005) *Narrative Therapies with Children and Their Families: A Practitioner's Guide to Concepts and Approaches*, Hove, Routledge.

Vincent, A. (1992) *Modern Political Ideologies*, Oxford, Blackwell.

Walter, C. A. and McCoyd, J. L. M. (2009) *Grief and Loss across the Lifespan: A Biopsychosocial Approach*, New York, Springer.

Watts, M. (2003) *Kierkegaard*, Oxford, Oneworld Publications.

Webb, S.A. (2006) *Social Work in a Risk Society: Social and Political Perspectives*, Basingstoke, Palgrave Macmillan.

Welsh, F. (2003) *The Four Nations: A History of the United Kingdom,* New Haven, CT, Yale University Press.

Wenger, E. (1998) *Communities of Practice: Learning, Meaning and Identity*, Cambridge, Cambridge University Press.

Westwood, S. (2002) *Social Power*, London, Routledge.

White, S., Fook, J. and Gardner, F. (eds) (2006) *Critical Reflection in Health and Social Care*, Maidenhead, Open University Press.

Wicks, R. (2002) *Nietzsche*, Oxford, Oneworld Publications.

Wicks, R. (2003) *Modern French Philosophy from Existentialism to Postmodernism*, Oxford, Oneworld Publications.

Wilkinson, R. and Pickett, K. (2009) *The Spirit Level: Why More Equal Societies Almost Always Do Better*, London, Allen Lane.

Williams, C., Soydan, H. and Johnson, M. R. D. (eds) (1998) *Social Work and Minorities: European Perspectives*, London, Routledge.

Wolf, C. (1990) 'Relative Advantage', *Symbolic Interaction*, 13(1), pp. 37–61.

Wrong, D. H. (1961) 'The Oversocialized Conception of Man in Modern Sociology', *American Sociological Review*, 26, pp. 183–93.

Yelloly, M. and Henkel, M. (eds) (1995) *Learning and Teaching in Social Work: Towards Reflective Practice*, London, Jessica Kingsley Publishers.

Index